ISBN: 9781314455434

Published by:
HardPress Publishing
8345 NW 66TH ST #2561
MIAMI FL 33166-2626

Email: info@hardpress.net
Web: http://www.hardpress.net

2971

Dr John Brodrington

Grace ascending

THE STORY

OF THE TWEED

ABBOTSFORD

T. & R. Annan & Sons

Photo.

THE STORY
OF THE TWEED

BY THE RIGHT HONOURABLE
SIR HERBERT MAXWELL, BART.

ILLUSTRATED

LONDON
JAMES NISBET AND COMPANY, LIMITED
22, BERNERS STREET, W.
1909

THE STORY OF THE TWEED
IS DEDICATED TO
ANDREW LANG
THAN WHOM
NONE IS MORE ABLE TO DISCERN ITS FLAWS
NONE MORE CERTAIN TO JUDGE
THEM GENTLY

INTRODUCTION

THE aim of the following chapters is to indicate some of the sources of interest which enrich the valley of the Tweed. In quoting from the ballads, in which this valley is more prolific than any other in the United Kingdom, the common and most familiar versions have been taken. From the year 1802, when Scott published the first volume of his *Border Minstrelsy*, down to the close of last century, when Mr. F. J. Child finished his monumental series upon English and Scottish ballads, this literature has never lacked diligent students and critics. Probably all that can be written usefully on the subject is within the reach of those who care to examine it critically.

As for history, the writer is human, and even in the slight sketch here offered some passages must be affected by his prepossession and prejudice, while other passages reflect what seemed to him the likeliest of two or more conflicting versions. The intention of the

INTRODUCTION

book is to provide what might be learned from the conversation of an intelligent native by one making a leisurely progress through the scenes described.

I am informed that Queen Mary's House in Jedburgh has lost the venerable appearance it presented when last I saw it many years ago. A slated roof has replaced the historic thatch, to the distress of the antiquary, but, let us hope, to the greater comfort of the inhabitants.

The quotations from Mr. James Brown's poems in chapter iii. are made by kind permission of his son and of Messrs. William Blackwood and Sons ; that from Mr. Lang's poem in chapter ii. by leave of Messrs. Kegan Paul, Trench, Trübner, and Co., and the verses by the same author in chapter iv. by leave of Messrs Longmans, Green, and Co.

HERBERT MAXWELL.

CONTENTS

LIST OF
ILLUSTRATIONS

CHAPTER I

THE greater part of the written history of every country consists of a narrative of its wars, and warfare most readily gravitates into the valleys of those rivers which serve as frontiers between nations. Hence *rivalis*, the dweller on a *rivus* or river-bank, came to be synonymous with an enemy, and has given us our word 'rival'—one who will not yield to that fellow on the opposite bank. During the long warfare between England and Scotland, which endured for three centuries, broken only by brief periods of precarious truce, the Tweed was recognised as the main boundary between the two realms ; the manhood and intellect of each nation were strained alternately in attacking and defending that line, and the valley of the Tweed became the chosen ground for feats of arms, the natural arena for chivalrous enterprise, the district above all others where, if men would live, they must keep their wits keen and their weapons handy. Practically during three hundred years one generation followed another on both sides of that river—born, living, dying in presence of an ever-watchful foe. Whence it has come to pass that there have gathered over Tweed and her tributaries such wealth of story, such mist of tradition, such glamour of ballad and song, as

1

invest no other river in Great Britain.   Both nations
have contributed their share, so there need be no
jealousy between them in awarding the palm to that
fair stream which laves English soil on the right and
Scottish on the left.

So powerfully has the imagination been moved—
so profoundly the interest stirred—by the lore of
Tweedside, that some persons, visiting the valley for
the first time, find the reality fall far short of their
expectation.   For the theatre of such intense and
varied human action and emotion they had conceived
a landscape of no ordinary kind.   This is especially
the case in these days of barbed-wire fences, tele-
graph-poles, railway whistles, and motor-cars ; but
it was much the same before any of these unlovely
products of civilisation had been dreamt of.   Eighty
years ago, when Washington Irving visited Walter
Scott at Abbotsford, and his host took him to the top
of the Delectable Mountains to feast his eyes upon
Lammermuir, Torwoodlee, Ettrick Forest, and Teviotdale, the American man of letters, nursed among
the stupendous forests and broad-bosomed rivers of
the New World, received but a chill impression.

'I gazed about me,' he wrote, 'for a time with mute
surprise, I may almost say with disappointment.   I beheld
a mere succession of grey, waving hills, line beyond line, as
far as my eye could reach, monotonous in their aspect, and
so destitute of trees that one could almost see a stout fly
walking along their outline ; and the far-famed Tweed
appeared a naked stream, between bare hills, without a tree
or thicket on its banks.   And yet such had been the magic
web of poetry and romance thrown over the whole, that it
had a greater charm for me than the richest scenery I had
ever beheld in England.'

At that time the land was bare enough. The days had been when these uplands of Tweed and Yarrow formed part of the great Caledonian Forest. The old woodland had been swept away, and Scott himself was one of the pioneers in replanting. At the present time the lower valley of the Tweed is rich in fine timber and broad woodlands. Much planting also has been done in Tweeddale proper and Teviotdale, although the effect of rectangular areas of immature wood upon the hillsides led Professor Veitch to sigh for the former bareness.—

' The heights of the district did not then show as if they had been curiously patched in needy places by bits of cloth different from their original garment, and they were free from shapes of wood that now look like arms *minus* bodies, again like bodies *minus* arms, now like a tadpole, and then like a soup-ladle. The people of last century were spared appearances of this sort, and instead of these they had simply hills, roads, and waters. ' [1]

Washington Irving had the priceless privilege of being presented to these scenes by one who has done more than any other to interpret their history and to codify (if such a harsh expression may be suffered) their romance. Readers, less fortunate, but tolerant, perhaps will suffer the leading of a humbler guide, equal only in one respect to the Wizard of the North —his unalterable love for the land and its people.

Whether the Tweed be an English river or a Scottish ' water, ' or whether each nation has an equal claim to the glory of possessing it, must be decided upon the following considerations. Taking the whole course of the river along its windings from

[1] *History and Poetry of the Scottish Border*, by Professor Veitch, i. 18.

source to sea at about ninety-seven miles, both sides of the channel are Scottish soil for eighty miles. From near Birgham downwards for fifteen miles the left bank is Scottish, the right bank English. For the last two miles below Paxton in its course to the sea the river is English on both banks, dividing Berwick-on-Tweed from Northumberland.

Thus a Scot may surely insist that birthplace and parentage are the true tests of nationality, and claim inalienable inheritance of the Tweed in virtue of its origin in the extreme south-west corner of Peebles-shire or Tweeddale, which was the ancient and better name for that country. And if a native of Peebles be not good Scots, then must ethnology be deemed but an idle fraud. To which the Englishman retorts that if the Tweed is born Scots it dies English. As Scotsmen from immemorial times have travelled south and become naturalised Englishmen, so the Tweed cannot live in its native land, and desert it for good and all.

Let the verdict be—Honours easy ! and let both nations enjoy their share of glory in this fair stream. It would be sheer waste of time to discuss the various interpretations which have been given to the name Tweed. Etymologists have become shy of assertion in these latter days, and are agreed to write off a large proportion of river names as of unknown origin. All that can be said with safety is that Tweed seems to be an abbreviated form of a name bestowed upon many rivers by the Brythonic or Cymric branch of the Celts, and may be compared with Taff, Teifi, Towy, Tavy, and Dovey in Wales, Tawe and Tavy in Devon, Tay and Teith in Scotland. This, too, may be added, that it is difficult to

believe that the Tweed and its principal tributary the
Teviot did not derive their respective names from a
common origin.   Above Hawick the Teviot invariably is called Water o' Teiott by the peasantry, who
are everywhere the only sure repository of the
pronunciation of place-names as they sounded before
they came to be written and printed.

So much for the speculative and elusive : now for
the tangible and demonstrable.

The accredited source of Tweed is a clear spring
known as Tweed's Well, rising in an upland meadow
some 1250 feet above the sea, near where the
marches of Peeblesshire, Dumfriesshire and Lanarkshire meet.   The accredited source, I say ; but
whereas the well lies between Corse Hill and Flecket
Hill, rising 450 and 400 feet respectively above the
level of the meadow, and sending down between
them the little Corse Burn which receives the outflow
of the well, it is in the said Corse Burn that the
Tweed first takes form and being.   Corse Hill and
Burn derive their name from Tweed Cross, a monument erected by pious hands 1632 feet above the
sea, to remind travellers of their Redeemer, and to
guide them withal across these desolate moors.   It
was destroyed, no doubt, by hands that one wishes
had not been so pious in that reforming zeal for the
obliteration of all tokens of Popery which has cost
Scotland so dear in the sacrifice of thousands of
works of art.

This upland is a prolific watershed, giving birth to
three chief rivers of the Scottish lowlands.—

'Annan, Tweed, and Clyde
Rise a' out o' ae hillside.

Tweed ran, Annan wan,
    Clyde brak its neck o'er Corra Linn. '

Admitted that some liberties are taken with actual topography in this rhyme; for, although Clyde's Burn draws its supply from a point not far distant from Tweed's Well and is reputed the parent stream, it is but a tributary of the Water of Daer, a much larger brook rising on Queensberry (2285 feet), which marks the watershed between Annandale and Nithsdale.

From its modest source, 'Tweed runneth for the most part with a soft yet trotting stream, '[1] to fulfil its destiny in draining a basin of about 1870 square miles, a larger area than any other Scottish river except the Tay.

Watch the mood of this solitude before you venture upon it, as narrowly as you would that of a jealous mistress. It is not always kind to wanderers. One summer day it may be all smiles, greeting you with

'The floating voices of the hill—
The hum of bees in heather bells,
And bleatings from the distant fells,
The curlew's whistle, far and shrill,
And babbling of the restless rill. '

So that, as you lie in the heather musing upon the countless associations of the scene—the riding and raiding, the driving and burning of the old Border days—you may get impatient with the languorous beauty of earth and sky, and murmur with the 'Scottish Probationer '—

[1] Dr. Pennecuik's *Description of Tweeddale.* Edinburgh, 1715.

' O western wind, so soft and low,
  Long lingering by furze and fern,
Rise ! from thy wing the languor throw,
  And by the marge of mountain tarn—
  By rushy brook and lonely cairn—
Thy thousand bugles take, and blow
  A wilder music up the fells. '

Well for you if your summons meets with no res-
ponse—if the raincloud, chill with the breath of Solway,
does not droop and wrap the landscape from your
sight. You are many miles from your supper, and,
though you like to think the path lies down hill, you
may learn, at the cost of aching shins, the difference
between wet heather and dry to travel over.

They carry their own peculiar charm, these bare
southern uplands ; yet few strangers would be at-
tracted to them, but for the human association which
has gathered in every hope and cleugh—every heathy
moss and grassy hillside. But for that, the monotony
would be oppressive. On every hand stretch out
smooth hills with easy gradients, ridge beyond ridge,
unbroken by bush or tree, parallel in their uniform ' strike ' from south-west to north-east, which
happens also to be the prevailing direction of the
never-tiring wind. The eye, without stimulus of
imagination and memory, would soon weary of such
sameness of outline and detail. The unread tourist
may grumble because the hills, rising to a height
which, in the Highlands, would ensure exciting
contours and varied scenery, here assume an aspect
as tame as if they had been artificially handled.

In truth they owe their appearance to a handling
more terrific than any human agency could apply.
The underlying rock is Lower Silurian, oldest of the

sedimentary beds, and containing the earliest known forms of life. Once these beds were subjected to fierce crumpling and contortion, thrust up into soaring crests, and cleft into darksome ravines, creating scenery of a kind to satisfy the most exacting sightseer. Then came a climatic revolution. For thousands of years not a drop of rain fell in Scotland : nothing but snow, snow, snow, to the depth of many hundreds of feet, solidified by its own pressure into a vast ice-sheet from sea to sea. Ice, being plastic, cannot remain stationary on a slope. Like water, which it is, it must find its own level. So this mighty field could not but move, as it is moving in Greenland at this day, creeping slowly, irresistibly off the higher ground to the sea-level. In its march it shore away every obstacle, pared off the hill crests, grinding the rocks of them into that boulder clay, which it piled in those gentle slopes so characteristic of the hill valleys in Upper Tweeddale. Much of this Silurian area had been covered by younger deposits, especially by coal-bearing strata; but these, with their contents of incalculable commercial value, the ruthless ice ploughed clean away, and we shall have to travel far down the Tweed valley before encountering even the Old Red Sandstone at Leader foot. For the treelessness of the scenery man alone is responsible. It is he who felled the oak forest of the valleys, the pines and birches of the higher ground, without a thought for the necessities of later generations. Local names bear indelible testimony to the wastefulness of our sires. Even the ground just below Tweed's Well is still called Tweedshaws, which means the wood of Tweed, though nothing could be less descriptive of its present appearance.

But we too, like the ice-field, must move forward, for we have a long road before us. Above all, let us forswear poetic quotation for the present, seeing that we are entering a country where verse has sprung up like wayside weeds, and every hanging shaw is as full of ballad as of the sound of birds. However, before leaving the site of Tweeds's Cross, mention must be made of a notable meeting which it is said took place at the summit of this pass of Erricstane six hundred years ago. Edward I had dethroned his puppet John Baliol, King of Scots, and had exacted oaths of fealty and homage from every Scottish baron. Among those whom he kept in prison was Sir William Douglas ' le Hardi, ' who had broken his allegiance, and joined Wallace in the abortive rising which ended in the capitulation of Irvine. Sir William died in the Tower of London about 1298, his eldest son, James, being an exile in Paris. James returned to Scotland some time after his father's death, and, his inheritance having been forfeited by King Edward, he became a page to Lamberton, Bishop of St. Andrews. In February 1306 took place the tragedy in Greyfriars' Church, Dumfries, when Robert Bruce, Earl of Carrick, slew his rival the Red Comyn; and, although nominally an official in King Edward's government of Scotland, proclaimed his title to the Scottish crown. Hearing of these events, young James Douglas announced to the Bishop his intention of joining him whom he believed to be rightful King of Scots. The Bishop gave him absolution: he gave him more : he gave him his own palfrey to ride forth on an errand whereof he so highly approved ; and James fell in with the new king at Erricstane, as he was riding to Glasgow on his way to be crowned at

Scone. A memorable episode in Scottish history, for this youth was soon to become known as ' the Good Sir James of Douglas'—King Robert's right-hand man. Douglas had never bowed the knee to King Edward ; there is no stain of perjury on his memory ; alone, among the leaders of that rising, he never owned allegiance save to the King of Scots.

For fifteen miles young Tweed holds her way through a pastoral land, gathering volume as she flows. If the feminine pronoun strikes strangely on English ears, let the reader note that in almost every part of Scotland the river of the district is so referred to, possibly because in Gaelic, once spoken all over the realm, *abhuinn* or *amhuinn* (avon), the generic term for rivers, is of the feminine gender. From right and left numerous burns hurry up their reinforcement to the suzerain stream. The Hawkshaw Burn flows from Falla Moss, of gruesome memory, for here one of Cromwell's outposts, sixteen horsemen, were surprised and taken by Porteous of Hawkshaw and a party of moss-riders. The prisoners were killed one by one in cold blood, and buried where they fell.

The next notable tributary is Talla Water, which joins the Tweed at Tweedsmuir Kirk. High among the hills, at the foot of Moll's Cleuch Dod (2571 feet), the Talla encounters some rocky barriers, which throw the stream into alternate cascade and deep pool. The place is known as Talla Linns, and here in the summer of 1682 was held an important gathering of Covenanters. There was a special reason for the choice of this place : it was just outside the jurisdiction of the dreaded John Graham of Claverhouse, Viscount Dundee, who, having been stationed for

some time at Dumfries in command of his troop of
dragoons, was appointed in January 1682 Sheriff of
Galloway, Dumfriesshire, and Annandale, and held,
besides, a commission of justiciary carrying powers of
life and death.   Claverhouse was thus virtually both
judge and general, a most vicious and unconstitu-
tional combination, for which he cannot be held
responsible.   A devoted royalist and an accomplished
soldier, he flinched not from carrying out the rigorous
measures of the Government against the disaffected.
'His not to reason why—his not to make reply';
yet his despatches contain frequent representations in
favour of making examples of lairds and leaders, and
dealing leniently with the peasantry.   It was an
odious task upon which to employ the most capable
soldier of the time, and it will take centuries before
the horror of 'the killing time' passes from those
lonely moors.   The memory of Claverhouse, as the
most active official, is held in execration to this day
among the hill shepherds.   Until lately, it was their
custom to destroy every nest of the pretty and
harmless peewit, whose shrill cries and aerial evolu-
tions betrayed the hiding-place of many a crouching
Covenanter to Claverhouse's dragoons. [1]

[1] An amusing story was told me among these hills in my youth. A
shepherd sat by the hearth, reading to his wife 'the chapter,' according
to pious custom, before going to bed. He had chosen Revelation xii.,
and began the third verse—'And there appeared another wonder in
heaven; and behold a great reid dragoon'—'Na, na, Tammas,' interrupted the wife, 'ye're wrang there. There never was a dragoon in
heaven yet.'—'It maun be sae, wife,' replied Tammas, 'for it's in the
written Word, ye ken.'—'Atweel,' was the resigned reply, 'if it's
there, it maun be sae; but there's ae thing I ken, it couldna been ane
o' Clavers's dragoons.' The reading proceeded, till Tammas came to
the ninth verse—'And the great dragoon was cast out, that old
serpent,' etc. Whereat the good dame broke in again—'I tell't ye
that, lad, I tell't ye that! I kent that nae dragoon wad bide lang in
heaven. It's nae place for the likes o' him!'

The Talla Linn convention, instead of taking measures of offence and defence, fell to arguing hotly upon points of doctrine, and separated without effecting anything; which betrayed a sad lack of carnal common-sense, seeing that in the previous year the Covenanters had declared war against Charles Stuart, as having forfeited 'all right, title to, or interest in, the Crown of Scotland.'[1] Luckily for my readers, in following the course of Tweed we shall leave behind us scenes darkened by the miseries of the Westland Whigs, and enter upon others, often drenched, indeed, with good blood, but mostly with blood shed in open fray.

Forward, then, along the lonely road, not so lonely as of yore, now that motors and bicycles have thrown open tracks long deserted by travellers. Opposite Tweedsmuir Kirk, to the left of road and river, remain the site and name, no more, of Oliver Castle, once the stronghold of a powerful Border baron. At the close of the thirteenth century Sir Simon Fraser, ancestor of the present Simon Fraser, Lord Lovat, was keeper of Ettrick Forest for Edward I., and bore arms under that monarch in the siege and capture of Caerlaverock Castle in 1300; but in 1302 he suddenly changed sides, joining the nationalist movement under Wallace, deserting from Edward's castle of Wark, and carrying off the horses and armour of his English comrade, Sir William de Dunolm [Durham].[2] He joined John Comyn, one of the three Guardians of Scotland, and with him inflicted a defeat on the English, under Sir John de Segrave, at Roslyn on

[1] Proclamation by Richard Cameron at the Cross of Sanquhar, 22nd June 1681.
[2] Bain's *Documents relating to Scotland*, ii. 334.

24th February 1303. Robert Bruce, the future king, was active in the English service at this time ; and on 9th February 1304 Comyn and his friends laid down their arms at Strathord. Sir Simon Fraser was ordered into exile for four years ;[1] better for him had he fulfilled the term. He was back in Scotland to join Bruce's rising in 1306, was taken prisoner, and on 6th September of that year was executed in London with all the rigour of Norman law against treason. First he was hanged ; then he was taken down alive, his entrails taken out and burnt before his eyes, and finally he was beheaded. All this, as a contemporary English chronicler complacently observes, *ut majores cruciatus sentiret*—that he might endure the greater torment.

This Sir Simon seems to have been the last of his line who owned land in Tweeddale, his lands of Oliver passing with his daughters to their husbands, Fleming of Biggar and Hay of Yester. Young Hay of Talla (part of Over Oliver barony) suffered death for his share with Bothwell in the murder of Darnley in 1567.

Passing the old wayside inn of Crook, a name denoting the former site of a cross, one perceives the alder and birch timidly beginning to fringe the stream. Polmood Burn comes in from the right here, flowing from the ample breast of Broad Law (2725 feet), reminding one by its name of the ancient forest fauna which has passed away. Polmood represents the Gaelic *pol madadh*, the wolf's stream.[2] That wolves survived the inroad of people of Saxon speech into

---

[1] Bain's *Documents relating to Scotland*, ii. 457.
[2] The name recurs in fuller form on the southern watershed of this range, Polmoody, a tributary of Moffat Water.

Tweeddale may be known by the occurence of such names as Wolf-hope Law, Wolf-field Craigs, Wolf Lee, etc. Before leaving the uplands for the low ground, it is interesting to note the recurrence of place-names derived from beast and bird. Hunt Law (2086 feet) stands suggestively on the north side of Polmood ; Glenmuck commemorates where the wild sow used to farrow (Gaelic *muc*) ; it is many a year since Hartfell (2651 feet) held either red stag or fallow buck ; Raecleuch has now scarcely cover for a mouse, let alone a roe-deer ; the erne or white-tailed eagle has been driven from Yearngill Head (1804 feet), but in 1845 shepherds were still complaining about the mischief wrought by these birds among their lambs. [1] Harecleuch, Hawkshaw, Tod's Knowe, and Ravencraig speak to us of creatures still resident—long life to them !

Polmood was the house of a family named Hunter in early days. One may catch a glimpse of the chase in a fragment of rhyme floating about the neighbourhood—

> ' The King rade round the Merecleuch Head,
>   Booted and spurred, as we a' did see,
>   And dined wi' a lass at Mosfennan Pett,
>   A little below the Logan Lee. '

Mosfennan, a farm-toun on the left bank of Tweed three miles below Polmood, between camp-crowned Wormal (1776 feet) and Glenholm Kirk, is the scene of another and later lyric, supplanting the old and forgotten one, and rehearsed to Professor Veitch by William Welsh, the Peeblesshire cottar-poet. From internal evidence Veitch was able to fix its date as

[1] *New Statistical Account.*

shortly after 1689, and as the ballad has never been printed except in his *Border History and Poetry*, space may be found for it here. It shows, at least, that the monotony of life was broken for dwellers in these wastes, not only by fire and sword, but by the gentler vicissitudes of courtship. The most notable thing about this ballad is that it is said to have been composed by the heroine herself, who was one of two joint-heiresses—Grizel and Janet Scott. Veitch, who died in 1894, had it from Welsh, who learned it from Jeanie Moffat, who died in 1874 at the age of ninety-nine. Jeanie averred that she learned the verses from a fellow-servant who had been serving-maid in the house of Mosfennan when the courtship was in progress, to whom her mistress, the Lady of Logan Lee, used to repeat them. It is not often that one can trace floating minstrelsy so directly to its source.—

MOSFENNAN, OR THE LOGAN LEE

There cam three wooers out o' the west,
    Booted and spurred, as ye weel micht see,
And they lichted a' at Mosfennan Yett,[1]
    A little below the Logan Lee.

Three cam east, and three cam west,
    And three cam frae the north countrie;
The rest cam a' frae Moffat side,
    And lichted at the Logan Lee.

'Is the mistress o' this house within,
    The bonny lass we've come to see?'
'I am the leddy o' this place,
    And "madam" when ye speak to me.'

[1] *Yett*, gate.

' If ye be the leddy o' this house,
　　That we hae come sae far to see,
　There's mony a servant lass in our country-side
　　That far excels the Leddy o' the Logan Lee.'

' Then it's no' to be my weel-faured face
　　That ye hae come sae far to see,
　But it's a' for the bonny bob-tailed yowes [1]
　　That trinle alang the Logan Lee.

' But be I black or be I fair,
　　Be I comely for to see,
　It maks nae matter what I be
　　While I've mony a yowe on the Logan Lee.

' I hae seven yowe-milkers in a bught,
　　Wi' their coaties kilted abune the knee ;
　Ye may seek a wife among them a ',
　　But ye 'll ne'er get the Leddy o' the Logan Lee !'

' Be she black or be she fair,
　　I carena a boddle what she may be ;
　I wad rather hae ane without a plack
　　Than wed the Leddy o' the Logan Lee !'

' Some says that I lo'e young Powmood,
　　Others some says he lo'es na me ;
　But I weel may compare wi' his bastard blood, [2]
　　Though I hadna a yowe on the Logan Lee.

' Graham o' Slipperfield and his grey mear,
　　Young Powmood wi' his greyhounds three,
　Charlie and his pistols clear—
　　Ye'll ne'er hae a yowe on the Logan Lee.

[1] Ewes.
[2] Robert Hunter of Polmood died in 1689, and his estate passed to his illegitimate son, George Hunter. The succession was disputed by Adam Hunter, tenant in Alterstane, in an interminable lawsuit, which lasted into the nineteenth century.

'But young John Graham is a weel-faured man,
  And a cunning[1] lad he seems to be ;
For he cam doun by the Langcleuch Fit,
  And *he'll* be the Laird o' the Logan Lee.'

At Kingledoors the valley broadens out, and at
Drummelzier[2] stand the ruins of Tinnis Castle,
where the family of Tweedie once held great sway.[3]
They own no land in these parts now, but they are
remembered for the length and violence of a blood-
feud between them and their near neighbours, the
Veitches of Dawick, whose lands also have passed
into other hands. The first Tweedie appears to
have succeeded to Drummelzier by marriage with
the daughter and heiress of Laurence Fraser, a cadet
of the house of Oliver. He and his successors, not
content with their duty in repelling English invasion,
and in lifting English cattle, set up as freebooters
on their own account, levying blackmail upon peaceable travellers and harrying their neighbours' lands.
With the Tweedies rode the Crichtons of Cardon
and Porteous of Hawkshaw. Two of them, 'William Twedy of Drummelzeare and Adam Twedy of
Dreva,' were among those arraigned for the murder of

[1] Clever.

[2] Note that the *z* in this and other Scottish names like Cadzow,
Dalziel, etc., does not represent the soft sibilant, but the consonantal *y*,
as in 'year' and 'yellow.' Drummelzier is pronounced 'Drummellyer,'

[3] The mythical origin of the name Tweedie is given in Scott's notes
to the *Lay of the Last Minstrel*. The Laird of Drummelzier, returning
from a prolonged absence as a crusader, found his wife with a fine
boy, 'whose birth did not by any means correspond with the time of
his departure.' She told him that she had been walking by the Tweed
one day, when the Spirit of the river appeared, and compelled her to
yield to his embraces. The indulgent husband accepted the explanation : the child grew into a very powerful man, and received the name
of Tweedie in virtue of his putative paternity. All of which recalls the
Homeric legend of the nymph Tyro, who, becoming enamoured of the
river Enipeus, was seduced by Neptune in the guise of that stream.

2

David Riccio in 1566. The feud with the Veitches
had been running long before that date. No one
knows its origin, but it is sure to have been a quarrel
about land. The frequent occurence in this district
of the place-name Threipland (Scots, *to threep, to
quarrel*) testifies to that common source of disagree-
ment. Anyhow, in the sixteenth century the Veitches
had for allies the Burnets of Barns, Geddes of Rachan,
and Lord Fleming of Biggar. In 1590 the head of
the Veitches was an immensely powerful man known
as the Deil of Dawick; his friend Burnet, called 'the
Hoolet, or the Owl, was his match in stature and
strength. Between them they managed to daunt
the tyrant Tweedie of Drummelzier. But one day
in June the 'Deil's' son, Patrick Veitch, being in
Peebles, was recognised by young Tweedie of Drummelzier. There were six Tweedies in the town
altogether, besides two Crichtons and a Porteous—
long odds against a single Veitch. No attempt was,
however, made against the young fellow in Peebles,
which was at that time a place of fashion and resort.
The nine rascals divided into two bands, one of
which galloped forward to Neidpath Castle ; the
other tarried in the town till they saw their victim
ride homewards alone. When he entered the gorge
of the Tweed at Neidpath the two parties closed,
and the young laird of Dawick was seen alive no
more. They swung for it, no doubt, these cowardly
assassins ? Not a bit. The extreme and unusually
vigorous step was taken of putting them in Edinburgh tolbooth ; but the Tweedies had no difficulty
in finding cautioners 'to satisfy pairties,' Scott of
Buccleuch standing forward for them, and the murderers went free. The feud was unappeased. Four

days after the slaughter of Patrick Veitch, two Veitches met John Tweedy, Tutor of Drummelzier, in
the High Street of Edinburgh, who presently was
lying in the kennel with Veitch of Syntoun's rapier
through his heart.

The last we can glean about this vendetta is in a
proclamation by James VI. and I., dated at Greenwich
the 10th March 1611, which, after reciting 'that the
deadly feid betwixt Veitches and Tweedies is as yet
unreconciled, ' calls upon the Privy Council to
summon before them ' the principalls of either surname, ' and force them to agree on pain of imprisonment. Such was one of the first effects of a strong
central government.

On Drummelzier Haugh the Tweed receives from
the west the Biggar Water. There is here no suggestion of magnitude or relative proportion : it is a
Norse name, from *bygg*, barley, and signifies simply
the *bygg garth*, or barley field, commemorating primitive agriculture. [1] Sir Archibald Geikie has drawn
attention to the singular fact that although the Clyde,
in its course from the Erricstane watershed, has run
twice as far as its sister Tweed, and has attained
more than double the volume, it passes Biggar within
seven miles of the Tweed at Drummelzier, and is
separated from it, not by a ridge or elevated ground,
but by a flat tract of loose sandy deposit. It would
require but a slight engineering effort, he says, to
throw the whole volume of the Clyde at Biggar into
the Tweed valley. [2] In fact, Tom Stoddart was long
puzzled by the appearance of salmon and their young

[1] The same name, less altered, appears as Biggart, near Beith, in
Ayrshire, and as Biggarts, near Moffat.
[2] *Scenery of Scotland*, 2nd ed., 349.

in this part of the Clyde, which is hopelessly closed against the ascent of these fish from the western sea by the falls of Cora Linn, eighty feet in height.——

'The fact is accounted for in this way. After passing Tinto Hill, the bed of the Clyde approaches to a level with that of Biggar Water. . . . On the occasion of a large flood, the two streams become connected, and the Clyde actually pours a portion of its waters into one of the tributaries of the Tweed.'[1]

Biggar was of old a burgh of barony of the Flemings. Here, in 1545, Malcolm, Lord Fleming, High Chancellor of Scotland, founded a collegiate church, and dedicated it to St. Nicholas, patron of Biggar. Of late pointed style, cruciform in shape, without aisles and with an apsidal east end, this building still serves as the parish church, and its square battlemented tower lends a sober dignity to the little grey town. It was probably the last church to be built and endowed in Scotland before the Reformation. In the manse of the Moat Park Church of the United Presbyterians, Dr. John Brown was born in 1810, kindliest of essayists, the author of *Horæ Subsecivæ* and of *Rab and His Friends*.

Drummelzier Haugh and the steep slopes of Scrape above it are full of misty memories of the wizard Merlin. A little below Drummelzier Kirk, says Dr. Pennecuik, writing in 1715, 'the particular place of his grave, at the foot of a thorn tree, was shown me, many years ago, by the old and reverend minister of the place.' The reputed burial-place is on the Powsail Burn—the stream of willows—just above its junction with the Tweed; but it must be

[1] *The Angler's Companion for Scotland*, 2nd ed., 346.

confessed that this clashes with the legend which assigns him a resting-place with King Arthur and his knights, in the enchanted halls under the triple Eildons, nearly thirty miles hence. An ancient prophecy—

'When Tweed and Powsail meet at Merlin's grave,
Scotland and England that day ae king shall have '—

is said to have been fulfilled on the coronation day of James VI. and I., 25th July 1603, when a tremendous flood caused the two streams to mingle their waters at this spot.

Much confusion exists about the identity of Merlin Wyllt or Caledonius, who was a different person from Merlin Emrys or Ambrosius, also a wizard, upon whom Vortigern, the Prince of south-east Britain, bestowed a town on the summit of Snowdon. This was in the fifth century; whereas the events in the life of Merlin Wyllt recorded by Gildas took place in the latter half of the sixth century. Professors Skene and Veitch laboured to unravel the puzzle, which is unintelligible unless one remembers that by his victory of Ardderyd[1] (Arthuret, near Carlisle) in 573, at which Merlin Wyllt was present, the Christian Rydderch Hael overthrew the pagan forces under Gwendoleu, and established himself as King of Cumbria or Strathclyde, a Welsh realm extending from the Derwent to Dunbarton.[2]

Merlin fled from the fatal field of Ardderyd, and, according to the statement in one of his extant poems, lived in the Caledonian Forest for fifty years. But whereas he admits that he was crazed with grief, his

[1] Pronounced Artheryd, with a soft dental, like *th* in 'this.'
[2] *Dun Bretan*, the fortress of the Britons or Welsh.

reckoning need not be taken literally. Possibly his 'ten years and forty' may signify ten years and forty days.

'Sweet apple tree, growing by the river !
Whereof the keeper shall not thrive on the fruit ;
Before I lost my wits I used to be round its stem
With a fair playful maid, matchless in slender shape. [1]
Ten years and forty, the sport of the lawless,
Have I been wandering darkling among sprites,
After wealth in abundance and entertaining minstrels.
I will not sleep, but tremble for my leader,
My lord Gwendoleu and the people of my country, [donia
After suffering from disease and despair in the forest of Cale-
May I become a servant of the Lord of Noble Retinues ! [2]

Rydderch Hael established Christianity in Strath-clyde, appointing the energetic Kentigern or Mungo as bishop, a state of things very disagreeable to the heathen Merlin. The lord of Drummelzier was one Meldred, whose name is probably preserved in the original form Dunmeller, the fortress of Meldred. Fordun, writing in the fourteenth century, records the tradition that Merlin met Bishop Kentigern *prope oppidum Dunmeller*—near the village of Drummelzier —and that Meldred's shepherds afterwards clubbed him to death.

Professor Skene suggested that this Haugh of Drummelzier was probably the scene of the seventh of King Arthur's twelve battles, which Gildas states took place *in silva Caledonis, id est, cat coit Celidon*—' in the forest of Caledon, that is, the battle of the Cale-donian Forest '; but Professor Veitch seems to be

[1] The Vivien of the legend and of Tennyson's idyll.
[2] *Black Book of Carmarthen*, xvii. See Skene's *Four Ancient Books of Wales*, i. 372, ii. 18.

nearer the mark in indicating Cademuir, formerly written Cadmore, as the true battlefield, to the east of Manor Water, six or seven miles lower down the Tweed, *cad* being the Welsh for a battle. Howbeit, the Caledonian Forest was a big affair, filling the whole of Strathclyde, whereof Ettrick, Selkirk, and Cadzow forests remained in the Middle Ages but the surviving fringe; wherefore it is not easy to determine the exact spot for this great combat.

The prehistoric remains of Upper Tweeddale are innumerable. Attack and defence were the primary business of primitive man, and almost every hill-top bears a stone fort of circular earthwork. They add to the interest of summer rambles among the hills; let him who, musing on the dim past, tries to reconstruct the scene in imagination, bear in mind that the land was densely wooded when its human occupants sought points of vantage for defensive works. No fewer than seventy-six of these ancient forts have been described with plans by Dr. David Christison in an exhaustive paper printed in the *Proceedings of the Scottish Antiquaries* for 1887.[1]

[1] The forts of Selkirkshire are dealt with by the same competent hand in the *Proceedings* for 1894-95.

CHAPTER II

FROM BIGGARFOOT TO ETTRICK WATER

AFTER its reinforcement by Biggar Water, although still more than 600 feet above the sea, the Tweed loses the irresponsible character of a mere upland stream, and takes on the airs and graces of a river. At this point, too, it parts with its pastoral surroundings and winds among well-tilled fields and hillsides, to which much of the original sylvan character has been restored. Notably at Dawick or Dalwick, the *wic* or dwelling in the dale, which the Veitches, perhaps broken by the long feud with the Tweedies, yielded to a lawyer, James Naesmyth, towards the close of the seventeenth century. This gentleman's grandson, Sir James Naesmyth of Posso, studied under the great Linnæus in Norway, and turned his studies to good and lasting account, for it is to him that the traveller owes that splendid prospect of forest which stretches behind the modern house far along the flanks of Scrape (2347 feet). It is said that Linnæus personally helped Sir James to lay out this fine wood, wherein the silver firs alone are worth a summer day's travel to behold. Dawick disputes with Dunkeld the honour of having been the first place in Scotland where larches were planted. [1]

Opposite Dawick extend the fine grounds and

[1] Dawick is now the property of Mrs. Balfour.

plantations of Stobo Castle, the centre of a large estate which once belonged to the Murrays, but was sold in 1767 to James Montgomery, Chief Baron of the Exchequer in Scotland. His grandson, Sir Graham Montgomery, was member for the county from 1852 till 1880, dying in 1901. The next baronet, Sir James, it may be remembered, fell from a night express travelling to London, and was thus killed in November 1902. The property has now been sold.

The parish church of Stobo is one of the very few in Scotland which escaped destruction or irreparable defacement in the fury of the Reformation. The structure is Norman, but the windows in the south wall have been reconstructed in sixteenth century pointed, and a porch of the same date has been put up in front of the Norman south door. It is to be regretted that when Sir Graham Montgomery was restoring the building in 1868 the Norman chancel arch was pulled down, and replaced by a modern pointed one. The 'jougs,' or iron collar for the correction of evildoers, still hung in the south porch a few years ago.

There are some remarkable trees at Dawick and Stobo. An oak at Dawick measured 80 feet high in 1880, with a clean bole of 42 feet, girthing 10 feet 8 inches five feet above the ground. Another oak at Stobo was the same height, with 35 feet of clean bole, and girthed 9 feet 4 inches at a height of five feet. A sycamore at Stobo, 63 feet high, girthed 17 feet 8 inches at five feet above the ground. [1]

Along the north-east border of Stobo parish runs the Water of Lyne, scene of an episode which ought to be read about in Barbour's *Brus* by anybody who

[1] *Transactions of the Highland and Agricultural Society*, 1880-81.

will be at pains to master the old northern English in which that delectable poet cast his verse. It took place in 1308. The noble, but terrible, Edward Longshanks had been dead for eighteen months : his ignoble, ill-starred son reigned as Edward II.; but the violent disputes with his own barons had diverted attention from Scottish affairs, and the cause of independence was waxing apace. Still there was a strong English party in Scotland, for the cross of St. George still flew over every chief fortress in that country. Sir James of Douglas had been busy for some months rousing the men of Tweeddale to action, and with good success, for King Edward forfeited the lands which Aymer de Valence, Earl of Pembroke, owned in that district, because his tenants ' had traitorously joined Robert de Brus. '

One summer night Douglas sought lodging at a house on the Water of Lyne, but found it was full of company already. Creeping under a window, he listened, and what he heard convinced him that those within were no friends to the good cause.

> Nerhand the hous, sa listnet he,
> And heard thar sawis ilke dele, [1]
> And be that persavit wele
> That tha war strange men. ' [2]

Douglas immediately took vigorous measures. He made his men surround the house, burst open the door, and surprised the company before they could get on their harness. Some were slain, some escaped in the darkness, but at least one prisoner of price

[1] ' Heard every part of what they said '—curiously misinterpreted by the transcriber of the Edinburgh MS. in 1489, who rendered the line—' Herd ane say tharin " the Dewill." '
[2] *The Brus*, lxxiv. 15.

remained in the person of Thomas Randolph, King Robert's nephew.

Randolph, a lad of mettle, hitherto most eager in pursuit of the King of Scots, was brought before his uncle, who received him kindly, and expressed a hope that he would now become a dutiful liege. But the young squire answered fiercely, taunting the king with having challenged open war and stooped to unknightly ruses. Back to prison with him, then! where a few weeks' reflection brought him to another mind. He took service under King Robert, and discharged it so well that he was created Earl of Moray, became the generous rival of Douglas in his king's confidence and favour, and after King Robert's death in 1329 was chosen Regent.

This bit of history seems to have associated itself with the Roman camp at Lyne, which goes by the name of Randal's Wa's or Randal's Trencher. A notable work it is, situated 700 feet above the sea, in the heart of the Peeblesshire hills, causing one to wonder why the Roman commanders should have chosen such a desolate, solitary region as the station of a powerful force, for the fortifications enclose a space of upwards of six Scots acres. But, as Chalmers pointed out, the position was one of considerable strategic importance, commanding the junction of the main routes from the south-eastern and south-western districts of North Britain with those from Strathclyde and Lothian. 'It was a fair inference, therefore, that the object of the Romans was to protect this important connection between the main east and west routes by which, from time immemorial, invading armies have penetrated into Scotland; and it is noteworthy that these connecting roads, although running through a hill country, encounter no high pass, and have such easy gradients that they are favourite cycling routes at the present day.'[1]

Another and later Regent of Scotland, upon whose deserts men cannot be got to agree so readily as upon those of the gallant Randolph of Moray, has left his memorial on the Water of Lyne. James Douglas, Earl of Morton, chose himself a fair site at the confluence of Lyne and Tairth whereon to build a mighty castle, where he might lodge when hunting in the royal forest. He lived to see it nearly finished on a fine scale—the great hall measures 50 feet long by 22 feet broad—but never did he lay his head therein. The Regent was summoned before the Council to answer for his part in the murder of Darnley, and on 2nd June 1581 his head was struck off by 'the Maiden,'[2] a kind of guillotine, which, it is said, Morton himself had directed to be used in Scotland, after seeing the clean work it wrought upon criminals in Yorkshire. Drochil Castle was never finished : it remains a massive and impressive monument of the vanity of human wishes.

The flat elevated tableland which fills the angle between Lyne Water and Tweed is called Sheriff's Muir or Shire Moor, not to be confused with Sheriffmuir, near Dunblane, where on 13th November 1715 the Duke of Argyll and the Earl of Mar fought a drawn battle. Sheriff's Muir in Tweeddale was so named as the spot where the sheriff of the county used to muster the local forces for service on the Border.

[1] *Proceedings of the Society of Scottish Antiquaries*, 1901, 154-186, where a full account may be found of the recent excavation of this camp.

[2] Now in the National Museum of Antiquities, Edinburgh.

The quaint little parish church of Lyne claims passing notice as a late-pointed building, probably of the early seventeenth century, measuring internally only 34 feet by 11.

About a mile below Lyne Water foot, Tweed receives on her right bank the Manor Water, and here we enter the very realm of romance, for in this solitude dwelt David Ritchie, a deformed recluse, whom Walter Scott saw in 1797, and handed down to fame as 'the Black Dwarf.' 'Bowed Davie' had the head, body, and arms of an immensely powerful man set upon legs so short that his only support seemed to be two enormous finlike feet. Early soured by the heartless derision which met him whenever he went abroad, especially from children, he built himself a cot in a secluded spot below Cademuir, where he lived till his death in 1811, a hermit, uncertain in his behaviour to strangers, but devoted to the beauties of nature and fond of poetry. Sir Thomas Dick Lauder describes 'Bowed Davie' reading aloud Shenstone's *Pastorals* and *Paradise Lost* in a most unmusical voice.

Follow Manor Water above the Black Dwarf's abode, and you find yourself once more, first in pastoral scenes, then amid the desolate hills.

Of old, one of a laird's privileges was the right of ' thirlage '—that is, of compelling his tenants to grind their corn at his own mill. Hence the satirical stanza—

> 'There stand three mills on Manor Water,
>   A fourth at Posso Cleuch ;
> Gin heather bells were corn and bere [barley]
>   They wad hae grist eneugh.'

Ruined peel-towers stud the course of the stream, once of great strength and, one would say, of greater discomfort. Castlehill, for instance, a stronghold of Veitch's ally, the Hoolet o' Barns, is a mere rectangular block, 37 feet 6 inches by 39 feet 6 inches, and with walls 7 feet thick. Domestic arrangements had to be conducted within a total free area of 23 feet 6 inches by 25 feet 6 inches. Posso Castle stands a couple of miles higher up the glen ; but we shall never get on with our journey if we pause to take note of all these towers, erected on every laird's land for alternate purposes of refuge and robbery. Messrs. MacGibbon and Ross have done incalculable service to historians, antiquaries, and architects by their admirable work on Scottish castles. [1] The humblest of these have not escaped notice and description, and readers curious upon such matters will find in the historical notes nearly all that need be told of these ghosts and skeletons.

Resuming the downward course of Tweed, a walk of a mile brings us within view of a castle which, by reason of the beauty of its site and its architectural interest, commands more than passing notice. Originally a keep above ordinary strength, the walls being over ten feet thick, it was much enlarged and beautified in the seventeenth century by the first Earl of Tweeddale, to whose ancestors, the Hays of Yester, Neidpath had belonged for centuries. The earl did not live to see the work finished ; in an evil hour the estate passed into the hands of the last Duke of Queensberry—the notorious ' old Q '—who wrecked the scenery by felling and selling the magnificent timber which clothed this gorge of the Tweed. One

[1] *Castellated and Domestic Architecture of Scotland.* 5 vols.

might have forgiven him, had he shown the grace to replant; but not he! All he cared for was to spite his heir, and to get cash to spend on pimps and prize-fighters in London. On doctors, too, for this wretched old debauchee endeavoured to prolong his worthless existence by paying the French physician, Père Elisée, a sum of money for every day he lived. In addition to this, one Fuller, an apothecary in Piccadilly, sued the duke's executors for £10,000, representing fees for 9340 visits and attendance on 1215 nights during the last seven years and a half of his patient's life, and actually obtained verdict for payment of £7500. Wordsworth visited Neidpath in 1803, eight years after the woods had been felled; and scourged the old reprobate with unaccustomed bitterness in the well-known lines beginning—

'Degenerate Douglas! oh the unworthy lord.'

This work of devastation is about all for which this heir of a noble name is remembered on Tweedside at this day.

A mile below Neidpath, Eddlestone Water joins the Tweed from the north, and at the confluence stands the royal burgh of Peebles, where a bridge of five arches was thrown across the river about the year 1467, and still remains, widened in accordance with modern notions of safety and convenience. Prettily situated, Peebles owes little beauty to the taste of its recent architects. The church of Holy Rood, or the Cross Church, was built by order of Alexander III in 1261, in gratitude for sundry miracles performed at a great cross which was dug up in that year. Fragments of the wreck of this church remain in a modern fir plantation on the west of the town.   It was 102 feet in length, and must have been a beautiful structure, but in 1784 it was dismantled, and used as building material for the present parish church ; an example of the dishonour that may be done by good men to grace and beauty.   The other church of Peebles, the collegiate one of St. Andrew, met with a less inglorious doom.   Erected in 1195, it was burnt irredeemably by the English in 1548, and nothing of it remains now but the tower, which Dr. William Chambers restored at his own charges in 1883—more honour to him had he been less successful in concealing the old work.   He is buried at the foot thereof.

The provost and town council, blind to the true interests of their burgh, have been sadly utilitarian in past years.   Of the city walls few vestiges remain. Even the ancient town cross they permitted Sir John Hay to transplant to his neighbouring park of Kings Meadows in 1807 ; but conscience smote their grandchildren, who obtained restoration of the cross to the town in 1859.

The days of glory for Peebles were those of the early Stuart kings.   It was the centre of a district famous for sport.   There was a royal castle there, now demolished ; it became the Balmoral of the royal family of the day.   Not only so, but it was a centre of gaiety and business for all classes throughout Tweeddale ; [1] so that the modern English joke which represents a Tweeddale man as exclaiming, 'They may talk o' Lunnun and o' Pairis, but for real pleasure—gie me Peebles ! ' was not far from the truth in old times.   At least we have the royal word for it—

[1] Tweeddale proper, as distinct from the Tweed valley consists of the shire of Peebles.

the word of James I. of Scotland, the most accomplished of his dynasty. In his poem *Peblis to the Play*, the king strikes a lower key than in *The King's Quair*, but strikes it with such truth and sympathy with the pleasures of his people that one cannot doubt his kindly nature and quick power of observation. [1]—

> 'At Beltane, when ilk bodie bownis
> To Peblis at the play,
> To heir the singin and the soundis,
> The solace, suth to say,
> Be firth and forest furth they found,
> They graythit tham full gay ;
> God wait that wold they do that stound
> For it was their Feist Day,
>   They said,
> Of Peblis to the play.'

The long poem which follows gives a description, minute as it is graphic, of the incidents of a gala day—rustic courtship, tavern scenes, and home-going—evidently painted from life by one who delighted *desipere in loco*.

Part of 'the play' was horse-racing, an important one, if we may judge from an order by the Lords of Council so late as April 1608, which prohibits the sport because of the risk of bloodshed owing to 'quarrels, private grudges, and miscontentment' existing between families.

The last monarch to visit Peebles was the ill-

[1] The authorship of the poem has been disputed on the high authority of Professor Skeat, mainly on philological grounds. The language and metre are considered to be those of a later date than 1437; but Professor Veitch thought that the discrepancy might be accounted for by oral transmission and the variants of later copyists (*Border History and Poetry*, ii. 55-63). 'The play' does not mean a dramatic performance, but a general festivity.

3

starred Darnley, who spent some time hunting there in 1565.

Five furlongs to the east of Peebles the Gatehope Burn crosses the road on its way to the river, marking the ancient boundary of Ettrick Forest.

In leaving the town the traveller has the choice of keeping to the left bank of the river, passing the towers of Upper and Nether Horsburgh, the ruined strongholds of an ancient family of that name, whose seat is now at the Pirn, on Gala Water, and so on to the pleasant little watering-place of Innerleithen ; or he may cross the bridge and enter Ettrick Forest by way of Traquair. But let him take which way he will, he cannot escape the spell cast upon all this land by Walter Scott ; for Innerleithen proudly claims to be the original of his St. Ronan's Well, and at Traquair one is confronted by the closed gates barring the long, straight avenue leading to Traquair House, flanked by pillars bearing aloft two stone bears, which do duty in the Tullyveolan of *Waverley.* Closed, these gates, and the avenue disused since 1796, when the seventh Earl of Traquair lost his countess, and decreed that the gates should not be opened until another Countess of Traquair should come to the old house. [1] But the title expired with the eighth earl, who died in 1861; on the death of whose sister, Lady Louisa Stuart, in 1875, wanting but four months to complete her hundredth year, the property passed by will to the Hon. Herbert Constable-Maxwell, who has assumed the additional name of Stuart.

The house itself is of great size and extreme

[1] Dr. John Brown says these gates have 'never been opened since the '45' (*Horæ Subsecivæ*—'Minchmoor ').

interest, preserving, as Mr. David MacGibbon has remarked, 'its antique aspect better than any other inhabited house in Scotland. Since the end of the seventeenth century, when the last additions were made, almost nothing seems to have been done to the building beyond the necessary repairs.'[1]

Quair Water rises upon Dun Hill (2433 feet), famous in old time for the quality of the falcons which were reared upon its crags. The memories connected with the Quair are less sanguinary than is usual in the Border land ; her Muse is distinctly of an amatory spirit. Robert Crawford of Drumsoy (died in 1733) was a native of Renfrewshire, but he drew his inspiration from Tweedside. The cream of his verse is *The Bush aboon Traquair*, which it is said he wrote to fit an old air, the words of which had been forgotten. This poem is less tainted with artificial classicism than most others of the seventeenth century, and is supposed to commemorate the unsuccessful wooing of one of the Stuarts of Traquair by young Murray of Philiphaugh.—

> 'My vows, my sighs, like silent air
> Unheeded, never move her.
> At the bonny bush aboon Traquair,
> 'Twas there I first did love her.'

Of the 'bonny bush' itself nothing now remains but a few decrepit birches inside a modern clump planted on a knoll about a mile above Traquair House. Principal Shairp of St. Andrews, visiting the spot in 1867, caught its spirit—

[1] *Castellated and Domestic Architecture of Scotland*, ii. 440.

> 'Now the birks to dust may rot,
>   Names of lovers be forgot,
> Nae lads and lasses there ony mair convene;
>   But the blithe lilt o' yon air
>   Keeps the bush aboon Traquair,
> And the love that ance was there aye fresh and green.'

Nay, the very minister of the parish must yield to the soft influence of the place. The Rev. James Nicol (1769-1819) 'gave himself away' in some very musical lines—

> 'Where Quair rins sweet amang the flowers,
>   Down by yon woody glen, lassie,
> My cottage stands—it shall be yours,
>   Gin ye will be my ain, lassie.
>
> For had I heir'd the British crown,
>   And thou o' low degree, lassie;
> A rustic lad I wad hae grown,
>   Or shared that crown wi' thee, lassie.'

Reluctantly leaving bonny Traquair, four miles or so lands us among the woods of Elibank, and under the walls of Elibank Tower, standing on the foot-slope of Elibank Law (1715 feet). Sir Gideon Murray, descended from Andrew of Blackbarony, who perished at Flodden, and ancestor of Lord Elibank, the present owner, built this castle in 1595; but it is now a wasted ruin, and the modern home of the family is on lower ground near the river.

This Sir Gideon, a person of much authority in the government of James VI., had a wife of a very practical mind, if the story by which she is remembered be well founded. The Murrays had been long at feud with the Scotts; they spent much of

their time lifting each other's cattle.   One night Sir
Gideon caught his enemies in the act, and was lucky
enough to capture young Scott of Harden, heir of
the famous Auld Wat o' Harden.   Now the Murrays
were blessed with three daughters, but never a
husband for any of them.   Under such circumstances
it behoved the prudent mother to be watchful.   She
asked her husband how he intended to deal with his
prisoner.

' Strap him up to the dule-tree,[1] wife,' quoth Sir
Gideon ; ' what else ?'

' Na, na,' replied the lady, ' ye can do better than
that, Sir Gideon, you that has three ill-faured lasses
to marry.   Hang the winsome young laird o' Hard-
en !   Hout na !'

Murray reflected a minute before answering.

' 'Shrew me !' he exclaimed at last, ' but ye 're no
far wrang, my leddy.   Young Harden shall wed wi'
mickle-mou'd Meg, or he'll strap for it.'

Scott was offered his life on these terms : he
vowed he preferred the gallows ; but he changed his
mind at the foot of the dule-tree.   He wedded
muckle-mou'd Meg, who made him an excellent
wife, and Sir Walter Scott traced direct descent from
their third son.   The only obvious discrepancy
between local tradition and history is that his bride's
name was really Agnes Murray, not Margaret.   His
second wife was Margaret Ker of Linton.

A couple of miles below Elibank stands Ashiestiel,
memorable for all time as the first home of Walter
Scott on Tweedside.   He had been appointed Sheriff
of Selkirkshire in 1799, but had hitherto kept his

---

[1] The hanging-tree, a necessary part of the establishment of a baron
who had ' power of pit and gallows.'

little country residence at Lasswade. 'I left,' he says, 'the pleasant cottage I had upon the side of the Esk for the pleasanter banks of the Tweed, in order to comply with the law, which requires that the sheriff be resident, at least during a certain number of months, within his jurisdiction,' and here the seven happiest years of his life were spent. Fruitful years, too ; for though *Waverley* was not yet, Scott was busily garnering that vintage of legend and history whence such an ample stream of narrative and romance should flow in later years. Moreover, it was at Ashiestiel that he composed *The Lay of the Last Minstrel* (1805), *Marmion* (1808), *The Lady of the Lake* (1810), and the introductory epistles to *Marmion.* When Scott resigned the lease of Ashiestiel in 1812 to enter upon possession of Abbotsford, a wider horizon opened before him, but it was crossed with clouds which never darkened his earlier and humbler sphere. The old oak still grows by the river where he had his seat, and the Shirra's Knowe, a little south of the house, has taken permanent rank among the place-names of the district.

Follow the Glenkinnen Burn up from Ashiestiel and you come to the secluded hill-farm of Williamhope, where on a day in 1803 rode together two men of note, Walter Scott and Mungo Park. Mungo, born in the farm of Fowlshiels on Yarrow, had already won fame by five years of African travel, had married the sweetheart of his apprentice days, and had resolved to settle in his native dale, to practise as a surgeon. But the wander-spirit had firm hold over him ; he had not the fortitude to resist proposals from the Government to undertake another exploration of the Gambia and the Niger,

and he was on the eve of departure. As they rode,
Park's horse stumbled. 'A bad omen,' observed
the sheriff. 'Freits[1] follows them that fears them,'
was the traveller's laughing reply ; he struck spurs
into his nag and rode away. 'I stood and looked
after him,' Scott used to say, 'but he never looked
back.' They met no more. Park was slaughtered
by some natives on the Niger some time in the
autumn of 1805.

Older and gloomier memories than this haunt the
ridge of Williamhope.[2] The place was once called
Galeswood, but it took the name of William's Cross
from a memorial stone set up to commemorate the
encounter of two knights named William Douglas.
The elder of these was known as the Knight of
Liddesdale, the son of Sir James Douglas of Lothian,
whose prowess against the English gained for him
the title of Flower of Chivalry. He won back from
them most of the Douglas lands on the Border, but
in 1346 he was taken prisoner, along with young
King David II., at the battle of Neville's Cross. Six
years' imprisonment in the Tower of London sapped
the integrity even of the Flower of Chivalry. He
betrayed the cause by which he had won his renown,
and 'became King Edward's man' on condition of
receiving extensive lands in Annandale and Moffat-
dale.

Meanwhile the younger William, nephew of the
'good Sir James,' and afterwards first Earl of
Douglas, had been educated in France since the
death of his father, Sir Archibald 'the Tineman,' at

[1] Omens.
[2] The suffix 'hope,' so common in Tweeddale and Ettrick, is the
Scandinavian equivalent of the Gaelic 'glen' which prevails in other
districts.

the battle of Halidon Hill in 1333. The Knight of
Liddesdale was his godfather and guardian during
his minority. Returning in 1351 to take up his
lordship, young William found that the Knight had
quietly annexed a good deal of his rightful inheritance, and had allowed his lands to be overrun by
Englishmen. He set to work to recover them and
expel the strangers, but no meeting took place
between godfather and godson until one day, in
August 1353, the young lord found the Knight
hunting in Ettrick Forest, where he had no right to
be. No man knoweth what took place; there would
be high words, followed by swift blades. Perhaps
Lord Douglas had the stronger following. Anyhow,
only one William Douglas rode away from that
meeting. The other lay stark in the greenwood.

Scott's nearest neighbour at Ashiestiel was Alexander Pringle of Whytbank, scion of an immemorial
Border race, who built the present house of Yair.
The name signifies a fish weir, is in fact the same as
the Anglo-Saxon *wer*, a weir or dam. This is one
of the loveliest parts of the Upper Tweed, and meet
tribute has been paid to its beauty by one of her
latest and most faithful lovers.

> 'Brief are man's days at best; perchance
>   I waste my own, who have not seen
> The castled palaces of France
>   Shine on the Loire in summer green.

> And clear and fleet Eurotas still,
>   You tell me, laves his reedy shore,
> And flows beneath the fabled hill
>   Where Dian drove the chase of yore.

And " like a horse unbroken " yet
    The yellow stream with rush and foam,
'Neath tower and bridge and parapet,
    Girdles his ancient mistress, Rome.

I may not see them, but I doubt
    If seen I'd find them half so fair
As ripples of the rising trout
    That feed beneath the elms of Yair.' [1]

Nearly opposite Yair stands the roofless house of Fernielea, once a fine example of seventeenth-century domestic architecture, and the seat of a branch of the Rutherfurd family. How such a charming residence came to be deserted is a puzzle—nobody seems to know—but reverence is its due for one reason, if for no other. It was here that Alison Rutherfurd (1712-1794), a daughter of the house, and afterwards Mrs. Patrick Cockburn, composed one of the two extant versions of that exquisite dirge *The Flowers o' the Forest.* It is remarkable that the other version should have been composed about the same time, say 1750, by Jean Elliot of Minto. The original words which went to the music that inspired both these ladies have been lost saving only the first line—

'I have heard them liltin' at the ewes milkin';'

another fragment—

'I ride single in my saddle,'

and the refrain—

'The Flowers o' the Forest are a' wede [2] away;'

[1] *The Last Cast*, by Andrew Lang.
[2] Withered.

but the air is preserved in the collection of John Skene of Hallyards (*d.* 1644).

Though these verses are so well known, a stanza of each may be quoted for comparison.

Alison Rutherfurd's, which is considered the elder version by a few years, referred to the financial disasters which had overtaken certain families in the neighbourhood of Fernielea.

> ' I 've seen the smiling
> Of fortune beguiling,
> I 've felt all its favours, and found its decay ;
> Sweet was its blessing,
> Kind its caressing,
> But now it is fled, fled—far, far away.
> I 've seen the Forest
> Adorned the foremost,
> With flowers of the fairest, most pleasant and gay ;
> Sae bonny was their blooming,
> Their scents the air perfuming,
> But now they are wither'd, and wede all away. '

Jean Elliot took for her theme a grander catastrophe—the crushing massacre of Flodden Field.

> ' I 've heard them liltin' at the ewe-milkin' [1]
> Lasses a-liltin' before the dawn of day ;
> But now they are moanin' on ilka green loanin',
> The Flowers o' the Forest are a' wede away.
>
> .   .   .   .
>
> Dule and wae for the order sent our lads to the Border !
> The English, for ance, by guile wan the day ;
> The Flowers of the Forest, that foucht aye the foremost,
> The prime o' our land, are cauld in the clay. '

[1] To secure the music of this line ' ewe ' must be pronounced in the Scottish manner ' yow.'

It is a curious literary coincidence that both these ladies, composing independently, should have used the same faulty rhyme—'forest' and 'foremost.'

There are some fine nuts for etymologists to crack in the place-names of Peeblesshire. Some of the farm names have been thrown into jingle by forgotten bards.

> 'Bonnington lakes and Cruikston cakes,
> Kademuir and the Rae ;
> And hungry, hungry Hundelshope,
> And skawed Bell's Brae.'

Again—

> 'Glenkirk and Glencotha, the Mains o' Kilbucho,
> Blendewan and the Raw, Mitchellhill and the Shaw,
> There's a hole abune the Threipland
> Has held them a'.'

The 'hole abune the Threipland' is a wet hollow in a hillside where there is a cave, connected by tradition with Covenanting times, and the rhyme indicates that the people in these farms found a refuge there.

CHAPTER III

ONE may be lightly beguiled into an excursion through Ettrickdale and Yarrow, but it is no easy matter to make escape from these upland vales, so thickly are they peopled with memories of the past.——

> ' There 's a far bell ringing,
> And a phantom voice is singing,
> Of renown for ever clinging
> To the great days done. '

Suppose we take that King of Scots for a guide, whose itinerary is so plainly set forth in the ballad of *The Outlaw Murray*. We may ford the river, as he did, at Cadonfoot, and hear the selfsame music of the shallows that has been sounding all through the centuries ; but after that how sorely changed is every furlong of the way !——

> ' The King was comand through Cadon Ford,
> And full five thousand men was he ;
> They saw the derke foreste them before,
> They thought it awsome for to see. '

Now the whole forest is one vast sheepwalk, and almost the only trees that greet the eye, except a few

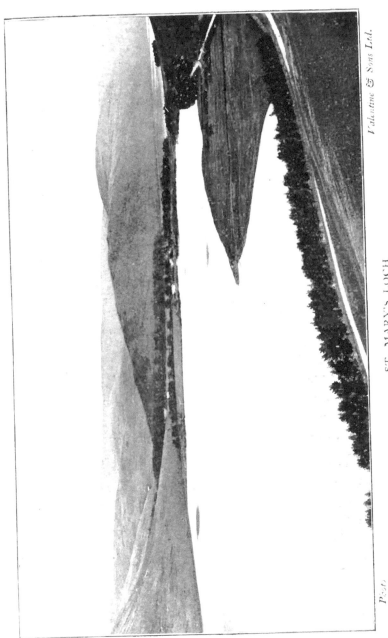

ST. MARY'S LOCH

Valentine & Sons Ltd.

Phot.

scattered birches in the steep cleuchs, are the fine plantations round the Duke of Buccleuch's modern house of Bowhill and Lord Napier's house of Thirlestane.

The king mentioned in the ballad is James IV., and the outlaw is probably John Murray, eighth laird of Philiphaugh, who claimed to hold Ettrick Forest independently of the Crown. King James sent a messenger to call the outlaw to account, who, having found Murray in his castle of Hangingshaw on Yarrow, received defiant answer as follows :—

> ' " Thir lands are mine ! " the Outlaw said,
>   " I ken nae king in Christentie ;
>   Frae Soudron[1] I this foreste wan,
>   When the king nor his knights were not to see. "
> " He desyres you 'll cum to Edinburgh,
>   And hauld of him this foreste free ;
>   And gif ye refuse to do this,
>   He 'll conquess baith thy lands and thee.
> He hath vow'd to cast thy castell down,
>   And mak a widowe o' thy gaye ladye ;
>   He'll hang thy merry men, payr by payr,
>   In ony frith where he may them find. "
> " Ay, by my troth ! " the Outlaw said,
>   " Then would I think me far behinde ;
>   Ere the king my feir countrie get,
>   This land that 's nativest to me,
>   Mony o' his nobles sall be cauld,
>   Their ladyes sall be right wearie. " '

To this challenge the king replied in person and in force, but before proceeding to strong measures he tried to win over his rebellious liege by diplomacy. Strange to say, he succeeded. Scotsmen had not as

[1] Southron, Englishman.

yet learned, as they did later, to mistrust the kingly word. Murray came out into the open, met the king in conference at Penmanscore, and flinched not from repeating his sole claim to be Lord of the Forest. King James knew a man when he saw him : here was one worth the winning. After a long palaver he said—

> ' " Will ye give me the keys of your castle,
>   With the blessing of your fair ladye ?
> I 'll make thee Sheriff of Ettrick Foreste,
>   Surely while upward grows the tree.
> Gif ye be not a traitor to your king,
>   Forfaulted sal ye never be. " '

On these honourable terms the outlaw bowed the knee, and became the king's man ever thereafter. After all, King James has not brought us very far on our way up Ettrickdale ; indeed, he has led us up the tributary Yarrow ; so it will be better to treat these streams in the same way as the others, and trace them rapidly from their sources.

Round the cradle of Ettrick Water, then, stand three majestic sponsors in a semicircle—Capel Fell (2223 feet), Wind Fell (2180 feet), and Ettrick Pen (2269 feet). Ettrick runs the usual course of hill burns for ten miles or more before it passes between the ruined tower of Gamescleuch on the right, built by Simon ' of the Spear, ' and Thirlestane on the left, where Simon's father, John Scott, had his abode. In 1699 William Scott, a lineal descendant of this John, married Elizabeth, heiress of the barony of Napier, who transmitted the title to her son as fifth Baron Napier, great-great-great-grandfather of the present Lord Napier and Ettrick, whose residence remains at Thirlestane.

A mile or so above Gamescleuch, Ettrick receives a burn called Tima, into which the little Red Syke tumbles in much haste from the bare brow of a hill on the east written in the ordnance survey Law Kneis, but pronounced by the shepherds Lan'ease.——

> 'When the Red Syke at e'en sounds loud,
> And the Lan'ease carries a cloud,
> And the corbie croups on the auld thorn,
> We're sure, Willie Wise, there'll be rain the morn.'

There is another stave connected with Tima, commemorating a solitary hag named Meg Linton, a reputed witch, who lived in a hovel called Bogle Sauch, and died of starvation there.——

> 'Auld Meg Linton, o' the Pool o' Midnight haugh,
> Is buried aneath the Bogle Saugh.
> Sae auld Meg Linton is cauld and dead,
> And nocht in her house but a pykit sheeps-head.'

Pool Midnight, an eerie basin in the Tima beside the Bogle Sauch, was the scene of the suicide of Wee Johnnie, a respectable weaver, with ill-fortune and a worse wife.——

> 'Let nane that gaes by the Gatecleugh foot
> Look east or west at the auld birk tree;
> For there, at e'en, will Wee Johnnie be seen,
> Wi' his neck twined round wi' loom-cords three.'

Tima has its source at Tamleuchar, the most desolate spot on Eskdalemuir. A cross stood there once, and many a weary treasure-hunt has been started on the strength of a rhyme connected therewith.——

> ' Atween the wet ground and the dry
> The gold o' Tamleuchar doth lie. '

The land between Tima and the Rankil Burn was the heritage in 1415 of Robert Scott, who exchanged part of it with the Monks of Melrose for the Moorland called Bellenden on the divide between Ettrick and Teviotdale.   The Scotts waxed apace in proportion as the Black Douglases waned, and added land to land in both valleys.   The head of the clan, Sir David Scott of Branxholm, appeared in James III.'s parliament of 1487 as *Dominus de Buccleuch*, a title derived from a farm on the Rankil Burn three miles above its junction with the Ettrick.   Sir Walter Scott, in his notes to *The Lay*, has lent sanction to a shadowy legend connecting this place with an incident of the chase in the days of Kenneth Mac Alpin, who reigned as first King of Scots, 844-859.   The progenitor of the family of Scott is said to have tackled successfully a buck which the king held at bay, and the ravine where this happened was known ever after as the Buck Cleuch.   Heraldry has endorsed the tradition, but has altered the buck into a stag trippant, with golden horns and hoofs, which is the crest of the Duke of Buccleuch in this twentieth century.   Readers may yield what credence they can—*se non è vero è venerevole*—this fact remains, that here is the cradle of a great family ; and further, that Bellenden, being on the ridge dividing Ettrick from Teviotdale, became the mustering-place of the clan, and ' Bellenden ! Bellenden ! ' its slogan or battle-cry.

A little lower down Ettrick Water was the tower of a scion of the house of Scott, Delorain, a name with which Sir Walter took poetic licence, throwing the stress on the first and last syllables. Ettrick men, having no exigencies of metre to serve, invariably accent the second syllable, which reveals the name as a Gaelic one—*dal Orain*, Oran's land.

The hoary ruin of Tushielaw, on the left bank of Ettrick opposite Rankil Burn, is fraught with gloomy memories. Here dwelt Adam Scott, whose lawless doings had earned him the title of 'King of Thieves,' and whose end has been the subject of a good deal of misrepresentation. It has been repeatedly stated that James V. himself apprehended and was present at the hanging of the Laird of Tushielaw and of William Cockburn, laird of Henderland on Meggat Water. The true facts are set forth in the Justiciary Records for 1530, proving that these two gentlemen were apprehended, brought to Edinburgh, tried, and duly beheaded on 18th May, a full month before King James set out upon his memorable excursion to the Borders.[1] Sir Walter Scott of Buccleuch, despite his kinship with both malefactors, was the direct agent, under royal warrant, in their apprehension.

One might linger long in Ettrickdale, musing and maundering over the past, but for considerations of space and time. It is impossible to quit this green upland without a passing tribute to one whose outward personality was thus vigorously sketched by Carlyle in 1832—

' A little red-skinned, stiff sack of a body, with quite the common air of an Ettrick shepherd, except that he has a highish though sloping brow (among his yellow grizzled hair), and two clear little beads of blue or grey eyes that sparkle, if not with thought, yet with animation. I felt interest for the poor " herd body, " wondered to see him blown

[1] Pitcairn's *Criminal Trials*, i. 145.

hither [to London] from his sheepfolds, and how, quite friendless as he was, he went along cheerful, mirthful, musical.'

In Scottish phrase, James Hogg had 'an unco guid consate o' himsel',' as well he might, for his poetical gifts were of no common order, and raised him far above the general run of rural bards. He was born near Ettrick Kirk in 1770, and was trained to his father's calling of shepherd. Like most other men of mark, he inherited his bright intellect from his mother, Margaret Laidlaw, who used to sing to him as a child the old Border ballads. It was her unrivalled knowledge of these that brought the Hoggs a visit from Walter Scott, in his search for material for the third volume of his *Border Minstrelsy*. By that time, 1803, Hogg had published a small volume of *Pastorals*, etc., which fell quite flat. He was at some field work when they brought him word that 'the Shirra and some o' his gang' were at the cottage, and wanted to see him. Mrs. Hogg delighted Scott by chanting the ballad of *Auld Maitland*. He asked her if it had ever been in print. 'O na, na, sir,' said she, 'there never was ane o' my sangs prentit till ye prentit them yoursel', an' ye hae spoilt them a'thegither. They were made for singing, an no' for reading, an' they'll never be sung nae mair.' Scott laughed merrily, and answered the dame by a couplet from Wordsworth. 'Ye'll find,' she persisted, 'that it's a' true that I'm tellin' ye.' And so it has proved; for, as James Hogg himself said, 'from that day to this, these songs, which were the amusement of many a long winter evening, have never been sung more.'

Few people read the Ettrick Shepherd now ; some love his verse—*When the Kye comes Hame*, for example—without any suspicion of the authorship ; but the late Professor Ferrier's judgment holds good, pronouncing him to be, 'after Burns, *proximus sed longo intervallo*, the greatest poet that has ever sprung from the bosom of the common people.' James Hogg was laid in the lonely kirkyard of Ettrick : fitting epitaph from his own hand might have been found in one of his early poems—

> ' Flow, my Ettrick ! it was thee
> Into life that first did drap me ;
> Thee I'll sing, and when I dee
> Thou wilt lend a sod to hap me.
> Pausing swains will say, and weep,
> " Here our Shepherd lies asleep. " '

Before quitting Ettrick, note must be made of yet another of those towers which stud all this Border-land so closely. Oakwood has fared better than many of them, being still wind and weather tight, although the upper floors are used only as a granary and storehouse, and the ground floor as a cartshed. As the property of Lord Polwarth, it remains in the family of Scott, who have owned it since 1517, when it was taken from Lord Home and granted by James V. to Michael Scott. Here, doubtless, is the source of that local tradition which affirms that in the thirteenth century the wizard Michael Scott of Balwearie was the lord of Oakwood. Sir Walter Scott has embalmed the following story among those notes to *The Lay* which some people find more to their taste than the poem itself.

When Michael came to live at Oakwood, he heard

a great deal about the Witch of Falsehope, a sorceress living on the opposite side of Ettrick Water.
Desiring to test her quality, he rode over one day,
dismounted, and, leaving his horse and greyhounds
in charge of his serving-man, entered the house.
The witch was jealous of the wizard ; would answer
no questions, and denied having any supernatural
power.   Michael having carelessly laid his wand upon
the table, the sorceress snatched it up and struck him.
Aware that mischief had been wrought upon him,
Michael beat a hasty retreat.   As he moved, his body
shrank, his ears lengthened, his raiment changed to
fur, and he crossed the threshold in the form of a
hare.   ' Haloo ! ' cried his man, ' haloo-loo-loo ! ' and
slipped the greyhounds upon the quarry.   Michael
ran a cruel course, finally escaping into the sewer of
his own tower, where he caught his breath, reversed
the spell, and reappeared in his proper habit.

Michael would have his revenge upon the male-
volent witch.   Riding one day in harvest to the brae
above her house, he sent his servant to ask her for
some bread for his greyhounds.   She was in the act
of baking for the reapers, but she told the fellow to
go to—some other place.   The man then acted as his
master had instructed him in the not unexpected
event of a refusal.   He placed a paper over the house
door, inscribed with cabalistic signs, and with the following couplet—

> ' Maister Michael Scott's man
> Sought meat and gat nain.'

Immediately the witch began dancing round the fire,
which, as usual in primitive households, was in the

middle of the floor, incessantly repeating the rhyme. Dinner-time arrived: the farmer sent down one of the reapers to fetch the food. The first messenger caught the infection, and joined in the dance; so did the next, and the next, until the house was full of dancing people, all shouting the rhyme at the top of their voices. Last of all came the farmer himself, who, hearing the din, looked cautiously through the window and beheld his wife in the last stage of exhaustion, dragged round the fire by his maddened workers. Instantly it occurred to him that she had offended the warlock. He made speed to Oakwood Tower, and besought Michael to reverse the spell upon his household.

'Go back to your house,' was the reply, 'enter it backwards, and with your left hand take the ticket from over the door.'

Which the agitated husband did, and all fell calm again, though the dinner was spoilt.

Though Michael Scott the Wizard probably never was at Oakwood, the adventure with the witch may have befallen his namesake; for that a witch there was is testified by a summit on Falsehope (properly Fauldshope, the glen of the sheepfolds), still called Witchie Hill.

As we took James IV. as a guide into Ettrick Forest, so we may follow his son James V. along the course of Yarrow. Like many a Stuart, this monarch, who made such a sorry end, began his reign with portentous energy. We have seen how he set Buccleuch to catch Henderland and Tushielaw. It was not enough: the Marches continued 'in grete ruyne and out of all gude order,' Buccleuch himself being the cause of much of the mischief. So in 1530 King

James clapped him in prison, and at the same time sent into durance the Lords Maxwell, Home, Bothwell, and other Border lairds, seeing that, in Sir James Balfour's words, 'they had winked at the willanies' constantly committed by their kinsmen and dependants.   Gathering a strong force, therefore, the king rode up Yarrow to Meggatdale, where he began his campaign with a great hunting.   Eighteen score of harts were slain ; poor sport, one would say, seeing that it was but the month of June, and the velvet was thick and tender on their horns.   All manner of small game, too, was taken by hawks.   Having provisioned his troops in this agreeable fashion, the king took in hand the grim part of the business.   He rode by what still bears the name of the King's Road, from St. Mary's Loch to Ettrick Water, across Bellenden Moor, and so into Teviotdale, where we shall take later note of his proceedings.

It cannot be the size of St. Mary's Loch that has earned it fame, seeing that it measures but three miles in length, and at no part exceeds half a mile in breadth ; and many another mere excels its unadorned beauty, albeit Wordsworth, gentlest but most unequal of poets, felt moved to utter this deplorable stanza—

> ' Throughout her depths St. Mary's Lake
>   Is visibly delighted ;
> For not a feature of those hills
>   Is in the mirror slighted. '

Neither can it be the quality of the angling that has made the name of this lake familiar to millions who have never looked upon its waters, for its trout were ever inferior in size and numbers to those of Meggat[1] and Yarrow. It was the solitude of hills and water and their message from an elder world that drew hither men like Christopher North, John Gibson Lockhart, and the Ettrick Shepherd, that endeared to them Tibbie Sheils's little tavern on the narrow neck of meadow separating St. Mary's Loch from the Loch of the Lowes. Here they argued, laughed, wrote, sang, and, it must be added, drank after a fashion that finds favour with us no more. *Noctes Ambrosianæ* had a brilliant day, but it is a day that is dead ; their boisterous pugnacity and forced style have lost the charm that fascinated our grandsires. Nevertheless the Ettrick Shepherd remains the *genius loci*. What Burns did for the West, and Walter Scott for all the North, James Hogg achieved for St. Mary's Loch : he made it known to all the world. It is meet, therefore, that his plaided figure, in good Denholm freestone, should preside over the scene. The statue was erected in 1860 at the foot of Chapelhope, on the far side of the loch from Altrive, where he farmed so badly and wrote so well.

On the north-west shore of the loch, opposite Altrive, is the graveyard and site of St. Mary's Church, which gave the lake its name. The destruction of this little shrine—*Sancta Maria de Lacubus*—was a characteristic episode in the blood-feud between the Scotts and the Cranstouns. In prosecuting this warfare, Janet, Lady Buccleuch, with two hundred spearmen, pursued the laird of Cranstoun on 25th June 1557, till he sought sanctuary in the kirk. Most unluckily for the fugitive, the parish priest was a

[1] There is another stream called Meggat Water, on the western watershed, a tributary of the Dumfriesshire Esk.

Scott, and took sides with the pursuers. Cranstoun, it seems, escaped with his life, for the parties were subsequently bound over to keep the peace (which assuredly they did not do), but the kirk was burnt down, and was never rebuilt.

Every step of the way down Yarrow is interwoven with song, generally breathing of sore hearts and severed lovers, sudden death and widowed hearths. Some of these ballads record the fortune or the fate of individuals whose names have been as clean forgotten as those of the bards themselves. Such is the tender dirge of *Willie*—

> ' Willie 's rare and Willie 's fair
>   And Willie 's wondrous bonny,
> And Willie hecht [1] to marry me,
>   Gin e'er he married ony.
>
> Yestreen I made my bed fu' braid ;
>   This night I 'll make it narrow ;
> For a' the livelong winter night
>   I lie twined [2] o' my marrow.
>
> O came ye by the waterside ?
>   Pu'd you the rose or lily ?
> Or came ye by the meadow green ?
>   Or saw ye my sweet Willie ?
>
> She sought him east, she sought him west,
>   She sought him braid and narrow ;
> Syne in the cleaving of a craig
>   She found him drowned in Yarrow.'

In the ballad known as *The Douglas Tragedy*, the identity of the actors cannot be established, but the

[1] Promised.
[2] Bereaved.

scene is laid with more than usual precision. In the old tower of Blackhouse, far up the Douglas Burn, a tributary of Yarrow, a certain—rather an uncertain—Lord Douglas is represented as living with his wife, seven sons, and two daughters. To judge of the scale of accommodation by the ruin that remains, it must have been a tight fit for so large a family, and difficult for any of them to accomplish anything clandestine. Howbeit, one night the elder daughter eloped with one Lord William, and her mother, discovering it, roused the family.—

> ' " Rise up, rise up now, Lord Douglas," she says,
> " And put on your armour so bright ;
> Let it never be said that a daughter of thine
> Was married to a lord under night.
>
> Rise up, rise up, my seven bold sons,
> And put on your armour so bright,
> And take better care of your youngest sister,
> For your eldest's awa the last night. " '

Lord Douglas and his seven sons set out in pursuit, and overtook the fugitives. Lord William slew the seven brothers, and turned upon the father.

> ' " O hold your hand, Lord William," she said,
> " For your strokes they are wondrous sair ;
> True lovers I can get many a ane,
> But a father I can get never mair. " '

Lord William bids her choose between father and lover ; she chooses the lover, of course ; down goes the father, and the lovers ride away.

'O they rade on, and on they rade,
    And a' by the light o' the moon,
Until they came to yon wan water,
    And there they lighted doun.

They lighted doun to tak a drink
    Of the spring that runs sae clear ;
And doun the stream ran his gude heart's blood,
    And sair she 'gan to fear.

" Hold up, hold up ! Lord William, " she says,
    " For I fear that you are slain. "
" 'Tis nocht but the shade o' my scarlet cloak
    That shines in the water sae plain. " '

But Lord William has got the death-stroke.   Just as
the lovers arrive at his mother's door he breathes his
last.

' Lord William was dead lang ere midnight,
    Lady Marg'ret lang ere day ;
And all true lovers that go thegither
    May they have mair luck than they. '

On the hillside above Blackhouse, 1180 feet above
the sea, stand what are called the Douglas Stones,
supposed to be seven in number, and to mark where
the seven brothers fell.   But, as Professor Veitch has
explained with heartless candour, there are not seven
stones, but thirteen, and these are ' obviously greatly
older than any reasonable date which can be assigned
to the story in the ballad. '[1]   They form, in short,
one of those prehistoric circles so commonly and so
unwarrantably termed Druidical.

One cannot pass away from Yarrow without notic-

[1] *Border History and Poetry*, ii. 177.

ing another of its lays, mournful though it be, like
all its early minstrelsy, and harping on a similar
theme—the violent death of lover or husband.
There has been much discussion about the chief actors
in the tragedy of the *Dowie Dens of Yarrow.* They
were both Scotts, you see; and though it be possible
to identify individuals in this most prolific clan so long
as they are fighting side by side against 'our auld
enemy of Ingland,' when they take to cutting one
another's throats—*passa!* This much seems pretty
clear, that in the early years of the seventeenth
century one Walter Scott eloped with Grizel Scott of
Thirlestane; and this more is certain, that on 22nd
October 1616 four gentlemen of the name of Scott,
kinsmen and allies of Thirlestane, were summoned at
the kirk of the Forest 'to hear themselves excom-
municat for the horrible slaughter of Walter Scott.'
The culprits put in no appearance, and there the
matter ends, so far as history is concerned. The scene
of the slaughter is traditionally laid in Deuchar
Swire, near the present parish kirk.

> ' " Yestreen I dreamed a dolefu' dream ;
>   I fear there will be sorrow ;
> I dreamed I pu'd the heather green
>   Wi' my true love on Yarrow.
>
> .   .   .   .   .
>
> But in the glen strove armèd men ;
>   They've wrought me dule and sorrow ;
> They've slain—they've slain the comeliest swain—
>   He bleeding lies on Yarrow. "

> She kissed his cheek, she kaimed his hair,
>   She searched his wounds all thorough ;

She kissed them till her lips grew red,
    On the dowie houms o' Yarrow.' [1]

All through the eighteenth and nineteenth centuries
the dirge-like strain flows on—Hamiltoun of Ban-
gour, John Logan, William Laidlaw, James Hogg,
John Wilson ('Christopher North'), Walter Scott,
Henry Liddell—how many more have yielded to the
spirit of this vale ! They may not be numbered ; but
that the spell is still potent let these stanzas, not many
years from the mint, testify—

' September—and the sun was low,
    The tender greens were flecked with yellow,
And autumn's ardent after-glow
    Made Yarrow's upland rich and mellow.

.   .   .   .

No sound, no word, from field or ford,
    Nor breath of wind to float a feather,
While Yarrow's murmuring waters poured
    A lonely music through the heather.

.   .   .   .   .

O Yarrow ! garlanded with rhyme
    That clothes thee in a mournful glory,
Though sunsets of an elder time
    Had never crowned thee with a story,

---

[1] Professor Veitch was of opinion that *Willie's drowned in Yarrow*
and the *Dowie Dens* had their origin in the same incident, and considered
these two ballads as variants of a single original version, which he
published for the first time (*Border History and Poetry*, ii. 194). Moreover, he inclined to identify the heroine with Mary Scott of Dryhope,
the Flower of Yarrow, who afterwards married Wat of Harden in 1576.
Veitch made a lifelong study of Border minstrelsy, and was far more
scrupulous than Scott in adhering closely to the current versions.
Passed from mouth to mouth and generation to generation, it is easy to
imagine how inextricably the characters and incidents in these ballads
became confused with each other.

Still would I wander by thy stream,
  Still listen to thy lonely singing,
That gives me back the golden dream
  Through which old echoes yet are ringing.

Love's sunshine ! sorrow's bitter blast !
  Dear Yarrow, we have seen together ;
For years have come and years have past
  Since first we met among the heather.

Ah ! those indeed were happy hours
  When first I knew thee, gentle river ;
But now thy bonny birken bowers
  To me, alas ! are changed for ever.

The best, the dearest, all have gone,
  Gone like the bloom upon the heather,
And left us singing here alone
  Beside life's cold and winter weather.

I too pass on ; but when I 'm dead,
  Thou still shalt sing by night and morrow,
And help the aching heart and head
  To bear the burden of its sorrow.

The summer flowers shall linger yet,
  Where all thy mossy margins guide thee,
And minstrels, met as we have met,
  Shall sit and sing their songs beside thee.'

These verses appeared in a volume entitled *Poems*,
by J.B. Selkirk, 1883. The real name of the poet
was James Brown, who was a partner in the firm of
J.H. Brown and Co., tweed manufacturers in Selkirk.
Born in Galashiels in 1832, he continued in the business of Messrs. J. & H. Brown until late in life, when

failing health compelled him to retire.   In July 1899
he received a testimonial locally subscribed, which,
with a grant of £150 from the Civil list fund
amounted to £440.   He died on 27th December
1904.   Five years previously he had chanted his swan-
song in *Blackwood's Magazine.*—

THE FALL OF THE CURTAIN

'The curtain's falling and the lights burn low ;
So, with God's help, I'm ready now to go.
I've seen life's melodrama—paid the price—
Have known its loves and losses, hopes and fears,
The laughter and the tears,
And now, God knows, I would not see it twice.

I've crossed life's ocean, faced its blinding foam,
But now, Heaven whispers, I am nearing home ;
And though a storm-tossed hull I reach the shore,
A thing of tatter'd sheets and broken spars,
Naked against the stars,
I soon shall be at peace for evermore.

For if again I pass these waters through,
I know the kingdom I am sailing to.
What boots it where I lie ?—beneath the sod,
Or down the dark impenetrable deep
Where wayward seamen sleep—
All gates are good through which we pass to God.'

One great treat that awaits the traveller through
this Border land is to watch a shepherd's collies at
work.   Collies were all the rage a few years ago as
pets for fashionable folk ; and very easily the rascals
became resigned to a life of compulsory indolence.

Now their reign is over, and Scots terriers are all the vogue; nor is that to be mourned, for it is but a sorry thing to see a collie loafing about the parks and streets of London, pampered and combed, with never a chance of putting to the test his fleet sagacity, his consummate understanding of an hereditary calling. In the showrooms collies still hold a favoured place; more than one fashionable sire has brought the exorbitant price of a thousand guineas. But here again it is not the peculiar qualities of the race that command esteem. The judges have decreed an arbitrary and fictitious standard of excellence, founded upon trivial points such as length of nose, colour of coat, and so on. Hear a note by Dr. John Brown, author of *Rab and His Friends*, as he was coming down off Minchmoor.—

'We now descended into Yarrow, and forgathered with a shepherd who was taking his lambs over to the great Melrose fair. He was a fine specimen of a border herd— young, tall, sagacious, self-contained, and free in speech and air. We got his heart by praising his dog "Jed," a very fine collie, black and comely, gentle and keen. "Ay, she's a fell yin; she can do a' but speak." On asking him whether the sheep dogs needed much teaching—"Whyles ay and whyles no. Her kind (Jed's) needs nane. She sooks't wi' her mither's milk." On asking him if the dogs were ever sold, he said—"Never, but at an orra [odd] time. Naebody wad sell a gude dowg, and naebody wad buy an ill yin."'

Yarrow loses itself in Ettrick Water below the meadow called Carterhaugh, the scene of the fairy-tale of *Young Tamlane*, which, altered and modernised though it be, is undoubtedly one of the most ancient pieces of Scottish minstrelsy. Whereas the ballad consists of more than sixty stanzas, it would be unprofitable to quote more than relates to the crisis. Tamlane, a corruption of Thomelin, or little Thomas, having been spirited away by the Queen of the Fairies at nine years old, grew no more in stature from that day, and as he was known to haunt the Carterhaugh, and to be of a dangerously amative nature, maidens were strictly cautioned to avoid that spot. This was quite enough to fire the curiosity of a certain wayward and beautiful Janet—

> 'She prinked hersell and prinned hersell
>   By the ae light o' the mune,
> And she's awa to Carterhaugh
>   To speak wi' young Tamlane.'

She met him, sure enough, and, as was more serious, bore him a son. Then Tamlane tells her his story, and explains how he may be delivered from Elfland. He bade her wait at Miles' Cross on Hallow E'en (31st October), when the fairy folk would ride past, and instructed her how she was to act for his deliverance.—

> 'Gloomy, gloomy was the night
>   And eiry was the way,
> And fair Janet in her green mantle
>   To Miles' Cross she did gae.
>
> Betwixt the hours of twelve and one
>   A north wind tore the bent,
> And straight she heard strange elritch sounds
>   Upon the wind that went.

About the dead hour of the night
　　She heard the bridles ring ;
And Janet was as glad o' that
　　As ony earthly thing.

And first gaed by the black black steed,
　　And then gaed by the brown ;
But fast she gripped the milk-white steed
　　And pu'd the rider down.

She pu'd him frae the milk-white steed,
　　And loot the bridle fa',
And up there raise an erlish cry—
　　" He's won amang us a' ! "

They shaped him in fair Janet's arms
　　An esk but and an ether, [1]
She held him fast in every shape
　　To be her bairn's father.

They shaped him in her arms at last
　　A mother-naked man ;
She wrapped him in her green mantle
　　And sae her true love wan.'

Then there is a terrible scene with the Queen of
the Fairies, who vows that had she known what was
coming she would have torn out Tamlane's eyes and
heart, and replaced them with wooden orbs and a
heart of stone ; but Janet has broken the spell, and
for aught that is known to the contrary, Tamlane
made her an exemplary husband.

The most notable ruin on Yarrow is that of Newark, a name borne by four other castles in Scotland,
besides several in England. This one, about a mile

[1] A newt and also an adder.

above Bowhill, on the right bank of the river, is referred to as the 'new werke' in a charter to Archibald, Earl of Douglas, in 1423, so it was probably built not long before that date in place of an older fortress. The Forests of Ettrick and Selkirk, being originally part of the private patrimony of the kings of Scots, were granted in free regality to the Good Sir James of Douglas by Robert I. in 1325, in token whereof the king placed an emerald ring upon his faithful baron's finger.[1] The kings of England continued to claim these forests so late as 1403, when Henry IV. granted them to Percy, Earl of Northumberland, with the significant proviso, 'so far as it was in his power to give.' The 'Black Douglas' retained the Forests until the fall of that house in the person of the last earl in 1455, when the lands were declared to be perpetually annexed to the Crown. In 1476 James III. bestowed Newark upon his queen, Margaret of Denmark, and although the 'Red Douglas' continued in favour during the next reign, and the chief of that branch, the Earl of Angus, was appointed Sheriff of Roxburgh, Selkirk, Peebles, and Lanark, James IV. retained the Forests as his patrimony, and Newark as his own house. He granted Ettrick Forest and Newark to his queen, Margaret Tudor, who, it will be remembered, married Angus within a year of her consort's death at Flodden. In 1522 she offered Angus a free gift of the Forest if he would consent to a divorce. These and many other events in the history of the old castle are brought freshly to mind by the royal arms sculptured on the west gable.

[1] 'The Emerald Charter' is printed in Robertson's *Index*, p. 10, No. 26, and in Sir William Fraser's *Douglas Book*, iii. 11.

It was in this massive keep, roofless now, and reft of all its fine freestone coigns, that the Duchess of Monmouth spent her widowhood after the execution of her husband in 1685. It was here that Walter Scott represented her receiving the Last Minstrel and listening to his Lay. It was 'new' no longer when Lord Grey captured it in 1548 for Edward VI.; still less so when it was garrisoned by Cromwell's troops after the battle of Dunbar in 1650.

Next to Newark lies Bowhill, on the slopes of Pernassie Hill, between the confluent streams of Ettrick and Yarrow. It is the manor-house of the great Forest estates, acquired by the Duke of Buccleuch no longer ago than the middle of the eighteenth century; but in the sixteenth century it was the property of a family of Scotts, cadets of Thirlestane; William Scott, brother of the laird of Bowhill or Bolhill, being one of the three-and-thirty stalwarts who rode with Buccleuch to the rescue of Kinmont Willie.

Scott of Bowhill was both cause and actor in a bloody tragedy in the year 1600. Young Archibald Napier of Merchistoun having complained to him that a valuable horse had been stolen from his house of Mure, Scott detected a covert insinuation in Napier's words, drew upon him, and bade him defend himself or die. Napier, having no ill-will against the other, avoided an encounter—in other words, took to his heels; but Scott dogged him all day, and 'at the evning focht him in the stret of the gait' [narrow part of the road] 'betwix low dykes, quhair he culd nocht flei.' Thus brought to bay, Napier fought gallantly, and slew his man. The case of aggression was so clear against Scott that

Napier was not put upon his trial. Nevertheless, blood for blood was the inexorable social code. The three brothers of the dead man, together with other Scotts, and young Crichton of Sanquhar, waylaid Napier beside his own house, the Wowmet, near Edinburgh, and there did him to death. For this atrocious crime no penalty was exacted. The murderers, indeed, were 'put to the horn' as rebels ; but their chief, the puissant Buccleuch, took up their cause, and tried to compromise with the Napiers for £1000. Alexander, brother of the murdered Archibald, would not hear of it. 'All is dishonorabell,' quoth he, 'quhair thair is not eie for eie and tuith for tuith.' The case was still unsettled when Alexander took his seat on the bench in 1626 as a Lord of Session (Lord Lauriston), and remained so until the two families were auspiciously united by the marriage of William Scott of Thirlestane to Margaret, Baroness Napier of Merchiston, in 1699.

Below the confluence of Ettrick and Yarrow is Philiphaugh, anciently Fulhophalch—the haugh or meadow of the foul hope, or boggy glen—a place which all Scotsmen must hold in memory, mournful or gladsome, according as their sympathies go with King or Covenant. It was here that the star of Montrose set, to rise no more. A series of brilliant victories in the north—Tippermuir, Aberdeen, Inverlochy, Auldearn, Alford, and Kilsyth—had wellnigh cleared the country of Covenanters : but he had parted with most of his Highlanders, always a difficult race to hold in hand after a spell of fighting. Three thousand had left him because he would not let them plunder Glasgow ; Colkitto had marched against Argyll in Kintyre ; the Gordons, taking offence at some fancied slight to their chief, went home in a body. Keeping his Irish levies together, Montrose marched to Kelso, where he had been promised fresh troops by the Lords Traquair, Home, Roxburgh, and others. These promises were indifferently kept by some of these gentry, and broken by the rest ; indeed, Traquair is suspected of having kept General Leslie, who lay at Berwick, informed of Montrose's movements, while Home and Roxburgh allowed themselves to be taken prisoners. Montrose then marched up the Tweed, pitched his camp on the flat ground to the west of Ettrick Water, [1] lying himself at Selkirk on the east bank on the night of 12th September 1645. Next morning Leslie, under cover of a fog, it is said, surprised the camp, coming round the north flank of Lingly Hill, falling on Montrose's left flank, and so obtaining an easy victory.

In a metrical account of the battle, which has more spice of a partisan ditty than lilt of an old ballad, Leslie is represented as picking up an old fellow at the Lingly Burn, who, having a good hatred of Montrose, offered to lead the way to where he was encamped.—

> ' " O were ye ever a soldier ? "
>   Sir David Lesly said.
>   " O yes : I was at Solway flow
>   Where we were all betrayed. '

---

[1] 'On the present cricket-ground of Selkirk,' says Mr. A. Lang (*History of Scotland*, iii. 157).

[2] If he meant the battle of Solway Moss, he must indeed have been an old man, for that was in 1542.

"Again I was at curst Dunbar
　　And was a prisoner ta'en ;[1]
And mony a weary night and day
　　In prison I hae laen."

"If ye will lead these men aright,
　　Rewarded shall ye be ;
But if that you a traitor prove,
　　I 'll hang thee on a tree."

"Sir, I will not a traitor prove ;
　　Montrose hath plundered me ;
I 'll do my best to banish him
　　Awa' frae this countrie."

He halved his men in equal parts,
　　His purpose to fulfil ;
The one part kept the waterside,
　　The other gaed round the hill.

The nether party fired brisk,
　　They turned, and seemed to rin ;
And then they a' came frae the trench,
　　And cried, "The day's our ain !"

The rest then ran into the trench,
　　And loosed their cannons a' ;
And thus, between his armies twa,
　　He made them fast to fa'.

Now let us a' for Lesly pray,
　　And his brave company !
For they hae vanquished great Montrose,
　　Our cruel enemy.'

[1] This is puzzling too, for the battle of Dunbar was on 3rd September 1650.

Montrose, with forty horse, rode to Traquair, where he did *not* find the perfidious earl, and thence escaped to the north. His Irish contingent made a fine stand : five-sixths of them fell ; the remainder surrendered upon promise of quarter, but when they claimed their lives it was explained to them that the promise was a personal one to their adjutant, Stuart. They were marched into a field at Newark, and shot down in batches, at a place still known as the Slain-men's-lee. [1]

A mile and a half below the junction of Ettrick and Yarrow stands the town of Selkirk, the Sele-chirche of the twelfth century—the church of the shieling, or shepherd's hut. Like Galashiels, the shieling on Gala Water, the chief industry of Selkirk has ceased to be that of shepherds and hunters ; an important woollen manufacture has sprung up, and this ancient burgh of David I. now has a population of more than 11,000.[2] The woollen mills have sup-planted another industry, that of shoemaking, for which the town was famous a couple of hundred years ago. In 1745 it supplied more than 3000 pairs of shoes to the requisition of Prince Charlie's Highland commissariat.

As the longbow was the national weapon of Englishmen, so the Scots relied on the pike, and never became decently proficient as archers. But the bowmen of Ettrick and Selkirk Forests were an exception. At the battle of Falkirk in 1298, where King Edward broke the power of Wallace, Sir John le Steward of Bonkill commanded a fine contingent

[1] This is the best that can be made out of contemporary accounts of this affair, which are very contradictory.
[2] Including the royal burgh and police burgh.

of them.   They were ranged between the ' schilt-
romes, ' or solid clumps of pikemen ; and when the
Scottish cavalry, taken in flank, galloped off the
field, the ' Flowers of the Forest ' were cut to pieces
with their leader.   Walter of Hemingburgh, a contemporary English chronicler, testifies to their
devotion, and to their fine stature and handsome
features. [1]

Selkirk was avenged at Bannockburn, where her
bowmen did timely service ; but of eighty ' souters '
who marched to Flodden it is said that only their
leader, William Brydone, town-clerk, returned to
the Forest.   The standard, which was long revered
as one which Brydone captured and brought home
with him, is still preserved in the old burgh ; but
the graceless lads who used to throw stones at it as
the ' Weaver's Dishclout ' were not far wrong in
the matter of its true origin, for there can be little
doubt that it was but a trade ensign.

William Brydone blamed the Homes for the loss
of his comrades by failing to support them in the
crisis of the battle.   Hence the well-known ditty—

THE SOUTERS O' SELKIRK

' Up wi' the souters o' Selkirk
    And down wi' the fazart ' Lord Home !
But up wi' ilka braw callant
    That sews the single-soled shoon.
And up wi' the lads o' the Forest
    That ne'er to the Southron wad yield !

[1] ' Homines elegantis formæ et proceræ staturæ.'
[2] Craven.

But deil scoup o' Home and his menzie [1]
    That stude sae abiegh [2] on the field.

Fye on the green and the yellow ! [3]
    The craw-hearted loons o' the Merse ;
But here's to the souters o' Selkirk,
    The elshin, the lingle and birse.
Then up wi' the Souters o' Selkirk !
    For they are baith trusty and leal ;
And up wi' the lads o' the Forest,
    And down wi' the Merse to the deil ! '

Purists have attempted to assign to this spirited stave an origin in a football match between Selkirk and the Merse. No doubt it was adapted, as much popular verse has been, to various events in the experience of modern burghers ; but the poem bears the genuine stamp of antiquity. The ' fazart ' lord was executed on a charge of treason three years after Flodden ; but it does not follow that the charge was founded upon fact.

In 1113 Earl David, afterwards King of Scots, founded in Selkirk a Tyronensian abbey, which was moved a few years later to Kelso. [4]

Two hundred years later, in September 1309,

[1] Men—pronounced ' menyie ', the z representing in Scottish orthography the consonantal y.
[2] Aloof.
[3] The liveries of the Homes.
[4] The signatures to the original charter to the Abbey of Selkirk are interesting as showing how many Norman knights David brought with him from the court of England. Out of twenty-eight names, eleven are Norman, including Robert de Brus, first Lord of Annandale, and ancestor of Robert I. of Scotland. There are also nine Saxon signatures and one Celtic, besides those of Queen Matilda, the Bishop of Glasgow, etc. The Gaelic etymology of Yarrow is well preserved in this charter, where the name is written ' Garua' = garbh, rough. Doubtless it would be originally amhuinn garbh, the rough water, the same as ' Garry ' in Perthshire and Inverness-shire.

Edward II. invaded Scotland by an unusual route. The accustomed lines of English invasion were by Berwick or Roxburgh on the East March, or by Carlisle and Annandale on the West March. This time Edward came by Selkirk, and penetrated as far as Linlithgow. Bruce pursued his usual strategy, avoiding a pitched battle, and driving off cattle and all manner of supplies, so that the English army was forced to retire before winter, in order to avoid starvation. Negotiations for peace having been opened, King Robert met the English commissioners at Selkirk before Christmas. A further meeting was fixed to take place at Melrose, but the King of Scots, warned that treachery was intended, avoided the same, and the war went on.

NEWARK CASTLE

Valentine & Sons Ltd.

Phot.

CHAPTER IV

ABBOTSFORD, MELROSE, AND EILDON

IN the year 1525 the Red Douglas, Archibald, sixth Earl of Angus, was appointed Warden of the East and Middle Marches, which did so well please Henry VIII. of England, that he directed Dr. Magnus to present the earl with a gift of £100. Angus had also been made guardian to his stepson, young King James V., in rotation with certain other nobles, each to hold office for one year in succession. The year of Angus ended on 1st November 1525, when his deadly rival, the Earl of Arran, should succeed him. To suffer this would be fatal to Angus's ascendency; nay, it would set him on the sure road to the scaffold; for the Red Douglas had as many foes in Scotland as he had friends in England. So he made use of power while it was his to hold the person of the King, and none dare say him nay. None, at least, save bold Sir Walter Scott—Wicked Wat of Branxholm, Lord of Buccleuch—who, it is said, received a secret entreaty from the young King for deliverance from the thraldom of his stepfather.

Accordingly, in the late summer of 1526, Buccleuch seized his opportunity when Angus was returning with King James from a perambulation of the Marches. The Court, on its way to Edinburgh, lay a night at Melrose. Next morning, when Angus and the King set forth with an escort of three hundred spears, they found the way to the bridge held by Buccleuch with a party of six hundred. Angus demanded a passage in name of the King. Buccleuch replied that he knew the King's mind better than Angus. Then Angus, committing the King to the custody of his brother, Sir George Douglas of Pittendreich, endeavoured to force a passage. A brisk encounter took place in the fields of Darnwick, and matters were going ill with Angus, when he received timely reinforcement. Lord Home, with the Kers of Cessford and Fernyhirst, had bidden adieu to the King in Melrose. Word of the affray was brought to them; they galloped out to Darnwick with a squadron of eighty horse, and charged the Scotts on their flank with such fury that they broke and fled. However, the Scotts were at all times awkward customers to follow; at a spot still called Turn-again they stood at bay, and one named Elliot slew Ker of Cessford, and so broke the pursuit. Lockhart has put on record how Sir Walter Scott's affection was early nailed to this spot.

'I have often heard him tell that, when travelling in his boyhood with his father from Selkirk to Melrose, the old man suddenly desired the carriage to halt at the foot of an eminence, and said, "We must get out here, Walter, and see a thing quite in your line." His father then conducted him to a rude stone on the edge of an acclivity about half a mile above the Tweed at Abbotsford, which marks the spot—

> Where Home and Douglas in the van
> Bore down Buccleuch's retreating clan,
> Till gallant Cessford's life-blood dear
> Reeked on dark Elliot's border spear.'

The result was that, so soon as Scott's pen had brought him affluence, he bought in 1811 the place originally known as Clarty Hole, that is, the Dirty Hole, subsequently modified euphemistically into Cartley Hole in 1811. 'The farm,' he wrote to his brother-in-law, 'comprehends about a hundred acres, of which I shall keep fifty in pasture and tillage, and plant all the rest. . . . I intend building a small cottage here for my summer abode.' Such was the beginning of Abbotsford (for that was the more romantic name with which Scott obliterated the homely one of Cartley Hole), which Dean Stanley justly pronounced to be a 'place to see once, and never again.' Architecturally it is the Strawberry Hill of Scotland, described by Ruskin as 'perhaps the most incongruous pile that gentlemanly modernism ever designed.'

Mrs. Hughes, writing from Abbotsford, gives the key to the whole scheme in a single sentence, when she lauds the plaster ceilings 'painted like oak with such exactness that it is impossible to detect it from the finest oak carving without scraping it.' *Quid plura?* Yet is this sorry sham endeared to all generations by a thousand memorials of one of the kindliest hearts and brightest natures that ever took the form of man. Yea, the very paint and stucco —the paltry battlements and senseless embrasures —are ennobled by remembrance of that brave struggle with, and victory over, adversity that must have broken any feebler spirit and less puissant hand. One may not grudge Abbotsford as the goal of its myriad tourists; for had Scott not fixed his affections upon Tweedside, where would have been the charm of all this vale?

" My first visit to the Tweed ", wrote William Scrope
long ago, " was before the Minstrel of the North had sung...
The scenery therefore, at that time, unassisted by story, lost
its chief interest... Since that time I have seen the cottage
of Abbotsford, with its rustic porch, lying peacefully on the
haugh between the lone hills... I have seen that cottage
converted into a picturesque mansion, with every luxury and
comfort attached to it ; the unproductive hills I have viewed
covered with thriving plantations, and the whole aspect of
the country civilised. But amidst all these revolutions, I
never perceived any change in the mind of him who made
them... There he dwelt in the hearts of the people,
diffusing life and happiness around him. He made a home
beside the Border river, in a country and a nation that have
derived benefit from his presence and consequence from his
genius. From his chambers he looked out upon the grey
ruins of the Abbey, and the sun which set in splendour behind
the Eildon Hills.[1]   Like that sun, his course has been run,
and though disastrous clouds came across him in his career,
he went down in unfading glory... Abbotsford, Mertoun,
Chiefswood, Huntly Burn, Allerley !—when shall I forget
you ? "

There were other attractions about Cartley Hole,
drawing Scott towards that particular reach of the
Tweed which, to the uninformed eye, offers less
charm than many fairer scenes on that river. Along
the south-east of the estate of Abbotsford runs the
Huntly Burn through the Rymer's Glen, so named
after True Thomas of Ercildoune, who is believed to
have lived from 1219 to 1299. He shares with the
shadowy Merlin and the dreaded Michael Scot the
fame of a prophet ; and if he claimed not, as they
did, to work enchantment, he was, at all events, the

[1] Just a trifle out of true reckoning here, seeing that the Eildons lie
to the east-south-east of Abbotsford !

subject of a very notable one. Before entering upon that let it be marked that Thomas was a genuine human being, appearing as " Thomas Rymor de Ercildoune" witnessing a charter of Petrus de Haga (Haig) of Bemersyde, between the years 1260 and 1270. That was at a time before men in general had fixed surnames ; his poetic gift no doubt gained Thomas the appellation of Rymor or Rhymer to distinguish him among other Thomases ; but local tradition is firm to the effect that the name of Thomas's family was Learmont. [1]

As to his prophecies, which were delivered from under a great tree on the north-eastern slope of Eildon (the spot now marked by a big stone), they are not worth much attention by reason of the numerous forgeries which were interpolated in later years to serve political ends. One only of the multitude of forecasts ascribed to him seems from its very simplicity to bear the stamp of Thomas—

" At Eildon tree, if you shall be,
   A brigg ower Tweed you there may see. "

Three bridges are visible from that place now ; but to span the Tweed seemed little short of a marvel in the thirteenth century. As Scott has observed, however, this prediction was not extraordinary for one who had " that sort of insight into futurity possessed by most men of a sound and combining judgment. "

It was on Huntly Burn, then, that Thomas laid the opening scene of the romance by which he is chiefly

[1] There is another Thomas Rymer (1641-1713), distinguished in literature as compiler of the Foedera, who is sometimes confused by the careless with him of Ercildoune.

remembered, a version of that "Sir Tristrem" which
has been rendered in so many lands.—

> 'In a mery mornynge of Maye,
> By Huntle bankkes my selfe allone.
> I herde the jay and the Throstylle cokke,
> The Mawys menyde hir of hir song, [1]
> The wodewale beryde as a belle, [2]
> That all the wode abowte me ronge.
> Allone in a loning [3] als I laye,
> Undyr-nethe a semely tree,
> I was war of a ladye gay
> Come rydyng owyr a fayre le. "

Note the exceeding tenderness for rural sights and
sounds breathed in these lines, which was almost lost
in the later versions.

Thomas's adventures began, as might be expected,
with the appearance of the "ladye gay." But this
was no earthly dame ; it was the Queen of Elfland,
who spirited the Rhymer away to her mysterious
realms beneath the Eildon Hills. The romance of
Sir Tristrem, considered to be, if not the oldest, at
least one of the oldest of extant Scottish poems,
was discovered by Ritson among Auchinleck MSS.
in 1744, and first edited and annotated by Sir
Walter Scott. But before this original had come
into his hands, he had published in the Border
Minstrelsy the following version of the story still
current among the peasantry a hundred years ago,

[1] The Mavis (thrush) moaned, wailed, in her song.
[2] Professor Veitch notes the "woodwale" as the woodlark, but
"woodwail" is still a local name for the green woodpecker which disappeared from Scotland with the fall of the forest. It would be a fair
exploit for any landowner to re-establish this beautiful and harmless
bird. I have failed in two attempts, but intend to persevere.
[3] A green glade.

which enables one to follow the narrative more easily than in the vernacular of the thirteenth century.

'True Thomas lay on Huntlie bank ;
A ferlie[1] he spied wi' his ee ;
And there he saw a lady bright
Come riding down by Eildon Tree.

Her skirt was o' the grass green silk,
Her mantle o' the velvet fine ;
At ilka tett o' her horse 's mane
Hung fifty siller bells and nine.

True Thomas he pu'd aff his cap,
And louted low upon his knee—
" All hail, thou mighty Queen of Heav'n !
Thy peer on earth I ne'er did see. "

" O no, O no, Thomas, " she said,
" That name does not belong to me ;
I am but the Queen of fair Elfland
That am come hither to visit thee.

" Harp and carp, Thomas, " she said
" Harp and carp alang wi' me ;
And if ye dare to kiss my lips,
Sure of your bodie I will be. "

" Betide me weel, betide me woe,
That weird shall never daunton me ! "
Syne he has kissed her rosy lipe
All underneath the Eildon Tree.

" Now ye maun gang wi' me, " she said
" True Thomas ye maun gang wi' me ;
And ye maun serve me seven years,
Through weel or woe, as chance may be. "

1 A marvel.

6

She's mounted on her milk-white steed.
　She's ta'en True Thomas up behind ;
And aye, whene'er her bridle rang
　The steed flew swifter than the wind.

O they rade on, and further on ;
　The steed gaed swifter than the wind ;
Until they reached a desert wide,
　And living land was left behind.

" Light down, light down now True Thomas,
　And lean your head upon my knee
Abide and rest a little space,
　And I will show you ferlies three.

" O see ye not yon narrow road,
　So thick beset with thorns and briers ?
That is the path of righteousness,
　Tho' after it but few enquires.

" And see ye not that braid, braid road,
　That lies across that lily leaven ?
That is the path of wickedness,
　Tho' some call it the path to heaven.

" And see ye not that bonny road,
　That winds about the fernie brae ?
That is the road to fair Elfland
　Whaur thou and I this night maun gae.

" But Thomas, ye maun haud your tongue,
　Whatever ye may hear or see ;
For if ye speak word in Elfyn land
　Ye'll ne'er get back to your ain countrie. "

O they rade on, and further on ;
　They wauded rivers aboon the knee ;
And they saw neither sun nor moon,
　But they heard the roaring o' the sea.

It was mirk night, there was nae stern light, [1]
　They wauded thro' red blude to the knee ;
For a' the blude that's shed on earth
　Rins through the springs o' that countrie.

Syne they came on a garden green,
　And she pu'd an apple frae a tree—
" Tak' this for thy wages, True Thomas ;
　It will give thee a tongue can never lee. "

" My tongue is mine ain, " True Thomas said ;
　" A Gudelie Gift ye wad gie to me !
I neither dought [2] to buy nor sell
　At fair or tryst, where I may be.

" I dought neither speak to prince nor peer,
　Nor ask grace from a fair ladye. "
" Now hold thy peace ! " the ladye said,
　" For as I say, so must it be. "

He has gotten a coat of the even cloth,
　And a pair of shoes of velvet green.
And till seven years were gane and past,
　True Thomas on earth was never seen. '

After seven years of sugared thraldom in Elfland,
Thomas was allowed to return to Ercildoune, and to
exercise among men the prophetic power he had
acquired. But he was bound to return when sum-

---

[1] Starlight.
[2] Preterite of ' to dow.' to be able.　If Thomas's tongue could not
lie he would cut a poor figure at fair or market !

moned by the Queen ; and so one day, when he was
entertaining guests at Ercildoune, they brought him
word of a great 'ferlie.' A hart and a hind had
come out of the forest, and were standing in the
village street. Thomas recognised the summons.
He rose at once, followed the wild creatures into the
depths of the forest and has never been seen since.
But we are told to look for his return some day,
when it shall please the Queen of Elfland to give him
fresh leave.

It may seem that time might be better spent than
over these childish legends ; yet it should be borne
in mind how firmly people believed them in what is
sometimes called the Age of Faith, and allowed their
actions to be controlled by that belief.

In 1586, for instance, a wretched woman named
Alison Pearson was arraigned on a charge of witch-
craft, one of the principal counts in her indictment
being as follows.——

'Item—for hanting and repairing with the gude neighbours (fairies) and Queene of Elfland, thir divers years past,
as she had confest ; and that she had friends in that court
which were of her own blude, who had gude acquaintance
of the Queene of Elfland... and that she saw not the
Queens this seven years, and that she was seven years
ill-handled at the court of Elfland ; that however she had
gude friends there, and that it was the gude neighbours that
healed her, under God.'

Upon this and pages of similar trash about the
'gude neighbours' (even her judges used this
periphrasis in referring to the fairies, lest that vin-
dictive race should take offence)—upon this and the

like, I say, Alison was convicted, condemned, and burned at the stake.

Half a mile below Abbotsford, Tweed receives the afflux of Gala Water, which runs a troubled course of twenty-one miles from the Moorfoot Hills in Midlothian, descending in that distance from an elevation of 1100 feet to one of 280. The early Saxons named this valley Wedale, or the Vale of Woe, and here, according to Professor Skene, took place King Arthur's eighth great battle against the pagans.

The name Wedale, which appears variously written in ancient manuscripts—Wedel, Wedhall, Weddale, etc.—became the surname of sundry of its inhabitants when they passed to other districts. With that lamentable indifference to grace in sound which is an infirmity of British ears, it has been allowed to assume the grotesque form of Waddell. There was a church in Wedale in very early times, where was treasured a piece of the true cross deposited there by King Arthur. It enjoyed the privilege of sanctuary, and Wyntoun makes the curious statement that the Black Priest of Wedale, the Thane of Fife, and the Lord of Abernethy were the only three persons entitled to the privilege of Macduff—that is, if any of them slew a gentleman in ' suddane chawdmellé, ' he should be held guilt-less on payment of 24 merks fine, and 12 merks for a yeoman. [1]

Writing about 1845, Sir Thomas Dick Lauder declared that, well as he was acquainted with most parts of Scotland, he knew none which was so ' com-pletely metamorphosed ' since the days of his youth as Gala Water.

---

[1] Wyntoun's Cronykil, VI. 19.

' The whole wore a pastoral character. Crops were rare, and fences hardly to be met with. Not a tree was to be seen, except in the neighbourhood of one or two old places, and especially at and around Torwoodlee and Gala House. Everything within sight was green, simple and bare ; the farmhouses were small and unobtrusive, and one or two small places of residence only, belonging to proprietors, were to be seen. The Break-neck road ran along the west side of the valley, being conducted in straight lines right up and down hill. '

Sir Thomas lived to see a new road with easy gradients engineered along the east bank of the water ; the valley fenced and ploughed, and thriving plantations clothing the slopes on either side. What would he think could he stand this day at Crosslee and watch the London express with its sleeping or dining car, thundering down the vale, leaping from this side to that of the patient stream, which once had to be taken into serious account by a maiden going to meet her sweetheart ?—

'Braw, braw lads o' Gala Water !
   Oh Braw lads o' Gala Water !
   I'll kilt my coats abune the knee
      And follow my love through the water.
         Braw, braw lads ! '

What would that excellent baronet exclaim could he visit Galashiels, which he lived to see develop from a cluster of cottages round a single woollen mill into a large and thriving manufacturing village of not less than 3500 inhabitants ? It now contains a population of over 13,000.

Thirteen thousand ' Sour Plums ' ; what a crop ! For the people here proudly claim the title of the

'Sour Plums of Galashiels,' from an exploit performed upon the English in the reign of Edward III.
A party of soldiers having taken up their quarters in
the hamlet, and seeing no signs of the enemy, began
wandering among the woods to gather wild plums.
One of the Scotts riding in with a clump of spears
perceived his opportunity, and vowed that these
should be the sourest plums men ever gathered. He
fell upon the scattered Englishmen, cutting them
down almost to a man. Some of them fled to a place
nearly opposite Abbotsford, which is still called the
Englishman's Syke. [1] To commemorate this exploit,
the arms of the town display a plum-tree 'fructed
proper'—that is, in full bearing—between two foxes,
which seem to have been added for some vague
association with the fox and sour grapes. The words
of the song 'Soor Plooms in Galashiels' are irretriev-
ably lost, but the air which fitted them remains. Sir
Walter Scott has told us how his uncle Thomas,
when he lay dying at the age of ninety, bade his son
James play him that tune, his favourite, on the pipes.

'No occasion,' wrote Ruskin, 'for death-bed repentance
on the part of this old gentleman ; no particular care even for
the disposition of his handsome independence ; but here is a
bequest of which one must see one's son in full possession—
here is a thing to be well looked after, before setting out for
heaven—that the tune of "Sour plums in Galashiels" may still
be played on earth in an incorrupt manner, and no damnable
French or English variations intruded upon the solemn and
authentic melody thereof.'

Whether it be because Galashiels lay further from
the English border than other dales, or that the swift

[1] Syke, a marshy rill.

uprising of manufacturers has unravelled the web of song and story, I know not; but there seem to be fewer memories of the olden time on Gala Water than may be recovered elsewhere. The very name of Galashiels—the shiels or cots on Gala—may be sought in vain among ecclesiastical records. The parish was formerly named Lindean, from a place on the south bank of Ettrick, where the Kers of Faldonside are buried.

Jealous as one must rightly be of any tampering with the ancient minstrelsy, Burns may not be blamed for his industry in setting new words to old music. He could not help it, any more than a lark can help singing.

> ' There's braw, braw lads on Yarrow braes,
>   That wander through the blooming heather ;
> But Yarrow Braes nor Ettrick shaws
>   Can match the lads of Gala Water. '

Yet what are these words without their inspiring melody, one of the sweetest in all the Caledonian repertory ?

Torwoodlee, on the right bank of Gala Water a couple of miles above the town, has been, and remains in possession of an ancient Border family of Pringle (formerly Hoppringle) since 1509. A modern mansion has replaced the house which, roofless and ruined now, was built by George Pringle in 1601 instead of a still older keep which was sacked by the Elliots and Armstrongs one winter night in 1568, when the laird was barbarously murdered. Redress against these dreaded marauders was out of the question before the union of the kingdoms. England and

Scotland being at war continually, it was easy for of-
fenders against the laws of one country to seek
protection in the other. There was nothing to
distinguish this outrage, and the impunity of its per-
petrators, from scores of similar cases, save this, that
thirty-nine years after the raid in January 1607, the
murdered man's grandchildren took advantage of the
union of the Crowns (1603) to endeavour to bring
the surviving malefactors to justice. The endeavour
failed ; at least it succeeded only so far as that John
Elliot of Capshaw was 'put to the horn' i.e. proclaimed outlaw, an infliction which he had long before
learned to regard with equanimity. As a typical
example of the incidents in a blood-feud, the 'dittay,'
or part of it, against the criminals will bear quotation.

'Foresamekill as the said Johnne Ellote of Copschaw.
Robert Ellote, callit *Marteinis Hob*, and Jok Airmestrang,
callit the *Lairdis Jok*, with thair complices, with convocation
of the haill Clannis of the Airmestrangis, Ellotes, Batiesones,
Grahames and remanent Clannis, duelland [dwelling] als-
weill on the Inglis as the Scottis Bordouris, all cowmone
thevis, outlawis and brokin men, to the number of thre
hundreth persones or thairby, boden in feir of weir [fully
armed] with jakis, speiris, steil bonnetis, lance-stalffis [staves],
hagbutis and pistoletis... in the moneth of December, the
yeir of God I^m V^c threscoir aucht yeiris, [did] come fordward
in hosteill maner, baith on hors and fute, to the Place of
Torwoidlie, and thair, under silence and clud of nycht with
foir-hammeris and geistis [joists, beams], dang up the zeittis
[broke up the gates] of the said place, and be force of
violence enterit within the samyn [the same] ; and tuik the
said George Hoppringill furth of his bed, and convoyit him
away as captive and prissoner with thame, to the Skaldeneise
within the Sherefdome of Selkirk ; and thair maist crewallie

and unmerciefully Murdreist and slew the said umq^le George. '

'Of course they carried off a great deal besides the unlucky laird. There follows a list of goods, which includes seventeen horses, one thousand pounds in cash, three pieces of silver plate, two dozen silver spoons, and so forth, whereof not a stiver was ever recovered for the heirs.

Old Gala House, the place of another branch of Pringles, stands deserted also, in favour of a spick-and-span example of the so-called Scottish baronial style. The old house stands on the site of one still older, which bore a stone with the date 1583, displaying the arms of Pringle—the five pilgrim's scallops on a black saltire—with the cinquefoils of Borthwick, being the scutcheons of Andrew Pringle and Marion Borthwick his wife. Andrew's grandson, David, married Margaret, daughter of Auld Wat of Harden and Mary Scott, the 'Flower of Yarrow.' They had no children, but David's sister Jean, having married Margaret Scott's brother Hugh, became heiress to her father, and that is the origin of the Scotts of Gala. A richer admixture of ancient Border blood could scarcely be contrived. Hugh's and Jean's arms are carved upon the same shield over the entrance to the family mausoleum in Galashiels kirkyard, with the date 1636.

On a wooded hilltop about half a mile behind the modern house of Torwoodlee is a circular camp of the kind which crowns so many similar uplands. This one is remarkable among others, because it seems to be the northern terminus of a

work which, under the various names of the Catrail,
the Pict's Wark, and the Deil's Dyke, has been the
subject of speculation and controversy among
antiquaries for generations past, and will be so for
generations to come. The identity of Junius of the
Letters has not called forth greater variety of suggestion than has this mysterious earthwork. It
consists of a ditch or fosse, flanked by two earthen
banks, running in a line, once continuous probably,
but now broken and defaced by agriculture, from
Peel Fell in the Cheviots, across the Slitrig to Pike
Fell (1516 feet), which it climbs, and down the
Teviot, where there are a number of prehistoric forts.
Crossing the Teviot, it may be traced over Commonside Hill, past Broadlee Loch, into the Rankil-
burn glen, and so to the summit of Corse Head
(1319 feet), where there has been a strong fort.
Thence it strikes across the dales of Ettrick and
Yarrow, over the Minchmuir, crosses the Tweed
near the mouth of Howden Pot Burn, passes
through the wood at Hollybush farm, and so by
Rink Hill and Mossilee to the fort at Torwoodlee,
completing there a total course of about forty-eight
miles.

'In most places now the work appears almost like
a brown benty road across the moorland . . . indeed
its line has been actually superseded here and there
by mountain roads . . . The old makers of the
ditch had worked down to the hard ground, and this
was utilised as a line of mountain road, and came to
be defaced from its former appearance as a ditch and
mound.' But it was not designed as a road originally.
Proof of that is that, in crossing streams, it is drawn
aside to no ford, but sometimes strikes the channel

where the banks are precipitous, reappearing on the opposite side. [1]

As to the purpose of such an extended work, the commonest and most obvious suggestion is that it was defensive, and the prefix of the name Catrail has been explained as the Welsh *cad*—Gaelic *cath*, a battle. But had the work been defensive, the ditch surely would not have been *between* the two mounds, but on the outer side of both, if two there were. Analogy with the Deil's Dyke in Galloway at once occurs ; but that well-known work, running, like the Catrail, over hill and dale sixty miles from the shores of Loch Ryan to the Nith near Sanquhar, was almost certainly a defence erected by the Picts of Galloway against their inveterate foes, the Britons of Strathclyde. In the Galloway work there is but one mound, to be strengthened by a stockade, with a fosse running along the outer or Strathclyde face thereof. A second rampart, outside the ditch, would greatly weaken the defence by affording shelter to an attacking force. Nevertheless, Professor Veitch, taking into account the apparent relation of the Catrail with the numerous hill forts along its line, was of opinion that this ditch was dug by the Britons of Strathclyde as a defensive boundary against the Angles of Northumbria about the beginning of the seventh century of our era. Having no alternative explanation to offer, I must be content to leave it so ; merely observing that if that was the origin and purpose of the Catrail, it is to be hoped that the Britons were better Christians than they were military engineers.

[1] This description is condensed from Professor Veitch's detailed account of the Catrail (*Border History and Poetry*, i. 183-209). He traversed and examined the work throughout its length.

A short way below Galashiels the Elwand or Allan Water crosses under the highroad in its haste to reach the Tweed. This little stream has been specially associated with the fairy folk, and passes through a narrow gorge called the Fairy Dean or the Nameless Dean. At the head of the glen is a remarkable group of three towers, ruinous now, standing within short distance of each other—Hillslap, Colmslie, and Langshaw. Colmslie was a strong house of the Borthwicks ; there is a fine lilt in the fragment of verse connected with it—just enough to make one wish for more.

> ' Colmslie stands on Colmslie Hill,
> The water it flows round Colmslie Mill ;
> The mill and the kiln gang bonnily,
> And it's up wi' the whippers o' Colmslie ! '

Hillslap is now known as Glendearg, because Scott so named the castle in *The Monastery*, the scene of that romance being laid on Allan Water. It bears the date 1585 on the door-lintel, with the initials N.C. and E.L., those of Nicolas Cairncross and his wife. The family of Cairncross has disappeared from the roll of landowners, and was never of much note. The said Nicolas went bail on 27th May 1591 for a kinsman, 'Robert Carnecroce callit *Meikle Hob*,' who, with three other rascals, was indicted for the forcible abduction of Jean Ramsay, Lady Warristoun.[1]

The Allan joins the Tweed in the grounds of the Pavilion, formerly the hunting-seat of the Lords Somerville, of whom the nineteenth and last died in

---

[1] Mother-in-law of the beautiful Jean Livingston, Lady Warristoun, who in 1600 was beheaded for the murder of her husband, and her nurse was burnt at the same time as accomplice.

1870, leaving his property to his daughter, the Hon. Mrs. Henry. An historic family that of Somerville, but notice of them may be deferred till we come to their ancient lands of Linton, which lay upon the very highway of English invasion.

Far as the fame of Tweed has run, and myriad as are those who travel from afar to visit its classic scenes, there is perhaps no place in all its valley which has such a wide renown as Melrose. I shall speak no word of disparagement ; yet it may be that disappointment is in the minds of some who see it for the first time, so busy has the modern builder been in its streets, so spruce are the villas which have sprung up in its suburbs. The abbey is there, unsurpassed in the beauty of death ; but all grace has fled from its environment. More closely interwoven with Scottish history than Dryburgh, the sepulchre of more of Scotland's great ones than Jedburgh, less marred in its main structure than Kelso, it has none of the sylvan seclusion of the first, and seems more closely elbowed than the others by the petty concerns of everyday life. Were it possible to transplant the abbey, together with its rich associations, to the site of the original foundation below Leaderfoot, then indeed Melrose would sit enthroned, peerless among the shrines of our northern land.

The Melrose of to-day—Kennaquhair of *The Abbot* and *The Monastery*—is not that *maol ros,* that naked headland in the wood, whereon Aidan of Lindisfarne, disciple of Colum of the Churches, financed by Oswald, King of Northumbria, built his church and monastery in 636, and appointed his beloved disciple Eata first abbot. That establishment, the site of which still goes by the name of Old Melrose, was wrecked in the ninth century by Kenneth Mac Alpin, first King of Scots. Drycthelm, converted by a vision of hell, purgatory, and heaven, became a monk there, and eventually head of the community. This paragon of austere piety used to bathe daily in the Tweed, summer and winter, without undressing before his plunge or changing his wet garments afterwards.

It was David I. who founded the new monastery in 1136 at a small village called Fordel, thenceforth to be Melrose for all time, and peopled it with Cistercians from Rievaulx in Yorkshire. The new building, which we may suppose to have been of the same exquisite late Norman design as Jedburgh Abbey, stood till 1322, when it was merged in the sacrifice incurred by the Scottish nation in their struggle for independence. The Earl of Warenne's English army, retreating from Edinburgh in that year, wreaked their wrath first upon Holyrood Abbey, which they burnt and sacked. Melrose they served in the same way, slaying the prior and two of the brethren who attempted to defend it, and then marched on to destroy the beautiful monastery of Dryburgh. Fair reprisal, it must be owned, for similar evil work wrought by the Scots when they were over the border earlier in the year. Three years later, at a Parliament held by Robert I. at Scone in 1325, the abbot and convent received a grant of £2000 out of the revenues of forfeited lands, with which they rebuilt their church and monastery. The finest part of the ruins as they remain to us date from this period. This includes the nave, from the crossing to the rood loft, and part of the transepts, together with the flying buttresses along the south front, and the south transept with its splendid window. Kemp, architect of the Scott Monument in Princes Street, Edinburgh, borrowed the dimensions and general plan of that work from the great transept arches of Melrose.

It is well known that King Robert the Bruce, when on his deathbed, charged 'the gentle knight Sir James of Douglas' to carry his heart to the Holy Land and present it at the Holy Sepulchre. But it is not so generally known that he did not intend that it should remain there. A few months before his death, Robert had written to his son and successor David, specially commending the abbey and convent of Melrose to his care, and desiring that his heart might be buried before the high altar. Which was duly performed, after the sorrowing comrades of the Black Douglas had brought the heart home in its silver casket, together with the body of their chief.

Edward III. respected the Scottish abbeys in his wars, and even restored to Melrose certain lands in England belonging of right to the convent. His successor, Richard II., confirmed the protection; but in 1385 he was so infuriated by the failure of his expedition into Scotland that, after sleeping a night in the abbey, he burnt it down. However, so great were the terrors of Holy Church in the fourteenth century, that in 1389 King Richard made atonement by remitting the duty upon a thousand sacks of wool exported by the monks from his harbour of Berwick. But the monks did not play fair. They were detected in trying to smuggle out twelve hundred sacks instead of a thousand, and the privilege was withdrawn. Howbeit, the lands of the monastery were extensive, and its revenue very great; so the monks had no difficulty in providing funds to erect the present east end of the choir, with its Perpendicular window tracery, which is the only conspicuous example in Scotland of that style of Gothic building. While English architects followed their own peculiar school of Perpendicular, Scottish designers borrowed the more graceful Flamboyant from the Low Countries.

The final ruin of this fair fane befell in the sixteenth century. Henry VIII., incensed at the rejection of his proposals for the marriage of the infant Queen of Scots with the Prince of Wales, vowed he would have Mary out of the strongest keep in Scotland, and sent Lord Hertford in 1544 to devastate the land. The campaign assumed a degree of ferocity unexampled since the sack of Berwick in 1296 by Edward I. The Merse and the Lothians were turned into a desert; the abbey and palace of Holyrood were gutted with fire, so was the abbey of Newbotle. Melrose, also, was practically destroyed, its tower probably being blown up; so that when the two knights, Eure or Evers and Layton, whom Hertford left to carry on the work of destruction, visited the abbey in the following year, there remained nothing of mischief for their hands, except to deface the tombs of the Douglases. They thought, perhaps, to quench the inexpugnable spirit of independence by obliterating the memorials of such champions as the victor of Otterbourne and the Knight of Liddesdale !

Eure and Layton lived not long to boast of their performance, yet long enough to rue it. The Earl of Angus, who most justly had been imprisoned on a charge of treason, had been released in 1544 that he might aid his country in her extremity. No doubt he had been in league with the English; but they had been so thoughtless as to raid and occupy some of

7

his lands. Nay, more : King Henry had conceived such well-merited distrust of his former confidant, that he set a price of two thousand crowns upon the head of Angus, and gave wide tracts of Douglas territory to Eure and Layton. Nothing short of this would have made Angus loyal to his country ; but he was in earnest now. He vowed that these knights should have the titles to his lands written upon their skins with sharp pens and bloody ink. Joining forces with his old enemy Arran, he marched to Jedburgh, Eure and Layton falling back upon Ancrum Moor. The Kers of Ferniehirst and Cessford were in the English force, with the red cross of St. George sewed upon their sleeves. Angus was reinforced by Buccleuch and Norman Leslie, famous fighters both, bringing up his strength to not less than a thousand spears; but still he was far inferior in numbers to the enemy. Acting on Buccleuch's advice, the Scots dismounted and went into ambush at Penielhaugh, sending their horses to the rear. Eure mistook this for a movement of retreat, and ordered an advance. Suddenly he came upon the Scots drawn up between him and the low February sun. The English charged in vain against the steady squares ; they wavered and broke. The Kers tore off their red badges, and joined their countrymen in the bloody pursuit. Eure and Layton were both slain with hundreds of their men ; a thousand prisoners were taken and twelve guns. 'Ah, welaway!' sighed Arran over Eure's body, 'that ever such slaughter and bloodshed should be among Christian men.'

With the name Lilliard's Edge, applied to a certain spot on Ancrum Moor, is associated the somewhat nebulous memory of a certain damsel of Teviotdale,

whose lover was slain by the English. To avenge
him, she marched with Angus to Ancrum Moor, and
her fate was recorded on a cross which, it is said, used
to stand on the spot, bearing the following inscription—

'Fair Maiden Lilliard lies under this stane ;
Little was her stature, but great was her fame ;
Upon the English loons she laid mony thumps,
And when her legs were cuttit off, she fought
[upon her stumps. '

If the monument was a genuine one, the rhyme should
have run ' Fair Maid o' Lilliard, ' for the place was
known as Lilliard's Edge long before the date of the
battle. In the twelfth century it was written ' Lili-
syhates, ' beside the streamlet ' Lilliesietburne, ' and
obviously the name owns a common origin with that
of the neighbouring parish of Lilliesleaf, formerly
Lillesclive.

After this last destruction came the Scottish Reformation ; the Earl of Bothwell, Douglas of Lochleven, and Sir John Ramsay were successively
appointed Commendators, and finally the lands of the
abbey passed into possession of the Scotts of Buccleuch. The building itself suffered the usual fate of
becoming a common quarry for building a tolbooth,
repairing mills and sluices, and erecting vulgar dwellings in the town. Finally, cruelest fate of all, in 1618
the nave was made to serve as the parish kirk, with
a new roof and square piers concealing the old ones
on the north side. It is amazing that through all these
vicissitudes so much remains of what must have been
an exquisitely lovely building.

The dominant feature in the landscape near Melrose, and for many miles around, is the triple crest of Eildon, which has drawn to itself enough legend, myth, and history to store the whole realm of Scotland withal. It is the isolation of this upheaval of porphyritic trap, and its peculiar three-cleft form, which have gained for it more notice and given it more powerful influence upon human imagination than the far loftier summits among which we took our way in Upper Tweeddale. [1]

'In the south of Scotland,' observed Walter Scott, 'any work of great labour and antiquity is ascribed, either to the agency of *Auld Michael*, of Sir William Wallace, or of the devil'; and, sure enough, Michael Scot is held accountable for the shape and position of the Eildons. According to one story, the wizard, happening to have no particular work for the familiar demon who served him, and being under superior obligation not to allow that restless sprite to join the ranks of the unemployed, bade him 'bridle the Tweed with a curb of stone.' He had underrated his auxiliary's power; the task was accomplished in a single night, and stands to this day—the *cauld* or weir across the river at Kelso. Next Michael ordered the demon to carve the single cone of Eildon into three; which was executed as easily and swiftly as the other job. Finally, the wizard hit upon the notion of setting the little devil to weave sea sand into ropes, which kept the creature quiet till his services were wanted in earnest.

The other story is more circumstantial, and Scrope quotes it as the more popular version in the district. Michael, being at constant feud with the monks of

[1] The three crests of Eildon rise respectively to no more than 1385, 1327, and 1216 feet.

Melrose, whose holy water and exorcisms interfered in the most exasperating way with his incantations, resolved to spite them by erecting a mountain between their monastery and the sun, and gave the necessary instructions to his familiar. The demon, with a single scoop of his shovel, carried enough material from the Cheviots to form one of the three Eildon, Hills ; another scoop supplied material for the second Hill ; but in his third trip he awkwardly spilt half his shovelful on the way back ; which accounts, not only for the lesser size of the third Eildon but also for the position of the lone peak of Ruberslaw (1392 feet) which stands so conspicuously in Teviotdale, representing the spilt half-shovelful. This was a lucky accident for the monks, interrupting the construction of a mountain which, if completed, must have thrown their pleasant abode into the shade. Michael, incensed at his demon's slovenliness, rushed at him to chastise him. The imp flew down to the river, embarked in his shovel, and sped downstream, Michael after him in a boat, forgetting that running water was fatal to his power of enchantment. Certain monks, enjoying the discord in the rival establishment, followed in a third boat to see the fun, and with them sailed True Thomas of Ercildoune, nothing loth. The chase went forward as far as Makerstoun, where dwelt a witch friendly to Michael. She flew out of the Corbie's Craig in the form of a raven, and her warning note reminded the wizard of the mistake he had made in going afloat. Landing at once, his power returned to him as soon as he stood on dry ground. He employed it to cast a bar of rock across the river, whereby the flow should be stopped and the demon's

boat be left adry.   But in his excitement Michael left
one foot in the water ; the whole force of the current
concentrated in that spot, forming the Trows, a
stream well known to many a salmon fisher, where
in very low water an active fellow might in former
times leap across the whole volume of the Tweed.
The demon finally made his escape to sea, was seen
no more, and a sandbank marks the place where he
left his shovel.

Let us turn from the visionary and unsubstantial
for a moment, and mark the change which occurs in
the solid earth under our feet at this point in the
journey.   Hitherto, ever since we left Tweed's
Well many a mile behind us and a thousand feet
above us, we have been travelling upon river gravels,
boulder-clay, and more recent peat, accumulated
upon the hard and twisted beds of Silurian rock,
most ancient of stratified deposits.   Now we enter
upon a newer, though still ancient, geological
horizon ; the soil changes in hue from hazel to brick
red ; the crags by the river are of softer material,
worn into outlines less rugged than those of the
uplands we have quitted.   From Melrose to the sea
the river channel is carved through the old red sandstone, which is torn and interrupted by volcanic vents
of the carboniferous or Permian age.   These ancient
vents, monuments of a bygone era of prodigious
volcanic activity, impart peculiar features to the
scenery of the valley, such as Eildon Ruberslaw,
Minto Craigs, Peniel Heugh, Bonchester, and
Dunian.

You may note a change in the climate, too, from
the soft air of the Westland.   Strained of sea damp
as it flowed over the high grounds, the atmosphere

EILDON HILLS

T. & R. Annan & Sons

Ph: t.

is more mellow in summer, more shrill in winter, than it is on the Atlantic seaboard. But plain prose is easily baffled in attempting to define the peculiar aura of Tweedside. Only to those who have the gift of song is it given to convey its subtle charm. Here is Twilight on Tweed, by one of her latest singers :—

> 'Three crests against a saffron sky
>   Beyond the purple plain,
> The dear remembered Melody
>   Of Tweed once more again.
>
> Wan water from the Border hills,
>   Dear voice from the old years,
> Thy distant music lulls and stills,
>   And moves to quiet tears.
>
> Like a loved ghost thy fabled flood
>   Fleets through the dusky land ;
> Where Scott, came home to die, has stood
>   My feet returning stand.
>
> A mist of memory broods and floats,
>   The Border waters flow ;
> The air is full of ballad notes
>   Borne out long time ago.
>
> Old songs they sung themselves to me
>   Sweet, through a boy's day-dream,
> While trout below the blossomed tree
>   Plashed in the golden stream.
>
> Twilight, and Tweed, and Eildon Hill,
>   Fair and too fair you be ;
> You tell me that the voice is still
>   That should have welcomed me.'[1]

[1] Andrew Lang.

CHAPTER V

FROM LAUDERDALE TO DRYBURGH

Two miles to the east of Melrose we come to Leaderfoot, where the Leader Water falls into the Tweed, after a course of twenty-one miles from its source on Lammer Law, in which distance it descends from 1375 feet above the sea to 215—a fall of 1160 feet. Its valley bears the name of Lauderdale, whence the family of Maitland derived their earldom. These Maitlands trace their descent from Sir Richard de Matulant or Mautland, who owned the lands of Thirlestane in the thirteenth century, and Thirlestane Castle remains the chief seat of the present Earl of Lauderdale.[1] It is a magnificent example of Scottish domestic architecture of the sixteenth and seventeenth centuries, built by Chancellor Maitland (created Lord Maitland of Thirlestane in 1590), and greatly added to and embellished by the Earls and Dukes of Lauderdale.

It is believed to stand on the site of Lauder Fort, built by the English under Edward I. The ballad of Auld Maitland, already referred to,[2] relates to a fruit-

[1] Like Thirlestane Castle in Ettrick, this place derives its name from a 'thirled' or perforated stone, which has passed from sight and memory. One such stone still exists in Kirkcowan parish, Wigtownshire, and is used by lovers for 'handfasting' i.e. clasping hands through the orifice in the stone.

[2] See p. 50 ante. 'This ballad,' said Professor Aytoun in the first edition of his Ballads of Scotland, 'if genuine' must be regarded as one

less siege of Thirlestane by Edward II., whereof all other record has perished.

> ' For fifteen days that braid host lay,
>   Sieging auld Maitland keen ;
> Syne they hae left him, hail and fair
>   Within his strength o' stane. '

The Maitlands seem to have been a quiet law-abiding race, for their names do not appear, like those of every other Border family, as frequent actors or victims in crimes of violence. Sir Robert Maitland of Thirlestane had a charter in 1345 of the lands of Lethington, now called Lennoxlove, in East Lothian: and from him was descended Sir Richard Maitland of Lethington (1496-1586), lawyer, statesman, and poet, one of the few admirable public characters in Scotland during the sixteenth century. He occupied his leisure in collecting early Scottish poetry, and it was after him that the Maitland Club, a literary society of the eighteenth century, was named.

Of his second son William, better known as Secretary Lethington, the record is not so unclouded. He acted in place of Huntly, the Chancellor, who refused to attend the Parliament which, in August 1560, put an end to the authority of the Pope and Church of Rome in Scotland. He was an

of the very oldest productions of the Scottish muse ;' and proceeds to give reason for doubting its authenticity. ' The ballad, ' he argues ' was never made for recitation. It is singularly deficient in the very quality which tends most to the preservation of ancient song.' He declares that nobody could learn it by heart and repeat it after an interval of two months. This is far from convincing. Tam o' Shanter was not composed for recitation : it has no refrain : yet I have heard a Wigtown lawyer recite it after dinner from beginning to end, with neither halt nor hover. Aytoun modified his opinion before preparing the second edition of his book.

accomplice with Bothwell in the destruction of Darnley in the House-o'-Field, and expiated the errors,
and worse, of a tortuous career, which earned him
the nickname of 'Mitchell Wylie' (Machiavelli), by
dying in prison at Leith in 1573.

The memories of Lauderdale reach far beyond
that date.   On the Headshaw Burn, four miles below
its source on None Cairn Edge (1479 feet) and a
couple of miles above its junction with Leader Water,
is the parish Church of Channelkirk, near Holy
Water Cleuch.   Here, close to a prehistoric hill-fort,
is St. Cuthbert's Well, among hill pastures where the
future saint, still bearing his Irish name, Mulloch,
served as a shepherd lad.   Bede describes how, in
651, Mulloch beheld the vision of Bishop Aidan
of Lindisfarne being borne to heaven by angels.
Straightway resolving upon a religious life, he presented himself at Old Melrose, was received by
Prior Boisil, submitted to the tonsure, and received
the new name of Cuthbert.   He spent ten years
there before entering upon his great missionary work.
Being appointed guest-master, he entertained an angel
unawares, who, in departing, presented him with
three loaves, ' such as the world cannot produce ;
excelling lilies in whiteness, roses in perfume, and
honey in sweetness.' [1]   (In these days of sugar boun-
ties and abundant confectionary, it profits to remember
that, before the discovery of cane sugar, honey was
practically the only direct source of sweetness).

Cuthbert's discipline at Melrose was of appalling
severity.   He used to recite the Psalms of David
from beginning to end standing in ice-cold water.
When Boisil died of the buidhe conaill or yellow

[1] Vita S. Cuthbert VII.

plague in 660, Cuthbert succeeded him as Prior of
Melrose. Four years later he was appointed Prior
of Lindisfarne, where he died in 687. His last
words to the brethren, as recorded by Bede, had
been more precious had they been fewer. 'Keep
peace one with another, and ever guard the divine
gift of charity. Maintain concord with other servants of Christ, and do not think yourselves better
than others'—one would fain believe that the
gentle Cuthbert stopped there, and that it was a
churchman of a later and sterner cast who added—
' of the same faith and manner of life. Only have
no communion with those who err from the unity
of Catholic peace.'[1] There spake the uncomprom-
ising ecclesiastic—there sounded the note of weary
centuries of intolerance and persecution to come.

After Cuthbert's death a church was built beside
the Holy Well in Lauderdale, and called Childes-
chirche (now corrupted into Channelkirk) to commemorate the boyhood of the shepherd saint. As
for his early patron Boisil, he too was canonised, and
his name has been borrowed for the neighbouring
parish of St. Boswells, formerly known as Lessuden.

The upper part of Lauderdale remains intensely
pastoral. Its chief town, Lauder, a royal burgh
under a charter of James IV. in 1502, nestles under
the park walls of Thirlestane Castle, with a dwindling population of eight hundred souls. ' Lousy
Lauther ' was a disrespectful title in the eighteenth
century, now happily inapplicable. Edward I.
lodged here on the Sunday after Ascension 1295,
returning from his invasion of Lothian. The town

[1] Vita St. Cuthbert XXXIX.

holds a foremost place in a rhyme still current about places in this district.

'The lasses o' Lauther ate mim and meek ;
The lasses o' Fanns smell o' peat reek ;
The lasses o' Gordon canna sew a steek,
But weel they can sup their crowdie. [1]

The lasses o' Earlston are bonny and braw ;
The lasses o' Greenlaw are black as a craw ;
The lasses o' Polwart are best o' them a',
And gie plenty o' meal for their crowdie. '

Tranquil and apart, Lauder dozes its life harmlessly away ; yet on a summer day long ago, it was the scene of a central event in Scottish history. The fifteenth century had run more than half its course before the revival of learning, spreading from its source in Italy through sympathetic France, began to make itself felt in Scotland. Among the readiest to yield to its influence was the dreamy and intellectual King James III. Careless of the scowls of his unlettered barons, he chose students and craftsmen as his favourites, with startling indifference to the claims of birth and feudal dignity. He spent whole days discussing matters of art and learning, allowing the Scottish nobles to nurse that bitterness and spirit of revenge which spring most surely from a sense of intellectual inferiority. Some of them took counsel with the King's brothers, Albany and Mar, who detested the upstarts as much as anybody, and readily joined in a plot for their expulsion. The conspiracy was made known to the King, whose all-powerful adviser, Thomas Cochrane, a builder or architect, caused the princes to

[1] Crowdie—milk porridge, hence meals generally.

be imprisoned. When Mar died in Craigmillar dungeon, his title and revenues were bestowed on Cochrane. Albany, escaping from Edinburgh Castle, made his way to France, whence he returned to England in time to join the army of the Duke of Gloucester (afterwards Richard III.) in its invasion of Scotland in 1482.

The bale-fires flew from height to height, from tower to tower, along the Border, summoning barons and yeomen to the accustomed task of national defence. King James rode from Edinburgh and put himself at the head of the assembled army, though Archibald Douglas, fifth Earl of Angus, having succeeded Albany as Warden of the East Marches, was the actual commander of the forces. The King had torn himself away from his beloved books and jewellery, true, but he had brought with him the detested Cochrane and his gang. Even in this urgent crisis he could not bear to part with them. And the danger was at the door; nay, it was over the doorstep, for had not Berwick fallen already, captured by the English, to be held by them, as it turned out, for all time?

Alas! Scotsmen were not united as of yore to repel the invader. Not a lance would these angry nobles lay in rest till the Court had been purged of those whom Angus classed as 'fiddlers and bricklayers.' He summoned a meeting of peers in the Kirk of Lauder. Lord Gray bitterly compared the assembly to the mice who determined that, in the common interest, a bell should be hung round the cat's neck. The difficulty was to find a volunteer who would carry out the delicate operation of hanging it.

'I WILL BELL THE CAT,' growled the Warden,

winning the name by which he is best known in history.

Another Douglas, Sir Robert of Lochleven, kept the kirk door during the conference. Cochrane, the new-made Earl of Mar, hearing that the barons were assembled within, rode down to claim admission, with a following of three hundred, dressed in his liveries of white doublets with black bands. He himself was gorgeously arrayed in a riding-coat of black velvet, a heavy gold chain round his neck ' to the awaillour ' (value) of 500 crowns and a baldrick of silk and gold across his shoulder. He wore a gold-mounted hunting-horn, too, with a large beryl set in it. All this we learn from old Pitscottie, who adds—' This Cochrane was so proud in his consait that he contit no lord to be marrow (equal) to him, thairfor he raschit (rushed) rudlie at the kirk dore.' [1]

Altercation arose between Cochrane and Sir Robert Douglas, when Angus, perceiving the opportunity, passed swiftly down the aisle, and bade the newcomer welcome. He was admitted ; but no sooner was he in the trap than the door was flung to and barred in the faces of his followers. Angus then facing his prey, tore the golden chain from Cochrane's neck. 'A rope would fit it better,' said he. Sir Robert taking his cue, pulled off the gay horn. ' Hunter of mischief he has been too long,' was his remark.

' My lords!' cried Cochrane, ' is this mows [acting] or earnest ?'

' Hard earnest,' quoth the Warden, 'and so you will find it.' They haled the wretched man to the king's tent, and there they seized the other objects of their hate, all but young John Ramsay, who clung

[1] Pitscottie, I. 174.

to the king's person. Him they spared because of his tender years. They put their victims through the form of a trial : before the summer sun had set Cochrane and his fellows were dangling lifeless over the parapet of Lauder Bridge.

The church in which the luckless Cochrane was entrapped was pulled down in 1617 to make way for the present pseudo-Gothic building.

Of later date and less lugubrious character is another story connected with the district. There lies in the Museum of the Scottish Antiquaries a curious silver chain known as Midside Maggie's Girdle, the gift to the society of Mr. Robert Romanes and Mr. James Curle. It weighs 7 oz. 11 dwt., and bears on the disc-shaped clasp the hall-mark for the year 1608-9, and its history is as follows :—

The farm of Tollis Hill was tenanted in the seventeenth century by three brothers of the name of Hardie, their landlord being John, second Earl, afterwards first Duke, of Lauderdale. The farm lies in the hill-country towards Lammerlaw, and the part of it named Midside was held by Thomas Hardie, whose wife, Margaret Lylestone, a thrifty, well-doing woman, was commonly known as 'Midside Maggie.' One bad winter Hardie lost most of his sheep in the snow, and was unable to pay his rent. Maggie went to the earl at Thirlstane Castle and laid the case before him. 'Very well,' said he, good-humouredly, 'as you say there is such wealth of snow on Tollis Hill, I'll forgive you the rent if you bring me a snowball in June.' One may fancy the anxiety with which this struggling couple watched the wreaths dwindling in the cleuchs. It happened to be a very backward season, and Maggie actually was able to carry a snowball to the castle on the first of June, and the earl was as good as his word.

Things went well with the Hardies after this, but ill with the earl. A staunch Royalist, he was taken prisoner at Worcester in 1651, and lay in the Tower for a number of years. The Hardies were as loyal to their lord as he was to his king. They carefully laid by the rent, and one fine day Midside Maggie put it all in gold pieces, baked them in a bannock, stepped it off to London, like Jeanie Deans in later years, and managed to convey the same to the pris-oner in the Tower.

Soon after this, Lauderdale, through favour of Monk, was set at liberty, went oversea to Holland, and returned with the king in 1660. He had not forgotten Maggie. She and her children sat rent free in Midside ever after, and the earl gave her the silver girdle as guerdon, saying, 'Every bannock has its maik but the bannock o' Tollishill.' The girdle, it will be remarked, was already fifty years old when it was given to Maggie. It descended to Maggie's posterity, the last of whom, Thomas Simson, went off to America in 1880, depositing the precious heirloom with Mr. Romanes of Lauder, who finally, in 1897, persuaded the owner to consign it to the National Museum of Antiquities.

Previous to the Maitlands obtaining ascendency in Lauderdale, there was another family of landown-ers there named de Lawedre or Lauder of that Ilk, ancestors of the present Sir Thomas Dick Lauder of the Bass. They had several towers in the district : the ruins of one may be seen on the left bank of Leader at Whitslaid, a couple of miles below Lauder. One of the family, William Lauder, '*vocatus* Wil-

liam-at-the-West-Poirt,' was Bailie of Lauder, and
lost his life when the tolbooth was burnt down by
his dangerous neighbours the Homes. Alexander,
Earl of Home, and a number of his clan, received
remission for this crime in 1607. [1]

The family gradually lost ground in this district,
the last landowner therein of that name being laird
of Carolside, below Earlston, known as Beau Lauder.
He must have been as great a dandy as the ill-starred
Thomas Cochrane, for he was a well-known figure
in the Edinburgh streets at the end of the eighteenth
century, figged out in scarlet, with lace ruffles,
embroidered waistcoat, satin shorts, white silk stock-
ings, and gold shoe-buckles set with stones.

At Earlston the old world and the new meet
again, for this little town of a round thousand inhabitants stands between a station of the North British
Railway on the one side, and a fragment of Thomas
the Rhymer's tower on the other. Its ancient name
of Ercildoune was transmogrified into the slipshod
Earlston when the burgh of barony passed into
possession of the Earls of Dunbar, and continues to
denote its ownership, now that it belongs to the Earl
of Haddington. But seeing that there are two other
places in southern Scotland called Earlston, it seems
a pity that the original form should be discarded,
even were there no historic reasons for resuming it.

From Earlston to Cowdenknowes the way is short
and the transition natural, so closely are the two
places associated in song.

'Ercildoune and Cowdenknowes,
    Where Home had ance commanding,
And Drygrange wi' its milkwhite ewes,
    'Twixt Tweed and Leader standing.

8

The bird that flies through Redpath trees
And Gladswood banks each morrow,
May chant and sing sweet Leader Haugh
And bonny houms o' Yarrow. '

Cowdenknowes, once the principal dwelling of the Homes (English readers will suffer admonition to pronounce the name as if written Hume), has passed into other hands now, but the interesting tower of the seventeenth century has been preserved and incorporated with the modern house, the ground floor having been adapted as an entrance hall. That the Homes were harsh rulers and hard riders is one of the clearest lessons of Border history, though some of their neighbours ran them hard in both respects. Dismal stories still float round the old tower of Cowdenknowes—stories of horrible cruelty passed upon prisoners in its dungeons, and of kindly Scots swinging on the ' burrow's tree ' before the door. There is a melancholy sough, too, in the name of Sorrowlessfield, a place on the opposite side of Leader, said to have been the abode of a family called Fisher, who were all slain on one battlefield, leaving none alive to mourn for them. But inasmuch as Robert Chambers tells of two brothers of the name who owned the property in succession in comparatively recent times, we may be inclined to substitute the matter-of-fact explanation of ' sorrel leas, ' *i.e.* the dry, brown field, or the field of sorrel (sour dock).

There are gentler associations than these about Cowdenknowes, which have shaped themselves, as seem inevitable in this valley, into melody and verse. There are three versions of *The Broom of Cowden-*

knowes ; the following lines form part of what is said
to be the oldest :—

   ' " O the broom, and the bonny, bonny broom,
     And the broom o' the Cowdenknowes "—
  An' aye sae sweet as the lassie sang
    I' the bught, [1] milking the ewes.
  The hills are high on ilka side,
    An' the bught in the lirk o' the hill ;
  And aye as she sang, her voice it rang
    Out o'er the head o' yon hill.
  There was a troop o' gentlemen
    Cam ridin' merrilie by,
  And one o' them has rode out o' the way
    To the bught, to the bonny May.
  " Weel may ye save and see, bonny lass,
    An' weel may ye save and see. "
  " An' sae wi' you, ye weel-bred knight ;
    An' what's your will wi' me ? "
  " The night is misty and mirk, fair May,
    And I hae ridden astray ;
  And will ye be sae kind, fair May,
    As come out and point the way ? "
  " Ride out, ride out, ye ramp rider !
    Your steed's baith stout and strang ;
  But out o' the bught I daurna come,
    For fear ye might dae me wrang. "
  " O winna ye pity me, bonny lass ?
    O winna ye pity me ?
  An' winna ye pity my poor steed,
    Stands trembling at yon tree ? "
  " I wadna pity your poor steed,
    Though it were tied to a thorn ;
  For if ye wad gain my love the night,
    Ye wad slight me ere the morn.
  For I ken ye by your weel-busket hat,

[1] Sheep-pen.

An' your merrie twinklin' e'e,
That ye follow the laird o' the Oakland Hills,
An' right aft in his companie. "
He's ta'en her by the middle jimp,
An' by the grass-green sleeve ;
He's lifted her ower the fauld dyke,
And speered [1] at her sma' leave.
O he's ta'en out a purse o' gowd,
And streek'd her yellow hair ;
" Now take ye that, my bonny May,
Of me till ye hear mair. " '

Then there follow several stanzas describing the usual period of suspense and deadly apprehension on the part of the maiden ; but it all comes right in the end. Fair May had grown pale and ill, when, eighteen weeks after her adventure, the knight rides that way again.—

' " Weel may ye save and see, bonny May,
Weel may ye save and see !
Weel I wot ye're a bonny May,
But whae 's aucht [2] that babe ye are wi' ? "
Never a word could that lassie say,
For never a ane could she blame ;
An' never a word could the lassie say
But—" I hae a gudeman at hame. "
" Ye lie, ye lie, my very bonny May !
Sae loud's I hear ye lie ;
For dinna ye mind that mirk, mirk night,
I was in the bught wi' thee ? "
Then he's leapt off his berry-brown steed,
An' he's set that fair May on.
" Ca' out the kye, gude father, yoursel,
For she's ne'er ca' them out again.

[1] Asked.
[2] Who owns.

I am the laird o' the Oakland Hills,
I hae thirty ploughs and three ;
An' I hae gotten the bonniest lass
That's in a' the north countrie. " ,

Drygrange, once the site of the granary of Melrose Abbey, now that of a conspicuous modern mansion, stands a mile below Cowdenknowes, on the right bank of Leader. Half a mile further on, the high road to St. Boswells and Jedburgh crosses the Tweed on a lofty bridge. From this point downwards as far as Kelso, the course of the river is one continuous, but changing, scene of beauty. Where its banks are steep, they are densely clad with timber, some of it exceedingly fine ; where they are flat, the surface is either rich pasture or scrupulously tilled. For some distance below the influx of Leader Water, the cliffs rise high on both sides of Tweed, with spaces of 'haugh' or meadow in the windings. The modern mansions of Ravenswood on the right bank, and Gladswood on the left, command views of river-reaches which it would be hard to exceed in loveliness. At Old Melrose the Tweed sweeps round three-fourths of a circle, enclosing the promontory—the *maol ros*—where Aidan founded his monastery in 636. As the Church grew in wealth and influence, so the clergy, secular and regular, became more fastidious about their comfort. They found the ground about Old Melrose inconveniently steep, and persuaded King David to transplant them to the level land at Fordel.

The loop in the river here, which encloses a fine haugh, as well as the height, bears an ancient descriptive name, well known to salmon-fishers. It is called the Cromwell, representing the Anglo-Saxon *crumb wyll,* crooked pool. 'Wele,' commonly written 'wheel,' is a frequent name in the south of Scotland for river pools with a bend in them.   Cromwell circles under a remarkable cliff on the left bank, where scattered pines maintain a precarious hold.   It is called the Gateheugh, from the road that runs along its brow ; another good Scottish word, for 'gate' has not here its modern restricted meaning, but signifies a road or way.[1]   Let no traveller who is not pressed for time decline to breast that 'gate.'   It is winding, it is exceedingly steep, and to describe the surface as indifferent would be to flatter it ; but in all the course of Tweed I know of no scene comparable to this for combined beauty and association with the past.

> ' More mighty spots may rise—more glaring shine—
> But none unite in one attaching maze
> The brilliant, fair and soft—the glories of old days.'

It was here that ' the Shirra' ' always reined in his horse to view his beloved Borderland.   Three hundred feet below, the broad river winds its course, now shimmering in the silver light, now reflecting the sombre hue of sloping woods.   Beyond the Tweed, over the massive oaks of Old Melrose, rise the mystic crests of Eildon, backed by the low, dim outlines of Ettrick and Selkirk Forests.   Due south, the solitary cone of Ruberslaw rears itself from the plain above the shaggy crest of Minto Craigs.   Here, almost at your feet, stands hoary Bemersyde ; beyond it, the peaceful girth of Dryburgh.   To the north you may trace the flowing lines of the Lammermuirs ; and

[1] The Scottish word for 'gate' is 'liggate,' the way into the 'lea' or field.

there stands the lonely tower of Smailholm, a lightless beacon against the eastern sky.

Conspicuous out of all proportion to its dimensions, this keep of Smailholm never fails to arrest a stranger's eye and to prompt the inquiry—What is that? Well, it is ' the outstanding sentinel of all the lower valley of the Tweed'; in other respects, just a Border pele, built, or rebuilt, by the Pringles of Gala in the sixteenth century, and distinguished among scores of its kind by its lonely and commanding position. You may watch from its summit the rainclouds gather on Slitrig and Ettrick to the west, or, turning east, perceive the glimmer of the North Sea beyond Berwick. It is less decayed than most deserted towers, for the steep roof still sheds off the rain and wards out the snow; but the chief renown of Smailholm is that here was the seed sown of that garden of historic fact and poetic fancy which was to be the delight of generations unborn. Six of Walter Scott's brothers and sisters had died in infancy; and he, a weakly child, seemed like to follow the same way. So his parents determined that ' Auld Reekie ' was no fit nurse for him, and sent him to country quarters at his grandfather's farm of Sandyknowe, close under Smailholm Tower. Here he remained, with the exception of twelve months at Bath, till he went to school at Kelso, listening to endless stories of Border raids and warfare from old Sandy Ormiston, the cow-bailie.

> ' And still I thought that shatter'd tower
> The mightiest work of human power ;
> And marvell'd as the aged hind
> With some strange tale bewitch'd my mind,

Of forayers, who, with headlong force,
Down from that strength had spurred their horse,
Their southern rapine to renew
Far in the distant Cheviots blue. '

He was close on thirty before he published his first original poem, *Glenfinlas*, which was followed by the *Eve of St. John*, the scene of which was laid in Smailholm.   The battlefield of Ancrum Moor lies in view on the southern horizon.   Scott's kindly face had been furrowed, his hair blanched, with the anxieties of twenty troubled years, before he had recourse to the same scenery once more, and represented young Graeme, in *The Abbot*, as rescued from drowning in the tarn which sleeps at the foot of the old tower.

At the summit of the Gateheugh, then, midway between the great abbeys of Melrose and Dryburgh, on a September afternoon in 1832, there paused to rest a band of mourners, silent with a sorrow deeper than moves many who meet ' to pay the last mark of respect. '

It was no common funeral this.   These men were bearing from Abbotsford to the prescribed resting-place in St. Mary's aisle of Dryburgh the mortal remains of the intellectual lord of all that land.

A band of mourners, did I say ?   Rather a band among mourners ; for in every hamlet through which they took their course the wayside was lined with folk, the very hillsides were peopled, and thousands of heads were bared to ' the Shirra'. '   Never man lived more universally loved than Sir Walter Scott ; never man dying left behind so many sorrowing hearts.   It was more than mere sentiment that caused Scott to choose Dryburgh Abbey as his last resting-place. The land had passed into the hands of the Haliburtons of New Mains, whose lineal representative was Sir Walter's paternal grandmother. Had Dryburgh remained in that family, he would have inherited it; but the owner having gone bankrupt, 'the ancient patrimony,' said Scott regretfully, 'was sold for a trifle, and my father, who might have purchased it with ease, was dissuaded by my grandfather from doing so, and thus we have nothing left of Dryburgh but the right of stretching our bones there.' The right of sepulture was granted to the Scotts by the Earl of Buchan in 1791.

Bemersyde, perched on a steep bluff overhanging the Haly Wele, a famous salmon pool whereof more anon, is distinguished by the fulfilment of a prophecy, which, if it was not spoken by True Thomas, as it is reputed to have been, at all events is of very high antiquity.

> 'Tyde, tyde, whate'er betyde,
> Haig shall be Haig of Bemersyde.'[1]

Of the great feudal families of Tweedside, how many have disappeared. Avenel and de Soulis, de Vipont, de Morville, and Comyn are blown clean out of remembrance; Douglas, de Vesci, and Maxwell have passed to other shires. Gone, too, are the once powerful religious communities, the Cistercians of Melrose, the Premonstratensians of Dryburgh, the Tironensian monks of Kelso, and the Canons Regular of Jedburgh, all extensive landowners in the valley of

---

[1] This rhyme was malignantly adapted long ago to another old family in the Tweed valley, Purves of that Ilk.
> 'Whate'er betyde, whate'er befa',
> There's aye be gowks at Purves Ha'.'

the Tweed ; but the modest heritage for which Petrus del Haga did homage to Malcolm the Maiden (1153-1165) still owns a good Haig as its lord.   Reckoning by centuries, the story is a venerable one : how much more so does it appear when note is taken of the change in manners and social order !   The aforesaid Petrus appears as witness to the instrument whereby, in 1166, Richard de Morville, Constable of Scotland, sold to Henry St. Clair the persons of Edmund the son of Bonda, and Gillemichel his brother, together with their sons and daughters and all their future progeny.   The price was not exorbitant—three merks, about forty shillings.   There was little concern in those days about allotments or labourers' dwellings.

Though the Haigs do not owe their permanence to their power—they were ever few in number and of small possessions—neither do they owe it to the indolence of the race.   The fifth laird fought under Wallace at Stirling Bridge ; the sixth was on the right side at Bannockburn, and met a soldier's death at Halidon Hill in 1333 ; the eighth and tenth both died in the hour of victory over the English—one under James, second Earl of Douglas, on the moonlit slopes of Otterbourne in 1388 ; the other, under William Douglas, second Earl of Angus, in 1435, when Percy was properly chastised at Piperdean for breaking truce.   Gilbert, eleventh laird, was with Douglas, Earl of Ormonde, when he routed the Percys once more at Sark in 1449.   The twelfth and thirteenth lairds fought on opposite sides at Sauchieburn in 1488 ; and William Haig, the thirteenth, fell at Flodden in 1513. His son Robert, fourteenth laird, distinguished himself in the destruction of the English force under

Evers and Layton at Ancrum Moor in 1544, receiving in reward remission of certain Crown duties due by him. The seventeenth laird had eight sons, four of whom fell in battle in the service of the King of Bohemia in 1629 and 1630. The fifth son, David, succeeding in 1638, left the estate to his eldest born, Antony, who began life in the Swedish army, but turned Quaker, and caused the children who were borne to him by his wife, Jean Home of Bassendean, to be christened Jacob, Zerubabel, Hannah, a second Zerubabel, Lazarus, Emmanuel—then comes a backsliding—Hibernia, William, and Joan. Further we need not follow the race, unless it be to add that the Quaker's brother William got into hot water for joining Lord Balmerino in his *Supplication against Parliamentary Bishops*, which the Lord Advocate of the day denounced as a 'scandalous, reproachful, odious, infamous, and seditious libel, most despitefully belched and vomited forth,' and called upon all good men 'to crush the cockatrice in the egg, and to abhor it as a pestilential clout!'

Bemersyde Tower itself is not nearly so venerable as the family of its lord. It consists of a fine keep erected not earlier than in 1535, doubtless upon older foundations, still inhabited, and, having received extensive modern additions, remarkably comfortable. Sir Walter Scott considered that, like the neighbouring Smailholm, this pele had been erected in compliance with an act of James V., calling upon every landowner on the Borders of £100 valuation to erect a tower as a refuge for his poorer neighbours in times of invasion.[1]

In front of the door stands ' the Covin' Tree, ' a

[1] *Border Antiquities*, vol. ii.

gnarled Spanish chestnut of great girth and age, but of moderate stature. In the flower-garden beyond are some enormous clipped hollies.

From Bemersyde an ancient and narrow paved causeway of bridlepath leads down past the monk's orchard to a loop of the river, embracing the quiet haugh where Dryburgh Abbey rears her shattered towers. The way slants through a sharply sloping wood, and as the stranger saunters down he becomes suddenly aware of a stupendous Presence—a colossal graven image towering above him on the crest of the brae. It is a statue of Wallace which the eleventh Earl of Buchan, living at Dryburgh in the early part of the nineteenth century, caused to be hewn out of red sandstone and set up here. The figure is twenty feet high ; of small artistic merit, yet impressive from its bulk and commanding position, fronting the Eildon Hills and the westering sun. The sculptor was one Smith of Darnwick.

Of all the abbeys in the Tweed valley, none is so sweetly placed as Dryburgh—none so reverently tended. Founded by Hugh de Morville, it was consecrated on St. Martin's day, 11th November 1150, 'that no demons might vex it,' and colonised by White Friars, or Premonstratensians, from Alnwick. Of the original building there are considerable remains, which formed the monastic buildings—sacristy, fratery, chapter-house, and so on—surrounding the cloister. These are in the transition style between Norman and pointed Gothic. This is well shown inside the chapter-house, which has an arcade of intersecting round arches, surmounted by pointed windows. The church is of later work, and has been a noble example of the best period of Gothic building. The nave and choir are roofless, but the arches and fine clerestory of the north transept and the vaulting of the side aisle remain to show what we have lost in the ruin of this splendid fane. It suffered at the same intervals as Melrose, being greatly injured in 1322 by Edward II., who camped in the grounds, and set the building on fire when he marched away. Rebuilt with funds provided by Robert I., it was destroyed again in 1385 by Richard II., and received its death-blow in 1544 from Evers and Layton, who carried off the internal fittings.

It is worth returning upstream from Dryburgh to cross the suspension-bridge, were it but for the bird's-eye view of the abbey and its charming environs as one stands on Braeheads, the crest of a lofty red cliff overhanging a right-angled turn in the river. The quiet little hamlet of Lessuden lies between the high-road and the Tweed, a mile apart from the parish church of St. Boswells, where stood the original village, containing sixteen 'bastel' or fortified houses. The place was ruined and burnt by Evers and Layton in their last fatal raid of 1544; and fragments of Norman carving are all that remain to lend interest to the church itself. Lessuden consists of a single street, ending on St. Boswells green, where are the kennels of the Duke of Buccleuch's foxhounds, and an excellent inn of the old coaching fashion. A new village, distinguished as Newtown St. Boswells, has sprung up round the noisy North British railway-station, a mile to the west of Lessuden, and is interesting only to farmers and salesmen, by reason of the importance and frequency of its cattle and sheep markets.

Bowden, the next parish, contains the burial-vault

of the Kers of the Roxburghe line. The sixth duke, who died in 1879, was the twenty-second chief of the clan in succession to be buried there. The seventh duke was laid in the south transept of Kelso Abbey in 1892. No explanation can be hazarded of a strange jingle connected with this place. It does not even rhyme, though it runs.

> ' Tillieloot, tillieloot, tillieloot o' Bowden !
> Oor cat's kittled in Archie's wig ;
> Tillieloot, tillieloot, tillieloot o' Bowden !
> Three o' them naked and three o' them clad.'

It is probably no more than a nonsense rhyme, representing the iteration of the song of a thrush.

CHAPTER VI

A<small>T</small> no part of its course does the Tweed wind so wantonly as between Dryburgh suspension-bridge and the woods of Merton. The river's destiny is in the North Sea, and eastward it must flow to meet it ; but it is ever turning back towards the beautiful abbey, as if unwilling to desert it. At first it runs an even course of two miles straight north-east. Presently it sweeps round under Clint Hill and turns back south-west almost to Lessuden again ; then comes another majestic loop which brings it to the rocks of Craigover, the first serious turmoil in its whole course from Tweed's Well. The river is now running due north, but, yielding to a red sandstone barrier, it bends gently away to the east close under Lord Polwarth's substantial mansion, graced with splendid trees.

Lord Polwarth is a Scott of Scotts, in direct descent from Auld Wat of Harden, whose ample lands he has inherited. A mile below his house, on the right bank of the river, stands the ruined castle of Littledean, a remarkable building, unlike any other of its class in Scotland. It was once the home of a branch of the Ker clan, though it belongs to Lord Polwarth now, and probably dates from the early part of the sixteenth century. The walls are fully six feet thick, those to the south and west being built in a semicircle (a very unusual feature), well furnished with shot-holes. The steep river-bank ensured defence from attack on the north, and a ravine on the east side—the 'little dean' which gives the place its name—made that aspect secure.

Rutherford, now in the peaceable possession of the English family of Antrobus, was once a place of importance in the Border annals, and through its proprietors in the twelfth and thirteenth centuries gave its name to a small clan famous for its fighting men.   From very early times there was here a church and hospital for the reception of strangers and the maintenance of poor and infirm persons, originally dedicated to the Holy Virgin, but consecrated afresh in the reign of Robert III. to St. Mary Magdalene. About the year 1820 the very sites of these buildings were obliterated by the plough, ' and the grave-stones were broken up and thrown into drains by an improving farmer. ' [1]   Before the Reformation the Kers of Littledean had obtained possession of the lands of Rutherford, and the family of the former owners had moved eastward into Jedworth Forest, where their descendants still own the estate of Edgerston.   Maxton, the parish containing the lands of Rutherford, probably derives its name from Maccus, the son of Undewyn, who obtained extensive lands in Roxburghshire in the twelfth century, and founded the house of Maxwell.

After passing Rutherford, Tweed enters the rocky defile of Makerstoun, from immemorial time the dwelling-place of a branch of the great Celtic family of Macdougal or M'Doual, long and still connected

[1] *New Statistical Account.*

KELSO ABBEY

Photo.

Valentine & Sons Ltd.

with Argyle and Galloway. Mention has been made above of Michael Scott's attempt to dam the Tweed, to which some attribute the formation of the cauld at Kelso;[1] but others, with at least equal confidence, assign that origin to the Trows of Makerstoun. These Trows (*Anglicé* Troughs) consist of a bar of trap rock 450 feet in width through which the river rushes in four narrow slits, descending 16 feet in the transit. Two of these channels are 35 feet deep, and they used to be so narrow that at low water an active man might leap from one to the other without wetting his feet. But one came to grief here on a day, so further mischance was avoided by artificially widening the channel.

Below Makerstoun, on the left bank, lies the stately demesne of Floors, the palace of the Duke of Roxburghe, whose ancestors, in days when chieftainship carried definite privilege and power, hotly disputed Ker of Fernihirst's claim to be reckoned head of the ' cappit Kers. ' It was one of those questions which can never be decided except by agreement, and agreement was hard to come by in feudal times. So luckless William Ker of Ancrum, grandson of the laird of Fernihirst, found to his cost in 1590, when Robert Ker, younger of Cessford, the rival house, ended the dispute by murdering him, being instigated, it is said, by his mother to adopt that conclusive form of argument. The Fernihirst branch, now represented by the Marquess of Lothian, spell their name Kerr, and are said to be descended from Thomas Ker of Fernihirst, a younger brother of Ker of Cessford in the fifteenth century. Sir George Mackenzie, however, declared that the Fernihirst Kers must be des-

[1] See p. 72 *ante.*

9

cended from the elder brother, because they carry the same arms as the Kers of England and France without any difference, namely a white chevron on a red field with three red stars on the chevron; and so the Marquess of Lothian displays them at this day; whereas the Duke of Roxburghe, as Ker of Cessford, carries his white chevron on a green field, with three black stars on the chevron. This difference Sir George accounted for in the following manner. In the reign of James IV. a laird of Cessford was killed fighting the English in a green meadow; wherefore the King directed that thenceforward the Kers of Cessford should display their chevron upon a green field instead of a red one, with the honourable addition of three unicorns' heads; which arms are now carried by the Duke of Roxburghe.

The battle of Melrose in 1526, where Ker of Cessford fell,[1] marked the outset of a deadly feud between the Kers of both branches and the Scotts, which ran its bloody course for thirty-eight years. When need arose, these families fought side by side to repel English invasion; but so soon as the Border was secure again they were at each other's throats. In 1535 the laird of Buccleugh was imprisoned and his lands forfeited for levying war upon the Kers, but he was restored by Act of Parliament in 1542. Ten years later Sir Walter Scott of Buccleuch was set upon by some of the Ker faction in Edinburgh and slain in the street, and so matters went on till the year 1564, when the Government made a determined effort to stanch the feud. The provisions of a contract, undertaken in that year before the Lords of the Council, between Sir Walter Ker of Cessford on the one part and

[1] See p. 56 *ante.*

Sir Walter Scott of Branxholm (Buccleuch) on the other, are of a singular kind. Each chieftain answered for his whole clan. First, Buccleuch undertook that neither he nor any of his people should take any action, criminal or civil, against the laird of Cessford 'for ony slauchter or blude committit in tyme bypast,' including the slaughter of Buccleuch's grandfather in 1552, and Cessford undertook the same obligation towards Buccleuch, including the slaughter of Cessford's father in 1526. Each family having bagged the chief of the other, they should now cry quits. But whereas the laird of Fernihirst, with that section of the Kers represented by the lairds of the Hirsell, Woodhead, Prymsydloch, Torbet, Graden, and Highton, had refused to stanch the feud, Buccleuch and his friends were declared to be 'na wayis prejugit [prejudiced] anent thair actionis quhatsumevir that thai haif intentit or may intent' against these gentlemen. Finally, the laird of Cessford undertook to come to St. Giles's Church in Edinburgh, and there, in presence of the congregation, 'reverently upone his kneis ask God mercy of the slauchter foirsaid [that of the laird of Buccleuch], and siclyk, ask forgevenes of the same fra the said Laird of Bukcleucht.' [1]

Fernihirst and his friends must have found the combination of Buccleuch and Cessford too strong to be withstood, for we find their signatures appended to a remarkable 'band,' concluded at Kelso in April 1569, between the barons, municipal officers, and others on the East and Middle Marches for the repression of crime on the Border. The signatories,

[1] Original in General Register House, Edinburgh, vol. vii. fol. 131. Also printed in Pitcairn's *Criminal Trials*, iii. 390.

thirty-two in number, represent the chief families of Scott, Ker, Home, Douglas, Turnbull, Cranstoun, Macdougal, etc., and the burghs of Jedburgh, Hawick, and Selkirk ; they bind themselves to put an end to 'the innumerabill slauchteris, fyre-rasings, heirschippis [plunderings], and detestabill enormities dalie committit,' and to that end declare war upon 'all personis of the suirnames of Armestrang, Ellot, Niksoun, Croser, Littil, Batesoun, Thomsoun, Irwing, Bell, Johnnestoun, Glendonyng, Routlaige, Hendersoun, and Scottis of Ewisdaill,' together with their wives, families, and tenants, who should not find surety before the Wardens for good behaviour within eight days of the completion of the 'band.' Those who could not find surety ' we shall persew to the deid [death] with ffyre, swerd and all vther kynd of hostilitie, and expone thaim and all thing in thair possessoun in pray to the men of weir [war].' Truly a formidable measure of police ; but it failed. The barons could not afford to put down those hardy moss-troopers, upon whom they relied as auxiliaries in quarrels among themselves and in the English war; so Armstrongs, Elliots, and others in Liddesdale, Eskdale, and the Debatable Land continued their system of rapine and blackmail until the union of the Crowns forced them into more orderly courses.

Meanwhile, however, the great feud between the Kers and Scotts was finally stanched ; and, in the same year that witnessed the completion of the above 'band, ' Sir Thomas Ker of Fernihirst married Janet, daughter of William Scott, younger of Branxholm and Buccleuch. The third son of this marriage was the well-known Robert Carre, James VI.'s favourite, created Viscount Rochester and Earl of Somerset.

Immediately opposite Floors on the right bank of the river is a low green ridge, with scattered groves, lying between the Tweed and Teviot above their junction. This Mesopotamia—this tongue of land between the rivers—must ever have powerful attractions for Scotsmen, apart from the grandeur of the landscape, for here stood the town and castle of Roxburgh, a name famous in our early annals. In the twelfth century the town was girt with wall and fosse; it contained three churches, schools, and a royal mint, was the fourth town of the realm in respect to population, and its castle was one of the four great national strongholds, the others being Edinburgh, Stirling, and Berwick. The total disappearance of this once important town, and the erasure, almost as complete, of the great fortress which gave it importance, is one of the most remarkable features in Scottish topography. Cities may dwindle and decay, but they seldom vanish altogether ; here was one where King Edward I., coming on the Monday after Ascension Day 1295, found good entertainment at the house of the Grey Friars ; on the following day he moved to the castle, where he lodged eight days. [1] Yet of this town not even the foundations can be traced ; and of the great castle only a few shapeless fragments of its massive walls remain.

Originally an integral part of the Saxon kingdom of Northumberland, Roxburgh town and castle became incorporated with Scotland when David I., hitherto Earl of Northumberland, ascended the throne in 1124. From the moment that Bruce drew the sword against King Edward in 1306, the possession of this key to the Middle Marches was the cause of

[1] *Voyage of Kynge Edwarde into Scotland* (Archæologia, xxi. 478).

incessant conflict. It was in English hands in that
year, James the Steward having surrendered it to
Edward on 13th May 1296, immediately after the
sack of Berwick.   In the autumn of 1306, when the
Prince of Wales captured the Queen of Scots and the
King's two sisters Marjorie and Marie de Brus in
Kildrummie Castle, Edward ordered that the two
princesses were to be confined in cages in the castles
of Roxburgh and Berwick ; the Countess of Buchan,
also, was to be caged in the Tower of London.   This
sounds a more barbarous doom than it really was.
Directions for the construction of these cages have
been preserved : they were made of wooden lattice
strengthened with iron, and were erected *inside* turrets
of the respective castles.   Moreover, English wait-
ing-women were provided to attend on the ladies, and
comforts denied to ordinary prisoners were attended
to *(et q la kage soit ensi fait q la contesse y eit essement de
chambre cortoise)*. [1]   Edward I.—*malleus Scottorum*—
showed no mercy to men among his enemies, but it
is an error to suppose that he inflicted indignity or
suffering upon the ladies whom he had to imprison in
pursuance of his policy.   He was a ruthless foe, but
a chivalrous one.

Roxburgh Castle remained in English possession
until 1314—the year of Bannockburn,—when it was
recovered by a neat stratagem of Good Sir James of
Douglas.   Choosing Shrove Tuesday, when he knew
the garrison would be merry-making on the eve of
Lent, he picked sixty stout fellows and made them
cover their armour with black frocks.   Then in the
dusk he led them to the green brae under the walls,

---

[1] *Documents, etc., illustrating the History of Scotland.*   Edited by Sir
R. Palgrave, p. 358.

where they scattered on all fours, so that the sentries should mistake them for browsing cattle. A crafty fellow named Sym of the Ledous (Leadhouse) had rigged up some rope-ladders with hooks to fling over the battlements, and was the first to scale the wall. Sym slew the sentry, and also another man who heard the scuffle and came to his comrade's help, before they could give the alarm; Douglas and his men followed quietly, forming up outside the great hall where dancing was in full swing. Suddenly the doors were flung open; the black-coated Scots rushed in crying 'A Douglas! a Douglas!' and we may imagine that the revellers got a short shrift, poor fellows! However, the governor, Sir William de Fiennes, a knight of Gascony, was in the keep, and managed to hold it all next day. Receiving a fearful wound in the face (of which he died not long after), he capitulated on condition of being allowed to march out with the honours of war and pass into England. King Robert caused the castle to be rased, according to his uniform strategy in this war.

The year 1332 is a black one in Scottish annals. The Regent, Randolph Earl of Moray, last of the famous trio who had accomplished the independence of their country, died suddenly, of poison, as was confidently affirmed. There was no hand firm enough to handle the reins except that of March, who betrayed his trust, and threw in his lot with the usurper, Edward Baliol. Roxburgh Castle must have been rebuilt by this time, for here Baliol acknowledged Edward III. as his feudal lord and alienated to him the towns, castles, and territories of Berwick and Roxburgh. [1] King Edward thereafter was often

[1] *Fœdera*, iv. 536, 538, 548 (folio edition).

in Roxburgh, twice celebrating his birthday there.
So matters remained till 1342.   David II. had not
long returned from his nine years' exile in France,
when they brought him word that Sir Alexander
Ramsay of Dalwolsey (Dalhousie) had taken Roxburgh Castle by a night escalade.[1]   The young King
showed his gratitude for this signal service by making
this gallant knight Sheriff of Teviotdale and Constable of Roxburgh Castle—fitting reward, indeed,
but, as it turned out, a fatal honour for Ramsay.

Experienced men foresaw the trouble, 'for few
were the things that King David did with mature
deliberation and the advice of wise men ; but his acts
were often headstrong, on his own judgment and
without counsel, as afterwards became plain.'[2]   For
Sir William Douglas, Knight of Liddesdale and
Flower of Chivalry, of whom we have heard before,
had recovered all Teviotdale from the English by his
own good sword, and held those offices which he was
now bidden to resign in favour of Ramsay.   Roxburgh Castle he had failed to win ; he could not brook
that the honour of taking it should be another's.
Ramsay was his old comrade-in-arms, yet he should
pay for this affront.   Douglas handed over his offices
to his successor with perfect outward show of friend-
liness ; but in his heart he cherished a horrible vengeance.

The new sheriff, having summoned a court to meet
in the church of Hawick, was waiting while it as-

[1] Sir Thomas Gray, the English writer of *Scalacronica*, expresses
himself as scandalised by the impiety of this act.   It took place on
Easter morning ' at the very hour of the Resurrection,' and he draws
the moral that all concerned therein came to an evil end (Leland's
synopsis : the original passage in *Scalacronica* having been written on
the missing folio).
[2] *Liber Pluscardensis*, ii. 222.

sembled, when *supervenit filius invidiæ*—'there arrived that brat of jealousy'[1]—the Knight of Liddesdale with a strong following. They seized Sir Alexander Ramsay, bound him in a saddle, and carried him off to the lonely castle of Hermitage, where this brave knight was flung into a dungeon (horse and all, they say), and literally starved to death.[2] *O inexterminabilis invidia diaboli !* 'O the unquenchable jealousy of the devil !' exclaims Bower in relating this tragedy,[3] and winds up with an appropriate quotation from Seneca ; but, after all, what shocked this pious Abbot of Inchcolm most in the whole affair was the sacrilege committed in Hawick Church. To King David, the worst part of Douglas's crime was that it was committed upon the person of his officer ; but he pardoned the offender and actually bestowed the offices rendered vacant by the murder upon the assassin himself! The first obligation upon the Crown of Scotland, overriding justice and humanity, was ever to keep in good humour enough powerful barons to overawe the rest. Among all the kings of Scots, after Alexander III., Robert the Bruce was the only one whose lords were made to feel that violence and treason did not pay.

Thenceforward, Douglas rose ever higher in favour with King David, receiving enormous tracts of forfeited lands : albeit there can be little doubt that he was in treasonable negotiation with the King of

---

[1] *Liber Pluscardensis*, ii, 222.
[2] In his notes to *The Lay*, Scott says that one 'digging for stones about the old castle of the Hermitage, broke into a vault containing a quantity of chaff, some bones and pieces of iron ; amongst others, the curb of an ancient bridle, which the author has since given to the Earl of Dalhousie, under the impression that it may possibly be a relic of his brave ancestor.'
[3] Bower's *Continuation* of Fordun's *Chronicle*.

England for the restoration of Edward Baliol.   The Flower of Chivalry held high command under David in the ill-starred expedition to Tynedale in 1346, and was taken prisoner with his king at the battle of Neville's Cross, near Hexham, on 17th October.   Where so many Scottish knights died in their harness, this Douglas might have found a fitting end.   But he had two strings to his bow.   King David entered upon eleven years of captivity in England ; but Douglas purchased his freedom by treason.   He bound himself by an indenture executed in London, 17th July 1352, to be the King of England's faithful liege, and to hold his lands of Liddesdale always open for the free passage of English troops into Scotland. [1]   It has been told in an earlier chapter how that foul compact was voided and the knight balked of his wages by the sword of another and a truer William Douglas. [2]

One of the evil consequences to Scotland of the disaster at Neville's Cross was that Roxburgh Castle passed once more into English keeping, and hither came the victorious Edward III. after the capture of Berwick in 1355.   Hither also came another Edward —Edward Baliol—and totally resigned to the King of England his kingdom of Scotland.   He laid his crown at the stronger Edward's feet, together with a portion of Scottish soil, and disappeared from history with a pension of £2000.

In 1435 James I. laid determined siege to 'the castell of Marchmound, that is to say, Roxburgh.... At last quhen the kyng had lyne at the sege foresaid XV. dayis and waistit all his munitioun and

[1] Bain's *Documents*, etc., iii. 286.
[2] See p. 29, *ante*.

powder, he returnit haim.'[1] Another attempt,
made by James II. in 1460, had a better issue,
though not for the King of Scots himself. He had
taken the town, and levelled it ; but on 3rd August
he was watching his gunners serve the great piece
called The Lion, when it burst and killed him on
the spot. His queen, Mary of Gueldres, nothing
daunted, brought young James III., a boy of eight
years, and allowed no respite to the garrison, who
capitulated shortly after. She then ordered the
complete destruction of the great castle, and although
Protector Somerset attempted to repair the ruins for
a garrison of five hundred men in 1547, it ceased to
be the place of strength to hold which had cost the
shedding of so much good blood. The land on
which town and castle had stood was granted by
James IV. to Walter Ker of Cessford in 1499, and
it remains the property of his descendant, the Duke
of Roxburghe.

The present village of Roxburgh, a couple of
miles further up the Teviot than the old town,
offers no temptation for lingering there.

Teviot and Teviotdale are too serious an enterprise for the middle of a chapter, so we will pass
the junction of the rivers, and so on to the good
town of Kelso. The handsome gateway standing
close to the bridge leads into Springwood Park, the
well-timbered demesne of Sir George Douglas, who
derives his descent from the ancient house of Cavers.
The name chosen for this place sounds sadly sub-
urban ; pity that the old one should have been
discarded. It was formerly called Maxwell, having
been granted, with the salmon fishery, by David I.

[1] Bellenden's *History.*

[1124-1153] to Maccus the son of Unwin. The fishery became known as 'Maccus' wele'; the lands took its name from the fishery, and the owners of the land, as was customary in feudal times, borrowed the name of the land as a surname, becoming de Maccuswell or Maxwell. The salmon cast below Kelso Bridge is still called Maxwheel, but the family of Maxwell had migrated to the western Border before the end of the thirteenth century.

In the absence of early scripts it would be vain to attempt an explanation of the name Kelso, so utterly does the modern rendering conceal what is probably its meaning. But in one of the Welsh bruts (*Book of Taliessin*, xviii.) the place is called Calchvynyd, which is plain Welsh—*calch mynydd*—for chalk-hill, and in the twelfth century it is written Calchou, referring, says Chalmers, to 'a calcareous eminence which appears conspicuous in the middle of the town, and which is still called the Chalk Heugh.'[1] Kelso, then, doubtless means simply Chalk Hill; for although there is no real chalk there, gypsum crops out on the face of the aforesaid brae, and gypsum is a calcareous deposit. The noble bridge of five arches spanning the united waters of Tweed and Teviot was finished in 1803 by young John Rennie, to replace one built in 1754, which was swept away by the mighty flood of 26th October 1797. Rennie's bridge was the first one ever carried on elliptic arches, a design which he afterwards repeated in Waterloo Bridge, London. The bridge of 1754 was a successor to a 'great stone brigge with arches' which the Scots broke down as a measure of defence against Protector Somerset in 1547.

[1] *Caledonia*, ii. 156.

Kelso, with its population of four thousand, is now but a cheerful market-town, well-to-do, bright, and favoured by a sylvan and richly cultivated environment. But it was once the great ecclesiastical centre of Scotland, in an age when ecclesiastical authority overawed all other in the realm. When David, Earl of Huntingdon, in 1113, transplanted thirteen Benedictine monks from Tiron in Picardy to his gloomy Forest of Selkirk, and bade them build a monastery at the ' schele chirche,' they little relished the grim skies and weeping soil of that upland. So when David became King of Scots he took pity on the shivering Frenchmen ; in 1126 he translated their abbey of SS. Mary and John to ' the place called Calkow,' and here in 1128 was begun the building of a magnificent conventual church. Immense possessions were granted to the monks by the pious David, yielding an annual rental of £3716, the value of which in modern money it is impossible to calculate ; but it may be mentioned that two hundred years later, in 1327, the total revenue on the King's ' great custom ' on merchandise exported from the kingdom amounted to only £1852.

The abbot of Kelso stood highest amongst the spiritual lords of Parliament, and in 1165 the Pope bestowed upon him the privilege of the mitre. The abbot also claimed precedence over the superiors of all other monasteries in Scotland ; but in 1420 James 1. awarded that eminence to the Prior of St. Andrews, in consideration of the greater antiquity of that foundation.

The Tironensian monks had a noble conception of what a great church should be. The fragments remaining testify to a structure in that late Norman and transitional style of Gothic which, in the judgment of some lovers of architecture, is more impressive even than the pointed order at its meridian. The tower has much of the external character of a Norman keep, with its massive corner protections or flat buttresses; indeed, it is to the military and strongly defensive nature of the building that we owe the survival even of those sorely defaced parts of the church which remain standing. Nothing short of the strongest construction could have saved it from effacement as complete as befell Roxburgh Castle. It is well that from the fourteenth to the seventeenth century no more powerful explosive than gunpowder was in use; one trembles to think to what purpose Dacre and Hertford might have employed dynamite or lyddite. This monastery was the first to suffer in Bruce's wars; the upper part of the tower dates from its repairs in 1344. In June 1523, a period when the war with England culminated in its ferocity, Lord Dacre, having captured 'Dand' Ker in the castle of Fernihirst, marched upon Kelso, sacked the town, gutted the monastery, fired the dormitories, and completely unroofed the abbey. The monks were scattered far and wide as mendicants, in reality as well as in name, wherever they could find shelter; and although James Stuart, the King's bastard, was nominal abbot—the last to hold that office—the glory of that great establishment was gone and its work wellnigh at an end. The lands and rents still remained, however; Melrose and St. Andrews were given also to the pluralist James, Holyrood and Coldingham to his brothers Robert and John respectively; the united incomes of these five great houses falling little short of the revenue of the Crown at that time.

In 1542 the Duke of Norfolk—better known north of the Tweed as Earl of Surrey, ' Scourge of the Scots '—crossed the Border, and in eight days burnt fourteen towns and hamlets, including Floors, with Fair Croft, and Kelso with its abbey. Next came Hertford's expedition in 1545. One would say that little more damage could be wrought at Kelso ; nevertheless twelve monks had gathered again round the desecrated altar, and collected a garrison of some seventy Borderers and townsmen. Summoned by York Herald to surrender, these gallant fellows defied the English lord, and repulsed an attack by Spanish mercenaries. Then Hertford bombarded the monastery, and the garrison retreated into the church tower, which was taken next day by assault. Some of the defenders had escaped in the night ; only forty-five remained, who were all put to the sword except five. Thereafter Hertford caused all the lead to be stripped from the roofs of the abbey buildings, and the towers and walls to be mined. On the Sunday following, to quote York Herald, who wrote a report upon this terrible campaign, ' the abbey of Kelse was razed and all put to royen [ruin], howsses and towres and stypeles, and the wittaieles cam, and [the] cartes [were] loden again w^t the leed [lead] of the said abbey. . . . Yesterday byng Satterday whas 3 Scottes men hang in thes campe and 9 schleyn in fild be the horshemen. . . . On Monday wy departyt from Kelsey abbey that was.' [1]

When Protector Somerset came to Kelso two years later, after the battle of Pinkie, he found the town deserted, the abbey much in the condition we

[1] From a MS. in Trinity College, Dublin, printed by the Society of Scottish Antiquaries, vol. i. pp. 271-276.

behold at the present day ; so he encamped in the Friar's Haugh below Roxburgh Castle, which he set his troops to fortify. Leaving a garrison of five hundred there, he marched into England, but not before the chief men of the Kers (both branches) and many other Border families had come in to make submission to him. Buccleuch and the Scotts, be it noted to their honour, were not among them.

And so ended the active history of the great Abbey of Kelso. Its lands and revenues were taken over by the Lords of the Congregation in the name of the Crown in 1559. In that or the following year a few monks who still clung to it were driven out by the Reformers, and their poor fittings and furnishings destroyed by the mob.

The town of Kelso, lying as it did in the fairway between England and Scotland, continued to witness a full share of what was stirring. In 1570 took place the last, but not the least destructive, inroad of an English army into Scotland, specially directed against the Scotts and Kers, as staunch adherents of Queen Mary. Sussex and Hundon were Queen Elizabeth's generals upon this occasion : they wound up their raid by a rendezvous at Kelso, with the comfortable assurance that they had burnt and destroyed fifty strong castles and peles, and more than three hundred villages.

In the next century General Leslie made Kelso the headquarters of the Covenanting army in 1639 ; and hither came Montrose in 1644, lured by the empty promises of the Kers, who were probably in direct communication with Leslie. Disappointed in his assurance of royalist support from both sides of the Border, Montrose marched up the Tweed to meet with disaster at doleful Philiphaugh. In 1715 Kelso was the appointed place of muster for the Jacobites of the West under Lord Kenmure, the Highlanders under Macintosh of Borlum, and the dalesmen of northern England under Lord Derwentwater and Mr. Foster. They lay there three days, and then marched on to Preston. Again, and lastly, in 1745, Prince Charlie lay at Kelso a couple of nights on his march to Derby.

CHAPTER VII

THE reader will now consent to quit the rich valley and gracious woods through which I have been leading him and ascend once more to the great water-divide of southern Scotland, in order to trace from its source Tweed's sister, Teviot, a stream as well dowered in song and story as the other.

The Teviot rises at a point 700 feet above the sea, a little more than thirty-seven miles from its junction with the Tweed at Kelso, Wisp Hill (1950 feet) and Todhope Hill (1961 feet) being its most conspicuous sponsors, marking the boundary between the shires of Roxburgh and Dumfries—Teviotdale and Eskdale. The scenery and land surface is of the same character as that of upper Tweeddale, and the sole industry in both places is sheep-farming ; but, of old, in proportion as Teviotdale lay nearer to the English border than Tweeddale, life and property in the first were even more precarious than in the other. Moreover, just over the ridge on the western watershed lay a district between the Sark and the Esk which, after Bruce won the independence of Scotland, was claimed by both nations, held by neither, and at last recognised as neutral, known as 'Batable or Threip Lands'

—the Debatable Land. This region became the haunt of both Scots and English, broken men, often of good family, who, ruined by the fortune of war, and incapable of extracting an honest living out of these uplands, frankly took to brigandage. From time to time the central government made spasmodic efforts to suppress these raiders, but in ordinary times the sole authority was vested in the Warden of the Marches. That high official had his own legitimate interests to serve in the protection of his lands from English inroads ; no more effective auxiliaries than these excellent irregulars. Far from being earnest in desiring to extirpate the Armstrongs, Elliots, and others, successive Wardens secured support and swelled their own following by taking bonds of 'manrent' or mutual service from the petty chiefs. In short, the Warden was usually pretty blind as to the means by which his neighbours maintained themselves, so long as they respected the property of himself and his friends.

Even the King's government willingly employed the men of the Debatable Land for offence or defence against England. They could put in the field a force contemptible neither in numbers nor quality. Every freebooter's house was a tower of defence, and the available force of the Armstrongs and others was estimated in 1528 by the Earl of Northumberland at three thousand cavalry. As to quality, these mosstroopers had fallen off no whit from Froissart's description in 1327.—

' They carry with them no provisions of bread or wine, being of such temperate habits that they will live for a long time on flesh half-sodden, without bread, and drink the river water for wine. They have therefore no use for pot or pans, for they dress the flesh of cattle in their skins, and being sure to find plenty of cattle in the country which they invade, they carry none with them. Under the flap of his saddle each man carries a broad plate of metal ; behind the saddle a little bag of oatmeal. When they have eaten too much of the sodden flesh, and their stomachs feel weak and empty, they place this plate over the fire, mix their oatmeal with water, and put a little of the paste on the hot plate, so making a thin cake, which they eat to warm their stomachs... They are mounted upon little hackneys that are never tied up or dressed, but turned to pasture on the heath or in the fields at the end of every day's march.'

Well might the rulers of Scotland hesitate to destroy such splendid fighting material during the long struggle against powerful England. But it went ill with the Armstrongs and their friends when there came a temporary suspension of arms, such as the triple treaty of peace concluded in 1515 between England, Scotland, and France. Special and stringent measures were arranged in that treaty for joint action between the English and Scottish Wardens to repress Border raiding. They did not take immediate effect ; but after young James V. had shaken off the thraldom of his stepfather Angus, he showed all the precocious energy of the Stuarts in dealing with the men of the Debatable Land. He imprisoned Lord Maxwell, the Warden, took matters into his own hand, and we do not follow Teviot far from its source before arriving at a scene which brings vividly to mind the rule of this monarch, not yet of full age, whose purpose was that of the first James when he swore that 'the key should keep the castle and the rush bush the cow through all Scotland.'

It was the climax of that midsummer hunting of 1530 in Meggatdale, which was described in chapter iii. of this volume. [1] Acting in concert with Lord Dacre, the English Warden, James rode over in force from Ettrick to Teviotdale, and encamped at Carlanrig, near the junction of the Frostly Burn, where there was a chapel and hamlet, to the south-west of the present kirk of Teviothead. It is alleged, and commonly believed, that the King had proclaimed indemnity to all broken men who should come in and make submission to him. Now the most dreaded of all freebooters of the Debatable Land at this time was Johnnie Armstrong of Gilnockie, brother to the Laird of Mangerton. Three years before, the English Warden had burnt Johnnie's tower of Gilnockie, in the church lands of Canonbie on the Esk ; but Johnnie still rode free, secure in the protection of the Scottish Warden, Lord Maxwell, who had received him as his vassal, and taken a bond of manrent from him. Now the King had taken the precaution to lay Maxwell in prison ; and Johnnie, threatened by the authority of both England and Scotland, began to find things getting too hot for him. It may well be that he was willing to abide within the law if only means of keeping body and soul together were open to him ; so, trusting to the royal word, he rode boldly into the King's camp at Carlanrig to make obeisance. Behind him rode four-and-twenty stout fellows, ' verrie richlie apparelled.' [2] They were brought before the King, who, displeased at their splendour, pointed at Gilnockie and asked angrily, ' What wants yon knave that a

[1] See p. 40, *ante*.
[2] Lindsay of Pitscottie.

king should have?' The ballad of *Johnie Armstrang*
tallies so closely with the sequel as told by contemporary chroniclers that no other version need be
given in this place.——

    'Some speak of lords, some speak of lairds,
        And sic-like men of high degree,
    But I shall sing of a gentleman,
        Sometime called Laird of Gilnockie.

    The King has written a loving letter
        Wi' his ain hand sae tenderlie ;
    And he has it sent to Johnie Armstrang
        To come and speak wi' him speedilie.

    The Ellots and Armstrangs did convene ;
        They were a gallant companie ;
    " We 'll ride and meet our lawful King,
        And bring him safe to Gilnockie.

    " Make kinnen [1] and capon ready then,
        And venison in great plentie ;
    We'll welcome hame our royal King ;
        I hope he'll dine at Gilnockie. "

    They ran their horse on the Langholm howm,
        And brak their spears wi' muckle main ;
    The ladies looked frae their loft windows :
        " God bring our men weel back again ! "

    When Johnie cam before the King,
        Wi' a' his men sae brave to see,
    The King he moved his bonnet to him,
        He ween'd he was a king as he.

    " May I find grace, my sovereign liege,
        Grace for my loyal men and me ?
    For my name it is Johnie Armstrang,
        A subject o' yours, my liege, " quo' he.

[1] *Kinnen, cuning* = a rabbit.

" Away, away, thou traitor strang !
Out o' my sicht soon mayst thou be !
I granted never a traitor's life,
And now I 'll not begin with thee. "

" Grant me my life, my liege, my King !
And a goodlie gift I 'll gie to thee ;
Full four-and-twenty milk-white steeds
Were a' foaled in ae year to me.

" I 'll gie thee all these milk-white steeds,
That prance and nicher at a spear ;
With as meikle gude English gelt
As four o' their braid backs can bear. "

" Away, away, thou traitor strang !
Out o' my sicht soon mayst thou be !
I granted never a traitor's life,
And now I 'll not begin with thee.

" Grant me my life, my liege, my King !
And a costly gift I 'll gie to thee ;
Gude four-and-twenty ganging mills,
That gang through a' the year to me.

" These four-and-twenty mills complete
Sall gang for thee throughout the year ;
And as meikle of gude red wheat
As a' their happers dow to bear. "

" Away, away, thou traitor strang !
Out o' my sicht soon mayst thou be !
I granted never a traitor's life,
And now I 'll not begin with thee. "

" Grant me my life, my liege, my King !
And a great gift I 'll gie to thee ;
Bauld four-and-twenty sisters' sons
Sall for thee fight though a' should flee. "

"Away, away, thou traitor strang!
  Out o' my sicht soon mayst thou be!
I granted never a traitor's life,
  And now I 'll not begin with thee."

"Grant me my life, my liege, my King!
  And a brave gift I 'll gie to thee;
All between here and Newcastle town
  Sall pay their yearly rent to thee."

"Away, away, thou traitor strang!
  Out o' my sicht soon mayst thou be!
I granted never a traitor's life,
  And now I 'll not begin with thee."

"Ye lie, ye lie, now King!" he says,
  "For all a king and prince ye be;
For I hae lo'ed naething in a' my life,
  I will daur say't, but honestie—

"Save a fleet horse and a fair woman,
  Twa bonnie dogs to kill a deer;
But England shuild find me meal and malt,
  Gif I had lived this hundred year.

"She suld hae found me in meal and malt,
  And beef and mutton in great plentie;
But ne'er a Scots wife could hae said
  That I had hurt her a puir flie.

"To seek het water aneath cauld ice,
  I trow it is a great follie;
I askit grace at a graceless face,
  And there is nane for my men and me.

"But had I kenn'd, or I left my hame,
  How thou unkind wad'st been to me,
I wad hae kept thy Border side,
  In spite o' a' thy peers and thee.

"Wist England's King that I was ta'en,
  O gin a blyth man he wad be!
For ance I slew his sister's son,
  And on his breast-bane brak a tree."

Johnie wore a girdle about his middle
  Embroidered o'er wi' burning gold,
Bespangled wi' the same metal,
  Maist beautiful was to behold.

There hung nine targats at Johnie's hat,
  And ilk ane worth three hundred pound—
"What wants yon knave that a king should have,
  But the sword of honour and the crown?

"O whaur gat ye those targats, Johnie,
  That blink sae brawlie abune thy bree?"
"I gat them in the field fechting,
  Where, cruel King, thou daur'st na be!

"Had I my horse and my harness gude,
  And riding as I wont to be,
It shuild hae been tauld this hundred year—
  This meeting o' my King and me.

"God be wi' thee, Christy my brother!
  Lang live thou, Laird o' Mangertoun!
Lang maist thou live on the Border side,
  Ere thou see thy brother ride up and doun.

"And God be wi' thee, Christy my son!
  Where thou sits on thy nurse's knee;
But an thou live this hundred year
  Thy father's better thou 'lt never be.

"Fairweel, my bonnie Gilnock-ha'!
  Where on the Esk thou standest stout;
Gif I had lived but seven year mair
  I wad hae gilt thee round about."

> Johnie murdered was at Carlinrigg,
>   And a' his gallant companie ;
> But Scotland's heart was ne'er sae wae
>   To see sae mony brave men dee.
>
> Because they saved their country dear
>   Frae Englishmen : none were sae bauld ;
> While Johnie lived on the Border side
>   Nane o' them durst cam near his hauld.'

Lindsay of Pitscottie breathes a kindly sigh for poor Johnnie, whose memory on the western Border is cherished much as Englishmen cherish that of Robin Hood.

'The king hanged Johne Armstrang, Laird of Kilnokie, quhilk monie Scottis menne heavilie lamented, for he was ane doubted [redoubtable] man, and als gude ane Christane as evir was vpoun the Borderis.   And albeit he was ane lous leivand [loose-living] man, and sustained the number of xxiiij weill-horsed able gentlemen with him, yitt he nevir molested no Scottis man.   Bot it is said from the Scottis border to New Castle of Ingland, thair was not ane of quhatsoever estate bot payed to this Johne Armstrang ane tribut, to be frie of his cumbir, he was so doubtit [dreaded] in Ingland.'

'Hereabouts, ' wrote Miss Wordsworth in 1803, 'Mr. Walter Scott had directed us to look about for some old stumps of trees, said to be the place where Johnnie Armstrong was hanged, but we could not find them out. '   One would fain disbelieve the statement that King James entrapped these men by a proclamation of pardon ; there can be little doubt that Johnnie rode in on the faith of it.   True, he and his men had been excommunicated ; all men were absolved from keeping faith with them ; but

should a king—the Fountain of Honour—stoop to
shelter behind priestly devices ? It is to be feared
that among his other Renaissance studies, James
had steeped himself in the principles of Machiavelli.
' A monarch's promises,' wrote the Duke of Alva
bluntly to Philip II. in 1573, 'are not to be regarded
as so sacred as those of humbler mortals.'

Six miles below Carlanrig, after Teviot has been
reinforced from the south-east by one of those
innumerable Allan Waters that are found all over
Southern Scotland, the road passes close by a house
famous beyond most others in Border history.
Those who chose the site of Branxholm Tower had
a keen eye for a military position, as was expedient
in this region. The Castle, which has been masked
by much modern building, stands on rising ground
at a sharp turn of the Teviot, and commands a clear
view up and down the glen. Sir Walter Scott has
repeated the tradition of how the lands of Branxholm
passed into possession of his ancestor, Sir William
Scott of Buccleuch, in the reign of James I. (1406-
1437). Half of the barony formed part of the
estate of Sir Thomas Inglis of Manor, a knight of
unwarlike habits, who complained bitterly of the risk
and loss he suffered from the proximity of Branxholm to the English border. Buccleuch had no
misgivings on that score, and offered to exchange his
estate of Murthockstone or Murdiestoun in Lanarkshire for Sir Thomas's share in Branxholm ; which
offer was gladly accepted. Buccleuch, in setting
seal to the bargain, observed significantly that Cumberland cattle were quite as good as those of Teviotdale, and began a system of raiding on English
ground, which became hereditary among his stout

posterity. In 1443 this Sir William's grandson, Sir Walter Scott, in reward for good service against the rebellious house of Douglas, received a grant from James II. of the other half of the barony of Branxholm, to be held in blench for the annual payment of a red rose.

The oldest part of the existing house of Branxholm has been so thoroughly incorporated with later work as to be past recognition. The ancient castle was burnt by the Earl of Northumberland in 1532, and the walls were blown up during Surrey's invasion in 1570. It was rebuilt in the years 1571-6 in a manner very unusual in the northern kingdom, the entrance door being an example, almost unique in Scotland, of the Tudor style. Between the arch of the door and the dripstone above is carved the following legend :—

'In warld is nocht nature hes wrought that sal last ay,
   Thairfore serve God, keip weil the rod, ' thy fame sal
                                           [nocht dekay.
      Schir Walter Scot of Branxholme, Knycht: Margret
                                     [Douglas 1571.'

In panels over the door are the arms of Scott and Douglas, with an inscription recording that Sir Walter began the work on 24th. March 1571, died on 17th. April 1574, and that ' Dame Margret Douglas his spous ' finished the building in October 1576. Lady Margaret was the eldest daughter of David Douglas, seventh Earl of Angus ; so that Branxholm, conferred upon a Scott for service against a Douglas, was completed by a lady of that house for a Scott.

¹ The road.

After the fall of the Black Douglas, Buccleuch was without peer in Teviotdale. A volume might be filled with a mere selection from the exploits and forays in which the family bore a part. Something has been spoken in earlier chapters of their doings in Tweeddale, but the scenes of some of Buccleuchs' most famous feats, such as the rescue of Kinmont Willie from Carlisle Castle, lie outside the limits of this sketch. Nothing illustrates better how completely the Scotts of Buccleuch had won the hereditary confidence of their weaker neighbours in Teviotdale and Liddesdale than the ballad of Jamie Telfer o' the Fair Dodhead. [1] So vividly does it set forth the conduct of a 'Hot Trod,' that is, the pursuit of marauders making off with booty—so clearly does it give the details of 'warning the water,' that, long as it is, I will venture to give it in full. These old ballads, rough in metre and shaky in rhyme, suffer more than other verse by being presented in snippets.

The incident is such an one as must often have interrupted the routine of a country gentleman's life on the Border. The characters in the ballad are touched so graphically, the localities are so accurately set forth, even the weather—' the gryming o' a new

[1] The deference paid to 'the bauld Buccleuch' has survived even into this democratic age. During the lifetime of the fifth Duke of Buccleuch I was in the Botanic Gardens of Edinburgh smoking a cigar in the open air. One of the officials came up, and said gruffly: 'There's nae smokin' allowed here.' 'Oh,' said I, 'I don't think my tobacco will injure your plants.' 'I don't know about that,' quoth he of the brass buttons, 'but I can tell ye there's nae smokin' allowed in the gardens.' 'All right', said I, 'if I meet Professor M'Nab (The Curator at that time) I'll square him.' 'Ye'll what?' exclaimed the man, eyeing me up and down, 'Ye'll square the Professor?' 'Yes,' I answered nonchalantly, 'he is a friend of mine.' 'God! I tell ye if ye were the Duke o' Buccleuch himsel' ye widna square oor Professor!' I collapsed at once, and threw away my cigar.

fa'n snaw'—is so carefully touched in, that one seems to be listening to one who took part in the events of that winter night. In fact in the sixth stanza from the end, the poet speaks as one of the 'Hot Trod'—

'There was a wild gallant amang us a'.'

JAMIE TELFER O' THE FAIR DODHEAD

'It fell about the Martinmas tide,
  When our Border steeds get corn and hay,
The Captain o' Bewcastle [1] bound him to ride,
  And he's ower to Tividale to drive a prey.

The first ae guide that they met wi',
  It was high up in Hardhaugh swire ; [2]
The second ae guide that they met wi',
  It was laigh down in Borthwick Water.

"What tidings, what tidings, my trusty guide ? "—
  "Nae tidings, nae tidings, I hae to thee ;
But gin ye'll gae to the fair Dodhead, [3]
  Mony a cow's cauf I 'll let thee see. "

[1] The office of Captain of Bewcastle was held by the chief of the Nixons.

[2] Swire, literally, 'the neck', hence the neck of a pass. Hardhaugh Swire is one of the passes between Liddesdale and Teviotdale.

[3] Identified by Sir Walter Scott with the Dodhead opposite Singlehill on Ettrick, where, he said, were remains of a tower. Despite his high authority, supported by Professor Veitch, it puzzles one to believe that Jamie ran first to Stobs, eleven miles in a bee line without taking hills into account, passing close to Branxholm on the way, and then six more to Coulthart Cleugh, making seventeen in all, before he got a mount. Moreover, when the Captain was overtaken, he had driven cattle up the Frostylee into the plain beyond, at least twenty miles from Ettrick, and no man can drive cattle much faster than two miles an hour. As he 'Lifted' them just before dawn ('the sun wasna up, but the moon was down ') it must have been nightfal before Willie Scott charged him. It seems far more probable that 'the fair Dodhead' was on the Dod Burn between Teviot and Slitrig Waters. There is no tower there now ; but there was a general demolition of these old strengths after the Union, and there happens to be a Peel Brae on this Dod Burn.

And whan they cam to the fair Dodhead,
  Right hastily they clam the pele ;
They loosed the kye oot, ane and a',
  And ranshackled the house right weel.

Now Jamie Telfer's heart was sair,
  The tear aye rowin' in his e'e ;
He pled wi' the Captain to hae his gear,
  Or else revengit he wad be.

The Captain turned him round and leugh,
  Said—"Man ! there's naething in thy house,
But ae auld sword without a sheath,
  That hardly now wad fell a mouse. "

The sun wasna up, but the moon was down,
  It was the gryming o' a new fa'n snaw ;
Jamie Telfer has run ten mile afoot
  Between the Dodhead and the Stobs Ha'. [1]

And whan he cam to the fair tower yett [2]
  He shouted loud and weel cried he,
Till out bespak auld Gibbie Elliot—
  "Wha's this that brings the fray to me ?"

"It's me, Jamie Telfer o' the fair Dodhead,
  And a harried man I think I be.
There's naething left in the fair Dodhead
  But a waefu' wife and bairnies three. "

"Gae seek your succour in Branxholm Ha',
  For succour ye'se get nane frae me !
Gae seek your succour whaur ye'se paid blackmail,
  For man ! ye ne'er paid aught to me. "

[1] Stobs Ha', now Stobs Castle, a house of the Elliots on Slitrig Water, where the War Office have lately established a camp of exercise.
[2] Gate.

Jamie has turned him round about,
    Wi' aye the saut tear in his e'e—
" I' ll ne'er pay mail to Elliot again,
    And the fair Dodhead I 'll never see.

" My hounds may a'rin masterless,
    My hawks may fly frae tree to tree,
My lord may grip my vassal lands,
    For there again maun I never be. "

He has turned him to the Tiviot side,
    E'en as fast as he could drie,
Till he cam to the Coultart Cleugh,[1]
    And there he shouted baith loud and hie.

Then up bespak him auld Jock Grieve—
    " Whae's this that brings the fray to me ?"—
" It's me, Jamie Telfer o' the fair Dodhead.
    A harried man I trow I be.

" There's naething left in the fair Dodhead
    But a greeting wife and bairnies three,
And sax poor cauves stand in the sta'
    A' routing loud for their minnie. "

" Alack a wae ! " quo' auld Jock Grieve—
    " Alack my heart is sair for thee !
For I was married on an elder sister,
    And you on the youngest o' the three. "

Then he has ta'en out a bonnie black,
    Was right well fed wi' corn and hay ;
He's set Jamie Telfer on his back
    To the Catslockhill to tak the fray.

[1] Coultherdscleugh is on the right bank of the Teviot a long mile below Teviothead kirk.

And whan he cam to the Catslockhill,
 He shouted loud and weel cried he,
Till out and spak him William's Wat [1]
 " O whae's this brings the fray to me ? "

" It's me, Jamie Telfer o' the fair Dodhead,
 A harried man I think I be !
The Captain o' Bewcastle has driven my gear,
 For God's sake, rise and succour me ! "

" Alack for wae ! " quo' William's Wat,
 " Alack, for thee my heart is sair ;
I never cam by the fair Dodhead
 That ever I fand thy basket bare. "

He's set his twa sons on coal-black steeds,
 Himsel' upon a freckled gray,
And they are on wi' Jamie Telfer
 To Branksome Ha' to tak the fray.

And whan they cam to Branksome Ha',
 They shouted a' baith loud and hei.
Till up and spak him auld Buccleuch,
 Said—" Whae's this brings the frae to me ? "

" It's me, Jamie Telfer o' the fair Dodhead,
 And a harried man I think I be ;
There's nought left in the fair Dodhead
 But a greeting wife and bairnies three.

" Alack for wae ! " quo' the gude auld laird,
 And ever my heart is wae for thee.
But fye ! gar cry on Willie my son,
 And see that he come to me speedilie !

---

[1] William's Wat was properly one of the Scotts.

"Gae warn the water, braid and wide !
  Gae warn it sune and hastilie !
They that winna ride for Telfer's kye,
  Let them never look in the face o' me !

"Warn Wat o' Harden and his sons,
  Wi' them will Borthwickwater ride ;
Warn Gaudilands[1] and Allanhaugh,
  And Gilmanscleuch and Commonside.[2]

"Ride by the gate[3] at Priesthaughswire,[4]
  And warn the Currors o' the Lee ;
As ye come down the Hermitage Slack
  Warn doughty Willie o' Gorinberry."[5]

The Scotts they rade—the Scotts they ran—
  Sar starkie and sae steadily,
And aye the ower-word o' the thrang
  Was—"Rise for Branksome readily !"

The gear was driven the Frostylee[6] up
  Frae the Frostylee unto the plain,
When Willie has looked his men before,
  And saw the kye right fast driving.

"Whae drives thir kye ?" 'gan Willie say,
  "To mak an outspeckle[7] o' me "—
"It's me, the Captain o' Bewcastle, Willie ;
  I winna layne[8] my name for thee."

[1] Now Goldielands, a tower commanding the junction of Teviot and Borthwick Water.
[2] All places inhabited by families of Scotts.
[3] The road on Borthwick Water to the North.
[4] A place on the Allan Water due south of Branxholm.
[5] Hermitage and Gorrenberry are in the watershed of Liddell, through which the Captain of Bewcastle must pass in returning with his booty.
[6] Up the Frosty Burn, where it joins the Teviot at Carlanrig, and so over into Liddesdale.
[7] A laughing-stock.
[8] Conceal.

"O will ye let Telfer's kye gae back?
  Or will ye do aught for regard o' me?
Or—faith o' my body!" quo' Willie Scott
  "I'se ware[1] thy dame's calf-skin on thee."

"I winna let the kye gae back,
  Nor for thy love nor for thy fear;
But I will drive Jamie Telfer's kye
  In spite of every Scott that's here."

"Set on them, lads!" quo' Willie then,
  "Fye lads! set on them cruellie!
For e'er they win to[2] the Ritterford
  Mony a toom[3] saddle there sall be."

Then till't they gaed, wi' heart and hand;
  The blows fell thick as bickering hail;
And mony a horse ran masterless,
  And mony a comely cheek was pale.

But Willie was stricken ower the head,
  And through the knapscap[4] the sword has gane;
And Harden grat[5] for very rage,
  When Willie on the ground lay slain.

But he's taen aff his gude steel-cap,
  And thrice he's waved it in the air—
The Dinlay[6] snaw was never mair white
  Than the lyart[7] locks o' Harden's hair.

[1] Waste or spoil.
[2] Win to, reach.
[3] Empty.
[4] Headpiece, steel bonnet.
[5] Wept. 'Auld Wat o' Harden' was fourth in descent from the second son of George Scott of Synton by a Scott of Robertson. He is the hero of the ballad The Flower of Yarrow, the heroine being his wife, daughter of Philip Scott of Dryhope. He died in 1629. Sir Walter Scott believed that "Willie" was a natural son of Buccleuch.
[6] Dinley Fell (1755 feet) overlooks the scene of this combat.
[7] Blenched.

" Revenge, revenge ! " auld Wat' gan cry ;
" Fye, lads ! lay on them cruellie !
We'll ne'er see Tiviotside again,
    Or Willie's blude avenged sall be."

O mony a horse ran masterless,
    The splintered lances flew on hie ;
But ere they wan to the Kershope ford,[1]
    The Scots had gotten the victorie.

John o' Brigham there was slain,
    And John o' Barlow, as I hear say ;
And thirty mae o' the Captain's men
    Lay bleeding on the ground that day.

The Captain was run through the thick o' the thigh[2]—
    O weel may his lady for him mak maen !
If he had lived this hundred year,
    He had never been loved by woman again.

" Hae back thy kye ! " the Captain said ;
    " Dear kye, I trow, to some they be !
For gin I should live a hundred years
    There will ne'er fair lady smile on me. "

Then word is gane to the Captain's bride,
    Een in the bower where that she lay,
That her lord was prisoner in enemy's land,
    Since to Tividale he had led the way.

" I'd sooner hae sewed a winding-sheet,
    And helped to put it ower his head,
Than hae seen him mained, as nae man shuild be,
    Whan he ower Liddel his men did lead."

[1] The Kershope Burn joins the Liddel Water from the left, three and a half miles below Newcastleton, and forms the boundary between England and Scotland—the March—throughout its course of nine miles.
[2] This line in the original was thus decorously paraphrased by the Scott. The Captain's injury was far more severe—teste loeva vulneratus—which explains the significance of the following three stanzas.

There was a wild gallant amang us a',
   His name was Watty wi' the Wudspurs, [1]
Cried—" On for his house in Stanegirthside ! [2]
   If ony man will ride wi' us."

When they cam to the Stanegirthside,
   They dang wi' trees and burst the door ;
They loosed out a' the Captain's kye,
   And set them forth our lads before.

There was an auld wife ayont the fire,
   A wee bit o' the Captain's kin ;
" Whae daur loose out the Captain's kye ?
   Or answer to his men and him. "

When they cam to the fair Dodhead
   They were a welcome sight to see,
For instead o' his ain ten milk-kye,
   Jamie Telfer has gotten thirty-and-three.

And he has paid the rescue shot, [3]
   Baith wi' gowd and white monie ;
And at the burial o' Willie Scott
   I wot was mony a weeping e'e.'

At the risk of outrunning all patience of readers, the picture must be completed by quoting from The Fray of Suport, [4] a modern ballad, in which an

---

[1] Wud, mad. Watty Wudspurs was the third son of Sir William Scott of Harden, who married 'Muckle mou'd Meg' of Elibank (see p. 28, ante), and grandson of Auld Wat o' Harden. He was ancestor of the Scots of Raeburn.

[2] On the English side of Liddel Water.

[3] This is an interesting line, showing that it was the custom to pay salvage for cattle and goods recovered from the enemy. 'Paying the shot' is commonly regarded as a term akin to slang, but in truth it is good and very old English. The Anglo-Saxon scot, sceot, softened into shot, signified 'payment'.

[4] Suport is on the English side, near the Kershopefoot, on the very Border.

Englishwoman who has been harried by a band of
Scotsmen summons her neighbours to the Hot
Trod. Breathless with speed, almost inarticulate
with rage, she chides Sim o' the Lambhill and
Jocko' Suport Mill for not turning out smartly to
her summons ; then, with all the volubility of her
sex, she tells her tale of woe. The iteration of the
yelling refrain is as startling as the warning shouts
of firemen in a street.—

'Fy, lads ! shout a' a' a' a' a'
My gear's a' gane.
Weel may ye ken,
Last night I was right scarce o' men ;
But Toppet Hob o' the Mains had guestened in my house
    by chance ;
I set him to wear the fore-door wi' the spear while I kept
    the back door wi' the lance ;
But they hae run him thro' the thick o' the thie and broke
    his knee-pan,
And the mergh [1] o' his shin-bane has run down on his spur
    leather whang ;
He's lame while he lives, and where'er he may gang.
        Fy, lads ! shout a' a' a' a' a' !
        My gear's a' gane.

. .   . .

Rise, ye carle coopers, frae makin' o' kirns and tubs
In the Nicol forest woods.
Your craft has nae left the value o' an oak rod ;
But if ye had had ony fear o' God,
Last night ye hadna slept sound
And let a' my gear be ta'en.
        Fy, lads ! shout a' a' a' a' a' !
        My gear's a' gane.'

[1] Marrow.

Borthwick Water, deriving from the bleak upland
of Eskdalemuir, runs a course of ten miles parallel
to the Teviot, at no point more than three miles
distant to the north-west ; then at Borthwick brae it
turns sharp to the east, and three miles more brings
it to a junction with its sister-stream. High up
among its headwaters is the great sheep-farm of
Howpasley, the scene in comparatively recent days
of a peculiarly revolting episode in a clan feud,
because the victims were not human beings struck
down in open mellay, but defenceless dumb animals.
It arose in 1618 out of a dispute between Sir James
Douglas of Drumlanrig and ' the Lady Howpaslet, '
the widow, apparently, of a deceased laird of Howpasley. About the year 1614 the estate came into
Douglas's possession, probably as the result of an
unredeemed mortgage. It had long been in possession of a branch of the Scotts ; and ' the Lady ',
having no intention of letting it go, summoned the
Scot clan to a meeting in Hawick to take measures
for her reinstatement. According to the ' band '
which every Scott obeyed under the chief Buccleuch,
each man was bound strictly to respect the ' room '
or possession of every other member of the clan.
Even Buccleuch himself, if charged with encroaching
upon the room of another, which might easily happen
in a wide, unfenced hill country, had to submit to
the judgment of four persons of the name of Scott.

The meeting, which seems to have been presided
over by the Lady Howpaslet and her kinswoman,
Jean Scott of Satchells, determined that Douglas
should be prevented from stocking his lands, and
adopted means described in the ' dittay ' of the trial
that followed as of ' sic monstruous and vnhard of

crewaltie as the lyk quhairof hes nocht bene hard amangst the wyld Irisch and savadge people, let be within any reformed and ciuile pairt of his majestie's dominionis. '   Four rascals were hired namely ' George Scott, cordiner in Hawick—the Souter, [1] called Marione's Geordie ; Walter Scott, son to Braidis Andro ; Ingrem Scott and Jok Scott, callit the Sukler, ' to slay such stock as Douglas had put on the land.   They went up Borthwick Water ' in the glomeing ' of an April night, and so to Howpasley, where they fell upon a flock of sheep and ' maist barbaruslie and inhumanely, as savadge and crewall beistis, destitute of natural reasone, with thair drawin suordis and utheris wappones, ran throw the haill flok of scheip, slew and menyet [2] to the number of threscoir, quhairof fouretir or thairby war slane be streiking of thair heids and cutting thame in tua throw thair bakis ; and the rest of thaim, thair spaldis [3] and legis wer strukin away fra thame in maist barbarous maner, and war sa left spreuling in thair deid-thraws vpone the grund. ' [4]

It may be noted in passing as something unexpected that the public prosecutor should have so much commiseration to expend upon the sufferings of mere sheep, in an age when witch torture had been brought to its highest perfection, and the burning of heretics had not passed completely out of vogue.

Howbeit, all the accused were hanged except Jock the Suckler, who saved his neck for the nonce by turning King's evidence.   But, being ' wanted '

[1] Shoemaker.
[2] Maimed.
[3] Shoulders.
[4] Pitcairn's Criminal Trials, iii. 380-396.

upon a charge of sheep-stealing committed four years previously, unlucky Jock was rearrested, tried before a jury whereof nine out of fifteen were Armstrongs, unfriendly to the Scotts, and sent to the gallows tree. The chief culprits, Lady Howpaslet and Jean Scott, got off free, although the dittay against their instruments admitted that these fellows had acted ' be the instigation, na dout, of sum persones of gritter qualitie and conditoun nor thame selffis. ' Lady Howpaslet recovered her estate from Douglas of Drumlanrig, which remains in the possession of Scotts to this day, and the story is rounded off by the fact that the present owner, the Duke of Buccleuch, is also Lord of Drumlanrig.

The most conspicuous feature alike in the scenery and history of Borthwick Water is the castle of Harden, [1] of which Tweedside's modern singer, John Leyden (1755-1811), has painted the winter aspect in a few vigorous lines :—

> ' Where Bertha hoarse, that loads the meads with sand,
> Rolls her red tide to Teviot's western strand,
> Through slaty hills whose sides are shagg'd with thorn,
> Where springs in scattered tufts the dark green corn,
> Towers wood-girt Harden far above the vale,
> And clouds of ravens o'er the turret sail.'

Readers a hundred years ago were less meticulous in the matter of ornithology than they are now ; else would Leyden never have substituted the impossible raven for the irrepressible jackdaw. Robert Scott, a cadet of the house of Synton, first acquired the estate from Lord Home in 1501, and it was his grandson, 'Auld Wat,' the chief's right-hand man in

---

[1] Not to be confused with a place of the same name in Liddesdale.

all his ridings, who has made the place famous in story. To his wife the 'Flower of Yarrow,' tradition ascribes the training of a certain lad whom Auld Wat brought home in one of his forays. This lad, whose name has been forgotten, is commonly believed to have composed many of the ballads which have been handed down to us in this day. Margaret, daughter of Auld Wat and the Flower, known for some obscure reason as ' Maggie Fendy, ' married Gilbert Elliot of Stobs, commonly called ' Gibbie wi' the gowden garters, ' perhaps the same from whom Jamie Telfer received such a heartless answer in his need. From the fourth of their six sons descended the family of the present Earl of Minto.

Phot.

Valentine & Sons Ltd.

BRANKSOME TOWER

CHAPTER VIII

FROM SLITRIG TO JED WATER

THE modern traveller is likely to be better acquainted with the Slitrig Water than with any other in this region, because, northward bound by the Waverley route, after passing the dreary brown moors about Riccarton, the train climbs the 'swire' of Whitter-hope Edge, drives through a couple of rock tunnels, emerges from the northern watershed, and runs close along the Slitrig Water to its junction with Teviot in the town of Hawick. About a mile to the north of these tunnels the line crosses that mysterious earthwork the Catrail, of which a length of four miles or so here has escaped obliteration in its winding north westerly course to Torwoodlee. The old Border 'makers' never shirked the local names, not they, but revelled in them, how harsh soever they might be ; and handed them on as they sounded from the lips of their own people. Scott was of that mind too, though he took occasional liberties, changing Carter-hole into Abbotsford, Burnsfoot into Chiefswood, and altering the stress on Dolorain to suit his metre, yet he held the old names in loving reverence. Not so his friend Leyden, who, affected by the classical craze, improved Borthwick into Bortha and Slitrig (which perhaps is more correctly written Slitterick, on the analogy of Ettrick) into Slata.

From the sixteenth century onwards, the Elliots were the chief family on Slitrig, firm adherents of the Scotts in all their feuds and fightings. Originally, it is believed the Elliots belonged to Forfarshire, taking their name from the Elliot Water, and transplanted to Liddesdale by the Earl of Douglas about the close of the fourteenth century. Redheugh or Lariston was their chief house in Liddesdale, where they throve but indifferent well, allying themselves with the Armstrongs and other broken clans of the debatable land, and brought trouble upon themselves in consequence. Before the end of the sixteenth century, however, a branch of the house of Lariston was firmly settled at Stobs, whence sprang a number of subsidiary lairds, who prospered amain under the shelter of puissant Buccleuch.

The ancient burgh of Hawick has lost all trace of the defensive character essential to a Border town in other days. The houses used all to be 'bastel' built, that is, with thick stone walls having no door to the street, but an entry to a back court, whence a stair gave access to the second floor. Now all is changed. The present population of 18,000 is housed just as in any other manufacturing town. When last I lay in Hawick about ten years ago, the sole conspicuous vestige of antiquity remaining in the form of stone and lime was the Tower Hotel— that part of it, at least, which was the castle of Douglas of Drumlanrig, as superior of the burgh. This building survived the last burning of the town by the English in 1570. But an oral relic of times far anterior to that has been preserved in what is called the 'Colour Song.' The ceremony of Common Riding takes place in June, when the Cornet precedes the magistrates in their perambulation to the burgh marches, after which the 'Colour Song' is chanted by the crowd assembled in the town. The words of this ditty are modern, the composition of James Hogg, the Ettrick Shepherd ; but the refrain seems to date from pagan times :—

> 'Up wi' Hawick's rights and common !
> Up with a' the Border bowmen !
> Teribus and Teri-Odin,
> We are up to ride the Common. !'

This has been interpreted as a battle-prayer to Odin, but its true origin is quite unknown.

'The Teviot,' says Dick Lauder, writing about 1840, 'is a peculiarly pure stream, while its purity is rendered more apparent by its pebbly bed.' Alas for this once fair water ! The growth of the hosiery and woollen industry of Hawick has taken grievous effect upon its current, which is now badly polluted, more's the pity, for it flows through a lovely vale, and is naturally an ideal salmon and trout stream.

The estate of Cavers, lying on the right bank of the Teviot below Hawick, remains in possession of the descendants of Archibald, the second illegitimate son of the second Earl of Douglas—he who perished at Otterburn in 1388. The earl left Drumlanrig to his elder natural son William, and Cavers to Archibald. There are some interesting relics preserved at Cavers, which are of undoubted antiquity, but the precise origin of which have been the subject of a good deal of amicable controversy.

The most important of these relics is a flag of sage green silk, 'about 12 feet long in its present shortened state, and about 3 feet wide at the staff end or " hoist ", narrowing to the ends, which seem to have been originally forked. ' [1] About this flag there are three various traditions current. The first of these is mentioned by Bishop Percy of Dromore in a memorandum preserved among the Duke of Northumberland's MSS. at Syon House. The Bishop was shown the flag when he visited Cavers in 1744, and says that ' the family of Douglas of Cavers, hereditary Sheriffs of Teviotdale, have long had in their possession an old standard, which they believe to be the very pennon won from Hotspur by the Earl of Douglas, to whom their ancestor was standard-bearer in the expedition (to Otterburn). ' Now, although we may accept Froissart's word for it that Douglas did encounter Hotspur in single combat before the gates of Newcastle, that he did capture the pennon from his adversaries' lance, and that it was to recover that pennon that Percy followed Douglas to Otterburn, it is clear that this Cavers flag cannot be the pennon. A pennon was a small pointed or forked affair, like that on a modern lancer's weapon. No knight in his senses would have gone into single or any other combat with twelve or thirteen feet of silk hanging to his lance.

The second variant of the tradition represents the flag as Percy's banner captured at Otterburn. The objection to this explanation is conclusive. The flag is not a knightly banner, which was square, and displayed only the armorial bearings of its owner. It is a standard, a variety of flag which came into

[1] The description is taken from the Earl of Southesk's paper on this relic in the Proceedings of the Society of Scottish Antiquaries for 1901-2, pp. 246-280.

fashion during the reign of Edward III., and, under the Tudor Kings, was of fixed dimensions according to the rank of him who displayed it, graduated from eight to nine yards long for a monarch down to four yards for a simple knight. But it could not have been the Percy standard, seeing that the devices painted upon it are the St. Andrew's Cross next the staff, a lion and the Douglas heart and stars, with the Douglas motto, Jamais arrière (written Jamais arreyre) on the tapering fly.

The third account (which, I believe, is the one accepted by the present family of Cavers) makes out that the flag is the Douglas standard carried at Otterburn by Archibald Douglas, founder of the Cavers line. To this there appear only two objections, either of which is fatal to the tradition. The second Earl of Douglas carried no lion on his shield, and the lion is conspicuous among the devices on this flag. The earldom reverted at his death to his relative Archibald the Grim, third Earl of Douglas, who, as Lord of Galloway, certainly quartered the lion of Galloway with the heart and stars of Douglas. The other objection is that, inasmuch as the Otterburn earl was only thirty when he was slain, his second natural son cannot have been of an age to act as standard-bearer in the battle. [1]

Another objection, which applies to all three of these variants, is that there is no instance of the motto Jamais Arrière in Douglas heraldry until it appears on the seal of Archibald, eighth Earl of Angus (1557-1588). Lord Southesk, sifting all the

[1] But he may have been ' the little boy, was near of Douglas kin, mentioned in the ballad of Otterbourne as announcing the approach of the English.

circumstances, came to the conclusion that the Cavers flag was a Douglas standard, dating not from 1388, but from some years after 1452, and belonging not to the Black Douglas branch, but to the Red. When George Douglas, illegitimate son of the first Earl of Douglas, became Earl of Angus in 1397, he quartered the lion of Angus with the heart and stars of Douglas, and so did all his descendants, including the fourth earl, who, on the fall of the Black Douglas in 1455, received a grant of all the lands belonging to that great house, and being Warden of the Marches in 1452, appointed Douglas of Cavers his keeper of Hermitage Castle. It is not improbable then, that the Cavers flag was the official standard displayed by the keeper on that fortress.

With the flag is preserved at Cavers an embroider-ed glove, supposed to have been taken by the Earl of Douglas at the same time as he captured Hotspur's pennon, and to have been a gage of that knight's lady. That may be so, but the initials K.P. worked upon the glove are difficult to identify, for Hotspur's wife was Elizabeth Mortimer, his mother Margaret Nevill and his only sister Margaret Percy. What fair lady answered to K ?

Hassendean Burn joins the Teviot from the north a short distance below Cavers, a name that was written of old Halstanedene, Hadestanden, and Astenesdene, and has been further altered in the modern song Jock o' Hazeldean. Of the tower that once commanded the junction of the waters, the only remaining fragment has been made to serve as the gable of a cottage. It was a house of the Scotts —Sir Alexander Scott of Hassendean fell at Flodden. In 1564 there occured a serious interruption in the alliance of the Scotts and the Elliots, probably arising out of the action of Martin Elliot of Braidley, a son of the laird of Redheugh, who claimed to be chief of the whole clan of Elliot in Liddesdale and Teviotdale. This gentleman was in constant intrigue with the English, received pay from Queen Elizabeth, undertook that his clan should become English with their whole surname, and their friends the Armstrongs, and pledged himself to deliver to the English Warden Queen Mary's castle of Hermitage for which he was ready to give four of the name of Elliot as hostages. [1] It may be supposed that such proceedings were odious in the eyes of the bold Buccleuch, the Scotts being perhaps the only Border clan untainted by traitorous dealings with the southern power, and especially devoted at this time to the cause of Queen Mary. Anyhow, the Elliots seem to have struck the first blow in a feud which raged with intense fury for a couple of years between them and the Scotts. On the 18th October 1564, they attacked Hassendean, and slew David Scott, the laird. Three days later six men named Elliot, and strange to say, James the son of Walter Scott, tenant in Hassendean, were put upon their trial in Edinburgh for the crime. Five of them were convicted ; three were beheaded by torchlight on the same evening ; while William Elliot of Horsliehill was condemned to banishment, a sentence which was remitted in the following year by Queen Mary at the instance of Ker of Fernihirst. But the family of Horsliehill never recovered their standing. The property was sold before the end of the century, and the feud having been stanched, Elliot entered the

[1] Scrope to Cecil 28th 1565 : Ms. Record Office.

service of Auld Wat o' Harden, who gave him a natural daughter in marriage, whence are descended the Elliot Lockharts of Wolfelee. [1]

Hassendean formed of old a separate parish, and the church, with some fine Norman work, stood at the junction of the burn with the Teviot, [2] but was dismantled on the suppression of the parish late in the seventeenth century. This was done during the minority of the chief heritor in the parish, Mary, Duchess of Buccleuch, and was so much resented by the people that they assembled in force and killed the first man who mounted the ladder to begin the work of demolition. Since then the Teviot has swept away the churchyard, and has so altered its own course that the site of the old kirk is now marked by a sandbank on the south bank.

This term ' dean ' representing the Anglo-Saxon denu, Middle English dene, a narrow wooded valley or glen, takes the place in lower Teviotdale of the ' hopes ' and ' cleughs ' of the upper country. It recurs again in Denhold, a village at the mouth of the Dean Burn, a short distance below Hassendean. More ancient than it appears, Denholm was burnt by Lord Hertford in 1545. An obelisk on the village green commemorates John Leyden, the poet, who was born here in 1775. Two miles to the south of the village Ruberslaw (1392 feet) rises abruptly from the plain, marking with its rugged cone the site of a volcanic shaft in the carboniferous age. On the opposite side of Teviot Minto Crags (729 feet),

---

[1] Pitcairn's Criminal Trials i. 456*, 466*. See also Proceedings of the Society of Scottish Antiquaries 1880-1, pp. 93-100, for the curious details of this sudden feud.

[2] There is an etching of it in Cardonnel's Picturesque Antiquities 1788.

thickly clothed with trees, and Minto ‹Hills (905 feet), form a beautiful setting for the modern seat of the Earl of Minto, chief of the Elliot clan. The estate was bought from the Turnbulls at the close of the seventeenth century by Gilbert Elliot (1651-1718), in whose veins the Border blood ran strong, for his grandsire, 'Gibbie wi' the gowden gartins' married, as aforesaid,[3] auld Wat Harden's daughter, 'Maggie Fendy.' A famous union this proved to be, for the energy of both families was perpetuated, and turned to good account in the service of the state. Gilbert, first of Minto, applied himself to the profession of ' writer '—the Scottish term for solicitor— and won early distinction in the trial for treason of William Veitch, the Covenanting divine (1640-1722), for whom he acted as agent so successfully as to obtain the commutation of the death sentence into one of banishment. This was in 1679.

Soon after Gibbie himself got into trouble through his Presbyterian zeal. For the active part he took in promoting Argyll's rising in 1685 he was condemned for treason and forfeited, but was pardoned. Admitted an advocate in 1688, he became clerk to the Scottish Privy Council in 1692, was made a baronet in 1700 and a judge in 1705, with the title of Lord Minto. His old client, Veitch, by this time was minister of Dumfries, and Minto never failed when his duties took him to that town to rally him about their early acquaintance.

' Ah, Willie, Willie !' he would say, ' had it no' been for me, the pyets had been pyking your pate on the Nether Bow port. '

' Ah, Gibbie, Gibbie !' was the minister's retort,

[3] See p. 170, ante.

'Had it no' been for me, ye would hae been writing papers yet at a plack the page !'

Gibbie's son (1693-1766), also, became Sir Gilbert first, and then a judge with the title of Lord Minto. It is told of him that each year, as he passed with the other Lords of Justiciary from Jedburgh to Dumfries on circuit, his friend Armstrong of Sorbietrees always brought out a large brandy bottle to refresh the cavalcade withal. On one occasion, when Henry Home, afterwards Lord Kames, accompanied the judges for the first time, Armstrong whispered to Lord Minto—'Whatna lang, black, dour-lookin' chiel's that ye hae amang ye in the front o' the coach ?' 'That,' replied Minto, 'is a man come to hang the Armstrongs.' 'Faith, then, Gibbie, it's time the Elliots were riding !' retorted Sorbietrees, as he shut the coach door.

Gibbie the second was succeeded by his son, Gibbie the third—Sir Gilbert Elliot (1722-1777), statesman, philosopher, and poet ; while the fourth baronet, also Sir Gilbert (1751-1814), rose to be Governor-General of India and first Earl of Minto. His son, second Earl of Minto and fifth Sir Gilbert Elliot in succession, was a Minister in Melbourne's Cabinet (1835-41) and in Peel's (1846). His son, succeeding in 1859 as third Earl, broke the spell, apparently from being named William instead of Gilbert, for he was the first of his line not to earn distinction in the public service. The tradition, however, has been well restored by the present holder of the earldom, who inherited the ancient family name of Gilbert, and, having carried it to great honour as Governor-General of Canada, was appointed Governor-General of India in the autumn of 1905.

Minto Crags was crowned by a remarkably well-preserved specimen of a Border pele, which has the curious name of Fatlips. It was the stronghold of Turnbull of Barnhills, a branch of the Bedrule family, whereof there will be more to tell presently when we enter the valley of Rule Water. A short way below the summit of the crags is a flat ledge called Barnhill's Bed, where the laird is supposed to have kept his outlook.——

> 'On Minto Crags the moonbeams glint,
> Where Barnhill hewed his bed of flint ;
> Who flung his outlawed limbs to rest
> Where falcons hang their giddy nest,
> ' Mid cliffs from which his eagle eye
> For many a league his prey could spy ;
> Cliffs doubling, on their echoes borne,
> The terrors of the robber's horn.'

Lower down are the remains of another tower, supposed to be Stanyledge, the house of another Turnbull. Both Fatlips, or Minto Tower, and Barnhills were wrecked by Lord Hertford in 1545. Of the history of this robber laird nothing is known but by vague tradition, but in the Justiciary Record it is stated that ' Hectour Trumbill of Stanyledge, Hector Trumbill of Barnehillis ; George Trumbill, his brother, and Gavin Trumbill their fadir-brother (uncle) ' were all outlawed in 1604 for the slaughter of William, James, Robert, John, Andrew and Thomas Grameslaw, sons of John Grameslaw in Little Newton. I have not found any other mention of this horrible massacre, and no particulars are given in the Records, but Barnhills must have been a disagreeable neighbour.

Three miles or little more to the north of Minto

another Turnbull had a castle at Belses.   This laird
was simply an atrocious villain, and met his doom
in 1602, when he was tried for the slaughter of John
Hamilton Cumnock in 1579, and of William Turnbull, younger of Rawflat, in 1600.   Also for seizing
Adam Turnbull, servant to Walter Turnbull, 'binding
him with fetteris, and hinging him be the feit and
schoulderis (shoulders) over ane balk (beam) for the
space of X days, quhairthrow (whereby) his feit rottit
fra him.'   Also for shooting William Turnbull,
younger of Rawflat, brother of the murdered William,
in the arm and thigh in 1602, besides a host of
minor crimes such as sheep and cattle stealing, burg-
lary, etc.   Evidence was defective against the accused, and he was acquitted on the main charges, but
convicted of 'weiring and schuting with hagbuttis
and pistolettis,' and was sentenced to be taken to
the Market Cross of Edinburgh, and there 'his
richt hand to be strukin fra his airme.'   This was
on 20th July.   A month later the mutilated wretch
was tried afresh on a charge of 'the filthie cryme of
incest and adulterir with Marioun Trumbill spous
to Jok Trumbill in Belsis, his brother sones wyfe,'
and being convicted was hanged forthwith. [1]

Opposite Minto Crags the Rule Water comes as
an important affluent to the Teviot, draining the
northern and eastward slopes of the range that sheds
Slitrig Water from its western face.   After the
confluence of the Lurgies and Wauchope Burns,
Rule enters its narrow main valley, passing the
kirk and manse of Hobkirk (properly Hopekirk),
where James Thomson spent some of his early years
and composed much of The Seasons.

Pitcairns's Criminal Trials ii. 421, 425.

The present spiritless parish church, built in 1858, replaced a wretched structure of 1692 or thereabouts, which was built of far nobler material. When it was taken down, the rubble-work was found to contain many carved stones from an earlier building, which were scattered and used as marks for graves. That excellent antiquary, Mr. A.O. Curle, has succeeded recently in recovering a few carved capitals—enough to fill one's heart with bitterness against the cruel hands that wrecked the ancient fane. For it is evident from the style of decoration on these stones, which is similar to that displayed in Edrom Church and on the east cloister doorway of Dunfermline Abbey, that here stood the original Ecclesia de Roule, an exquisite example of Norman building dating from the first half of the twelfth century. Mr. Curle also discovered in a gamekeeper's garden at Harwood, a mile and a half from Hobkirk, the mutilated head of a cross, not Celtic but mediaeval, which had been built into the wall of a byre. Earlier than that, it was ascertained that this stone had been unearthed from the foundations of Appotsyde, once the tower of the family of Loraine, now extinct. The hill road to Slitrig and Liddesdale lay past this tower, and Mr. Curle suggests that this cross stood by the wayside, citing the analogy of other wayside crosses of similar peculiar design, the limbs of the cross being of the patée or Maltese form, strengthened by a circular band left in the solid stone. The meaning of such crosses is explained in Wynkyn de Word's Dives et Pauper (1496) : 'For this reason ben crosses be the waye ; than whan folke passying see the cross they shoulde thynke on hym that deyed on the croysse

and worshippe hym above àll thynges.' [1] Less
sordid reminders, surely, than the field-signs of
soaps and patent pills with which we suffer our
routes of travel to be defaced nowadays !

Close to Bedrule, a tiny hamlet beside the kirk
of the parish so named, may be traced the foundations of that tower where once the chief of the
lawless little clan of Turnbulls held sway. The
entire race has passed away ; none of the name is
numbered now among the landowners of Scotland ;
but all up and down this water they have left their
mark on the landscape in the shape of ruins, or at
least foundations, of their strongholds—Wauchope,
away up among the moors ; Hallrule, in the pleasant
haugh below Bonchester ; Fulton, a well-preserved
house on the right bank fronting dark Ruberslaw,
and so forth.

The chief of the Turnbulls, a giant in stature and
strength, met his death in single combat before the
battle of Halidon Hill on 19th July 1333. The
English army was drawn up awaiting the ill-judged
attack of the Scots under Archibald Douglas, 'The
Tineman,' Regent of Scotland, when Turnbull stood
forth leading a huge mastiff on a leash, and challenged any English knight to single combat. Sir Robert
Benhale or de Venale, a young cavalier of Norfolk,
accepted the challenge, though greatly inferior in
height and strength to the Scottish champion.
Turnbull loosed the mastiff at the Englishman,
who, stepping nimbly aside, caught the beast such a
swinging blow on the loins as severed its hind
quarters from the fore. Then he faced Turnbull,

[1] See Mr. Curle's paper, Proceedings of the Society of Scottish
Antiquaries, 1903-4 pp. 416-421.

whose mighty bulk put him at a disadvantage. Benhale was too quick for him, parried his attacks, leapt out of reach of his mace, until the giant was completely blown. Then Benhale went in : first he shore off Turnbull's left hand and then his head.

The Turnbulls were a clan formidable out of all proportion to their size, and seem to have been at feud with all their neighbours in succession. After making up their quarrel with the Scotts, they did not shrink from attacking the powerful Kers. In 1601 six of them, including Thomas of Minto and Hector of the Firth, together with the five Davidsons and 'Jaquie' Laidlaw of Rawflat, were tried for the murder of Thomas Ker, brother to Sir Andrew of Fernihirst, and of his servant George Glaidner. This was a most daring outrage, committed in broad light on Holy Cross Day (4th May) at Jedburgh Fair. The Turnbulls attacked Ker's house with a force of thirty men. Ker's brother Sir, Andrew, Provost of Jedburgh, gave chase, overtook the murderers, and slew two of them, to wit, Robert Turnbull of Bewlie and William Middlemas of Lilliesleaf. For this rough and ready reckoning he was tried formally with eighteen others ; but there was no miscarriage of justice. Proceedings against the Kers were not pressed ; but of the Turnbulls four were sentenced to death, though only one seems to have been brought to the gallows— Andrew, brother to the 'Gude man of Bewlie,' slain by the Kers.[1] Little is heard of the Turnbulls in local history after this.

The name of this parish, Bedrule, carries us far back into Celtic times for it is said to commemorate

[1] Pitcairn's Criminal Trials, ii. 370-381.

Bethoc, the wife of Radulph, the son of Dunegal, who was joint proprietor with her husband, and had probably been heiress, of the manor which appears in the thirteenth century as Rulebethock, and in the fourteenth as Bethokroule.

In this tuneful Border land there is no deed so dark, no life so obscure that it may not be embalmed in song ; and thus it happened that a drunken brawl between two strolling fiddlers furnished Allan Cunningham with the theme of one of his best-known lays. William Henderson lived at Priesthaugh in Teviotdale in the seventeenth century, earning a livelihood by his skill on the violin. The liveliness of his strains combined with his convivial habits to earn him the byname of ' Rattlin', Roarin' Willie'. He had a rival, Robin of Rule Water generally known as ' Sweetmilk ' from the place of his abode. These two were drinking together in Bedrule one day, when they fell to disputing about their respective merits as musicians. Words would not settle the matter ; they adjourned to the river bank to fight it out with swords ; Willie ran Robin through the heart, and went into hiding. Had Sweetmilk been without powerful friends, a few months in retreat might have absolved Willie from the consequences of his act, at so light a ransom was mere human life reckoned in those days. But Sweetmilk was the special minstrel of the Elliots of Stobs and Falnash ; so it came to pass that when Willie rashly put in an appearance at the Rood Fair of Jedburgh the Elliots recognised him, chased him to Oxnam Water, brought him back to Jedburgh, and hanged, or had him hanged, on the same day. Willie was the popular favourite, and seems to have had all the sympathy of the countryside with him.—

    'Our Willie's awa to Jeddart
      To dance on the Rood-day,
    A sharp sword by his side,
      A fiddle to cheer the way.
    The joyous tharms o' his fiddle
      Rob Rule has handled rude,
    And Willie left Newmill banks
      Red wat wi' Robin's blude.

    Our Willie's awa to Jeddart—
      May ne'er the saints forbode
    That ever sae merry a fellow
      Should gang sae black a road.
    For Stobs and young Falnash
      They followed him up and down
    In the links o' Ousenam Water
      They found him sleeping sound.

    Now may the name o' Elliot
      Be cursed frae firth to firth !
    He has fettered the gude right hand
      That keepit the land in mirth.
    That keepit the land in mirth,
      And charmed maid's hearts frae dool ;
    And sair will they want him, Willie,
      When the birks are bare at Yule.

    The lasses o' Ousenam Water
      Are rugging and riving their hair,
    And a' for the sake o' Willie,
      His beauty was so rare.
    His beauty was so fair
      And comely for to see
    And drink will be dear to Willie
      When Sweetmilk gars him dee.'

We must now leave the banks of the Teviot in order to follow from its source a very important tributary flowing in from the left—the Ale. To do so takes us back into a neighbourhood where we have spent much time already, for the Ale Water rises in the same upland as gives rise to the Rankil Burn in Ettrick, besides some minor affluents of Borthwick Water. It flows past Bellenden to within three miles of the Ettrick of Selkirk, so thoroughly watered is all its pleasant land. The name Ale is one of a puzzling group. Originally written Alne, it is obviously the same word as the Aln at Alnwick, and the root may be recognized in Allan Water, a feeder of the Tweed near Melrose, which used to be written Elwand, and in the Elvan Water, a tributary of the Clyde, which used to be written Elwan. The preposterous derivation from the Gaelic aluinn, beautiful, may be dismissed with a wish that people would give up darkening judgment with wild shots like this. The Ale is a bonny stream, but not one whit more so than scores of others : besides, primitive races don't name natural features from emotional impulse. Probably all these names are worn forms of a vocable signifying ' water ' in some forgotten language.

For the first five miles of its course the Ale is a mere mountain runner, leaping over innumerable cascades in its haste to reach a smoother channel. Presently, passing under the hill road from Hawick to Ettrick, it finds repose in Alemuir Loch, a nearly circular basin with a diameter of 450 yards, reputed as the abode of the water kelpie, and affirmed to be thirty fathoms deep. Issuing from Alemuir, the stream skirts Ettrick Forest in a seven miles course to Ashkirk, passing by Salanside and Sinton, ancient fortresses of the Scotts, and so on to the lands of Riddell, which seem to have been known in the twelfth century as West Lillesclive. At all events Gervase of Rydale, Sheriff of Roxburgh in the reigns of Alexander I. and David I., died before 1153, and Walter of Rydale, his son, was confirmed in the lands of Lillesclive by the latter king. Rydale or Riddell, therefore, seems to have been an imported name, conferred by the early owners upon this property to distinguish it from Lillesclive proper, which was a barony of the Bishop of Glasgow. [1]

The Riddells, in common with many others in this district, suffered from proximity to the troublesome Turnbulls, who in 1502 burnt the house about their ears and drove away five hundred sheep. [2] After eight centuries of possession the family recently parted with their ancient heritage.

The older name Lillesclive remains in the modified form of Lilliesleaf, which designated the parish in the twelfth century, and no doubt earlier, if we knew it. One groans in spirit on hearing that the ancient church was replaced by a new one ; but it is a matter of indifference that this in turn has been much pulled about by a later generation. Visitors who have learnt by mournful experience to wince as sorely at the work of restorers as at the waste of reformers, know what to expect in the announcement of the *Gazetteer* that 'recent improvements have

[1] In like manner, a younger son of Sir Walter Riddell (*c.* 1660), obtaining property in Dumfriesshire, called it Glenriddell, and became the progenitor of Robert Riddell, the friend, correspondent, and *convive* of Robert Burns.
[2] Pitcairn's *Criminal Trials*, i. 34.

changed this church from a plain, barnlike edifice to one of taste and elegance.'

Within this parish, measuring about six miles by five, there remained at the close of the eighteenth century no fewer than fourteen castellated houses of the Turnbulls, Scotts, Riddells, and Kers. Of the last two families the names are united in the person of the present owner of Cavers-Carre, who is descended in the female line from Ralph, second son of Sir Andrew Ker of Fernihirst, and in the male line from a second son of Sir Walter Riddell of that Ilk.

All this upper part of the Ale Water suffered periodical devastation in common with the rest of the Border land. In one of his reports to the English Privy Council, Lord Dacre states that 'the watter of Ale, fro Askrige [Ashkirk] to Elmartour [Alemuir Tower] in the said Middilmarchis, wherupon was fifty pleughes, lyes all and every of them waist now, and noo corne sawne upon none of the said grounds.'

The Ale pursues a generally eastern course through miles of pleasant meadow land until about a mile from its junction with Teviot, when it turns sharply to the south and then nearly due west, enclosing the promontory whereon is built the ancient village of Ancrum, that is Alne-crumb, the crook of Alne or Ale. The stream here has wrought itself a deep and tortuous channel through the red sandstone beds, leaving steep cliffs picturesquely clad with wood wherever trees may find a footing. In these cliffs are hewn many caves of unknown antiquity, reminding one of the rock-dwellings still inhabited in the Loire valley. One of the Ancrum caves is still associated with the name of Thomson, the poet of *The Seasons*, who made it his frequent summer resort.

The manor and barony of Alnecrum or Ancrum formed part of the possessions of the Bishop of Glasgow as early as 1116, and the old house of Ancrum was an episcopal palace until the Reformation. Then it passed to Ker of Fernihirst, who is stated to have rebuilt it after its destruction by the English in 1544. That was by no means the first time it had suffered at their hands, for in 1513, after the battle of Flodden, they burnt down the village, as well as the Templar's 'spital' or hospital. In 1670 the property was acquired by Sir John Scott of Kirkstyle, who traced lineal descent from the wizard, Michael Scott of Balwearie. The old house of Ancrum was finally and totally destroyed by fire in 1873, though the English cannot be suspected of the mischief this time. Having been rebuilt on the former lines, the work had scarcely been finished when, by a strange fatality, fire broke out again and consumed it. It was erected a third time in the form it bears at present. This long series of evil vicissitude has effaced all vestiges of the architecture which must once have adorned this ancient ecclesiastical site. As for the parish church, it is vain to seek for beauty there : what can be expected from a structure built in 1762 and subjected to alteration in 1832 ?

The Ale never recovers its easterly course after its abrupt wheel to the south at Ancrum, but joins the Teviot at a right angle opposite Timpendean, a ruined tower of the Douglas family. On the left bank of Teviot, to the east of the Ale, lies the ample and well-wooded park surrounding Monteviot House, the modern seat of the Marquis of Lothian, who is descended from Mark Ker, the brother of

Walter, ancestor of the Dukes of Roxburghe. Mark was Abbot of Newbottle, but having accepted the reformed religion, took unto himself a wife, begat several children, and died in 1581. His eldest son, Mark Kerr, was created Earl of Lothian. Note the double *rr*, please ; for although Kers of the Roxburghe line are content with a single consonant, those of the Lothian branch insist upon their right to a pair.

Immediately below Monteviot park the Teviot receives an important tributary in the shape of the Jed Water, a stream which has witnessed more bloodshed and violence than most others of its dimensions. It rises on the flanks of the Carlin Tooth (1810 feet) and Hartshorn Pike (1789 feet), within a few hundred yards of the head waters of the Liddel. Another branch flows from Dand's Pike and farseen Carter Fell ; while a third tributary, furthest to the east, is most famous of all, for its channel forms the road to the Reidswire—that red ' swire ' or pass which witnessed one of the last acts in the long tragedy of the Border.

But before describing the Raid of the Reidswire, of which the crisis took place in the pass itself, let us recall a drama enacted nearly two centuries earlier, half the actors in which passed by this road to a theatre that they were to make for ever famous. There had been peace on the Border for two years after the young Earl of Douglas had raided the rich lands of Cockermouth in 1386. No counterstroke had followed on the part of the English, for King Richard's hands were full with domestic quarrels ; while Percy and Nevill, the two great powers on the East March, were nearly at civil war about the

Wardenship. Clearly it was a great opportunity for an expedition ; but blear-eyed Robert III., King of Scots, was a hopelessly pacific person, and could not be got to perceive the enormous advantage of burning his neighbour's houses and crops, and slaying the Tynedale peasants. So his barons, headed by his pugnacious son the Earl of Fife, took matters into their own hands, held a meeting in Aberdeen, and arranged secretly all the preliminaries of a great invasion. A strong force—Froissart puts it at 50,000, but we may safely strike off two-thirds from that estimate—was appointed to muster at Southdean on Jed Water early in August. Warden Percy was duly warned by spies of what was impending : one young English gentleman acting that hazardous part very near came to disaster. He tied his horse to a tree, entered Southdean Church, where a council of war was sitting, heard enough to serve his purpose, and slipped out to get his horse. The horse was there no longer, 'for a Scot—they are all thieves, these Scots—had stolen him.'[1] The spy set off on foot for the Border, but his boots and spurs excited suspicion. He was stopped at the outposts and brought before Douglas, who found means to extract the admission from him that Percy was well aware of what was afoot, and intended to make a counter-raid so soon as the Scots should enter English soil. Hearing this, the Scottish leaders determined to go one better. They had troops enough for *two* raids : the Earl of Fife should lead the main body upon Carlisle, while Douglas should take a flying column and harry Northumberland.

Douglas and Moray, therefore—names how shi-

[1] Froissart, iii. 124.

ning in the story of Scottish independence !—rode
forward through the Reidswire at the head of 300
or 400 spears and 2000 bowmen.——

> ' It fell about the Lammas tide,
>   When the muir men win their hay,
> The doughty Douglas boun' him ride
>   Into England to drive a prey.
>
> He chose the Gordons and the Graemes,
>   With them the Lindsays light and gay ;
> But the Jardines [1] would not wi' him ride,
>   And they rue it to this day.
>
> Then they harried thc dales o' Tyne,
>   And half o' Bambroughshire,
> And the Otterdale, they burnt it haill
>   And set it a' on fire. '

They passed by Ottercop and Rothley Crags,
pushing forward as far as Brancepeth on the Yorkshire border. Then they wheeled to the left and
marched for Newcastle, where Hotspur and his
brother Ralph were in force, while the old Earl of
Northumberland lay at Alnwick, hoping to take the
Scots in flank as they returned from their enterprise.
Douglas encamped on the rising ground outside the
walls of Newcastle ; Hotspur had but to lie within
his defences, for his enemy had no cannon or siege
engines. But such was not the chivalrous custom
of the time. Challenges to single combat were
offered and accepted on both sides. Douglas met
Hotspur *à outrance ;* the famous English knight
went down before the spear of the young earl, who

[1] Probably a late interpolation made after the Jardines had risen in
the world. In the fourteenth century they were of little note, being
but respectable vassals of Annandale.

tore Percy's pennon from his lance, and, as he left the lists, boasted that he would carry it to Scotland and display it from his highest tower.

'By God!' cried Hotspur, 'you shall never leave Northumberland alive with that.'

'Then you must come and take it this night,' retorted Douglas. 'It shall stand before my tent, for him to take it who dares.'

Thus Froissart, though the ballad gives a different version of the fact. It represents Hotspur fixing a tryst with Douglas.—

> 'Now gae ye up to the Otterburn
>   And bide there dayis three,
> And gin I come not ere they end,
>   A fause knight ca' thou me!'

Anyhow, the Scots moved off in a leisurely way, burning Portland Tower, about five miles out of Newcastle, on the first day, and on the third day laying siege to Otterburn Tower in Redesdale, about thirty miles from Newcastle. Douglas knew well enough that if Hotspur's scouts brought him word that the Earl of Fife's column was busy at a safe distance, his chivalrous enemy would not fail to redeem his pledge.—

> 'They lichted high on Otterburn
>   Upon the bent sae brown,
> They lichted high on Otterburn
>   And pitched their pallions [1] doun.
>
> And he that had a bonnie boy,
>   He sent his horse to grass;
> And he that had nae bonnie boy,
>   His ain servaunt he was.

[1] Pavilions, tents.

Then up and spake a little boy—
Was near of Douglas kin [1]—
" Methinks I see an English host
Come branking us upon.

" Nine wargangs [2] beiring braid and wide.
Seven banners beiring high ;
It would do any living gude
To see their colours fly ! "

" If this be true, my little boy,
That thou tells unto me,
The brawest bower o' the Otterburn
Shall be thy morning fee.

" But I hae dreamed a dreary dream
Ayont the Isle o' Skye ;
I saw a deid man win a fight,
And I wot that man was I. " '

Douglas had pitched his camp in a wood, as a
protection from archery, preferring that situation to
the stronger, but treeless, one near at hand— the
old Roman station of Bremenium.

The Scots were at supper when their pickets were
driven in by the English skirmishers. They stood
to arms at once, gaining some valuable minutes by
reason that Percy, in the dusk, mistook the baggage
bivouac, outside the entrenchment, for the real camp.
While he was so occupied a detachment of Scots
crept through the wood and fell upon his flank.
After a fierce tussle the Scots began to yield ground,

[1] Perhaps one of his two natural sons, William or Charles, lords, in
later years, of Drumlanrig and Cavers. In the version of this ballad
given by Scott in the first edition of the *Minstrelsy*, the little boy slew
Douglas with his own hand treacherously, an obvious device to ensure
fulfilment of the dream about the dead man winning a field.
[2] Columns.

being heavily outnumbered ; then Douglas thrust
forward into the thick of the mellay. In his haste
his armour had not been braced rightly.——

> ' He belted on his gude braid sword,
>   And to the field he ran ;
> But he forgot his hewmont[1] strong
>   That should hae kept his brain. '

The ballad represents Percy as the slayer of the
Douglas—for poetic symmetry, no doubt, for Froissart merely says that the earl fell with spear wounds
in shoulder, belly, and thigh, and that as he went
down an axe gashed his skull. He sent his page to
bring his nephew Sir Hugh Montgomerie,[2] and if
the verses that follow be not history, they are ballad
poetry at its finest.——

> ' " My nephew gude, " the Douglas said,
>   " What recks the death of ane ?
> Last night I dreamed a dreary dream,
>   And I ken the day's thine ain.
>
> " My wound is deep—I fain would sleep—
>   Take thou the vanguard o' the three,
> And bury me by the bracken bush
>   That grows on yonder lily lea.
>
> " O bury me by the bracken bush
>   Beneath the blooming brier ;
> And never let living mortal ken
>   That a kindly Scot lies here. " '

[1] Helmet.

[2] ' And fetch my ae dear sister's son,
        Sir Hugh Montgomerie.'
Not very intelligible. Douglas had but one sister, Isabel, Countess of
Mar, who first married Sir Malcolm Drummond, and afterwards Alex-
ander Stuart.

He lifted up that noble lord,
 Wi' the saut tear in his e'e,
And he hid him by the bracken bush
 That his merry men might not see.

The moon was clear—the day drew near—
 The spears in flinders flew;
And many a gallant Englishman
 Ere day the Scotsmen slew.

The Gordons gay in English blude
 They wat their hose and shune;
The Lindsays flew like fire about
 Till a' the fray was dune.

The Percy and Montgomerie met,
 That either of other was fain;
They swakkit swords and sair they swat,
 And the blude ran down between.

" Now yield thee, yield thee, Percy," he cried,
 " Or else I'll lay thee low ! "
" To whom maun I yield ? " Earl Percy [1] said,
 " Since I see that it maun be so."

" Thou shalt not yield to lord or loon,
 Nor yet shalt thou yield to me;
But yield thee to the bracken bush
 That grows on yonder lily lea ! " [2]

This deed was done at Otterburn
 About the breaking of the day;
Earl Douglas was buried at the bracken bush,
 And Percy led captive away. '

[1] A mistake; he was not Earl Percy, his father having only been
created Earl of Northumberland in 1377.

[2] A handsome concession, for it would have freed Percy from the
necessity of paying ransom; but such a concession never was made.
Percy was held to ransom at £3000, to which the English Parliament
voted £1000.

If Douglas was indeed buried at the bracken bush, his body was afterwards removed to Melrose Abbey. Percy's brother Rafe, being sore wounded, yielded to Sir John Maxwell. It was so dark he could not distinguish who was his captor. ' I am Rafe Percy, ' said he. ' Sir Rafe, ' answered Maxwell, ' rescue or no rescue ? I am Maxwell. ' ' Well, ' quoth Sir Rafe, ' I am content ; but I pray you take some heed to me, for I am sore hurt ; my hosen and my greaves are full of blood. ' He was allowed to go on parole to Newcastle, ' to seike him leiches that were fine and gude. '

The English version of the story is given in the ballad of *Chevy Chace,* in which apparently some other episode has got jumbled up with the affair of Otterburn, for the story does not tally so closely with history as the Scottish verses.

Whether the dying Douglas made any such speech as is reported may never be known. Poets (and Froissart was poet as well as chronicler) never allow that heroes should die mute like foxes. Wyntoun says the earl's fate was not known in the Scottish army till next morning. Likely enough, as the Scots were in hot pursuit of the enemy, capturing Sir Matthew Redman, Governor of Berwick, after a long chase. But whether Douglas spoke those words or not, they have received a tender claim upon our regard from an incident mentioned in Lockhart's *Life of Scott.* Broken in fortune, shattered in health, the gallant old ' Shirra ' was industrious to the last. He travelled with Lockhart to visit Douglas Castle, the model for Castle Dangerous in his last romance. Silent he stood, viewing the green vale and dark moorland under a lowering summer sky. Tears gathered under his aged lids, for he felt that he must soon take his last look upon the land he loved so well ; then, striking his stick into the turf, he repeated slowly the words of the dying Douglas at Otterburn—'My wound is deep,' etc.

The scenery round the upper part of Jed·Water is of the usual wild pastoral kind. The march between England and Scotland runs along the crest of the Cheviots. Every drop that falls north or west of the water-divide finds its way to the Tweed: rain that falls south or east of it runs into the Tyne. A burn that flows in from Wolflee Hill on the west goes by the name of Peden's Cleuch, and doubtless was one of the many shelters frequented by the dauntless and much hunted Alexander in the 'killing time.' But it is about the eastern affluents of this water that memories cling most closely, for of old, as at the present day, one of the chief riding roads into England lay at a height of 1450 feet over the foot of Catcleuch Shin—the pass known as the Reidswire. It became famous through a bloody encounter which arose out of what was meant to be a friendly conference, and which forms the subject of one of the best-known of Border ballads. The Raid of the Reidswire took place during the regency of the Earl of Morton. It was in June 1575 that Sir John Forster, the English Warden, met Sir John Carmichael, the Scottish Warden, at the Reidswire, for the settlement of sundry Border claims of the usual kind.

It did not conduce to the peaceful transaction of judicial business that each Warden appeared at the head of several hundred men.

'Carmichael was our warden then,
    He caused the country to convene ;
And the Laird's Wat, that worthy man,
    Brought in that sirname weel beseen. [1]
The Armestranges, that aye hae been
    A hardie house, but not a hale, [2]
The Elliot's honours to maintain
    Brought down the lave [3] o' Liddesdale.

Then Tividale came to wi' speed,
    The Sheriff brought the Douglas down, [4]
Wi' Cranstoun, Gladstain, good at need,
    Baith Rule Water and Hawick town.
Bonjeddart [5] bauldly made him boun,
    Wi' a' the Trumbills, [6] strong and stout ;
The Rutherfoords, with grit renown,
    Convoyed the town of Jedbrugh out.

Of other clans I cannot tell,
    Because our warning was not wide.
By this our folks hae ta'en the fell
    And planted pallions [7] there to bide.
We lookit down the other side,
    And saw come breasting o'er the brae,
Wi' Sir John Forster for their guide,
    Full fifteen hundred men and mae.

[1] *Weel beseen* = well appointed. Sir Walter Scott was in doubt about the identity of the leader of the Scotts on this occasion, but inclined to suppose it was the young laird of Buccleuch, he who afterwards delivered Kinmont Willie from durance in Carlisle.

[2] Referring to the frequency with which the Armstrongs, being outlaws, were found fighting under English colours.

[3] The rest.

[4] That is, Douglas of Cavers, Hereditary Sheriff of Teviotdale, brought down his following.

[5] Douglas of Bonjedward.

[6] Turnbulls.

[7] Pavilions, tents.

It grieved him sair that day, I trow,
　Wi' Sir George Hinrome o' Schipsydehouse ; [1]
Because we were not men enow
　They counted us not worth a louse.
Sir George was gentle, meek and douce,
　But he [2] was hail and het as fire ;
And yet, for all his cracking crouse, [3]
　He rued the Raid o' the Reidswire.

To deal with proud men is but pain,
　For either must ye fight or flee ;
Or else no answer make again,
　But play the beast and let them be.
It was na wonder he was hie——
　Had Tynedale, Reedsdale at his hand,
Wi' Cukdaill, [4] Gladsdaill [5] on the lee,
　And Hebsrime [6] and Northumberland.

Yet was our meeting meek enough,
　Begun wi' merriment and mowes, [7]
And at the brae aboon the heugh
　The clerk sate down to call the rowes.
And some for kine and some for ewes,
　Called in of Dandie, Hob and Jock ;
We saw come marching o'er the knowes
　Five hundred Fenwicks in a flock,
Wi' jack and spear and bows all bent
　And warlike weapons at their will ;
Altho' we were na weill content
　Yet, by my troth, we fear'd na ill. '

[1] Sir George Heron of Chipchase.
[2] Forster.
[3] Loud boasting.
[4] Coquetdale.
[5] Perhaps Glaisdale, a parish in the north riding of Yorkshire.
[6] Hebburn or Hebron, a village near Morpeth.
[7] Acting, mummery.

With so much combustible lying about, it is not surprising that the gathering soon parted with its judicial character. A true bill having been found by the joint court against an English freebooter called Farnstein, or, as some accounts have it, Henry Robson, Carmichael, in accordance with Border law, claimed delivery of him pending satisfaction being done to the injured party. Forster declared that Farnstein had absconded: Carmichael, believing this to be an evasion of justice, bade the English Warden 'play fair.' Forster made an insulting retort, and the two knights were in a fair way to coming to blows, when the Tynedale men let fly some arrows among the Scots. Then the mellay became general; the Scots were having the worst of it, Carmichael himself being felled and made prisoner, when suddenly the rocks resounded with the well-known battle-cry 'Jethart's here!' announcing the timely arrival of a force from Jedburgh. 'To it, Tynedale!' shouted the English in reply, but Jedburgh's onset turned the day. Sir George Heron was slain, with four-and-twenty Tynedale bowmen, and the Warden himself with several English gentlemen were taken prisoners. It was a complete triumph for the Scots.

> ' But little harness had we there,
> But auld Badreule had on a jack ; [1]
> And did right weel, I you declare,
> Wi' a' his Trumbills at his back.
> Gude Ederstane [2] was not to lack,

[1] Sir Andrew Turnbull of Bedrule, a notorious freebooter, had on an iron jack or cuirass.

[2] Rutherfurd of Edgerstone, a very ancient family, represented by the present owner of this property.

Nor Kirktoon, [1] Newtoun, [2] noble men !
Thir's a' the specials I of speake
By [3] others, that I could na ken. '

The bard, it will be noticed, throws all the blame
for this untoward fray upon the English, and
specially on Sir John Forster's overbearing temper.
No doubt the other side could have given a different
version ; but the Scots seem to have made out a
good case, judging by what followed. Carmichael
took his prisoners to Edinburgh, much to the dis-
quiet of Regent Morton, inasmuch as Scotland and
England happened to be enjoying one of those rare
intervals of peace which broke the wasteful routine
of war. Queen Elizabeth would not be slow to
exact vengeance for such an outrage upon her
Warden ; wherefore Morton ordered the immediate
release of the prisoners without ransom, and sent
Carmichael to explain matters at the English Court.
Apparently he made good his case, showing that his
party had only acted in self-defence, for he was not
detained by the irascible Queen.

Sir John Carmichael was not a Borderer, and his
appointment as Warden by the Regent had been
bitterly resented by Angus, the Kers, Scotts, and
Maxwells, but he proved himself such a vigorous
and useful official that, although his patron Morton
was executed in 1581, Carmichael was continued as
Warden till 1591, when he resigned in favour of
Lord Maxwell. Better it had been for Carmichael

[1] Doubtful whether it was Douglas of Kirkton or Kirkton of
Stewartfield. The former, I think.
[2] Grameslaw of Little Newton, fighting this day side by side with
the Turnbulls. It was twenty-nine years later that the family of
Grameslaw were massacred by the Turnbulls (see p. 181, *ante*).
[3] Besides.

had he never resumed the office, for he had made
himself many enemies among the broken clans.
Lord Maxwell was slain by the Johnstones in the
battle of Dryfe Sands, 6th December 1593. His
kinsman, Lord Herries, having been appointed to
succeed him in the wardenship, was also beaten in
an encounter with the Johnstones in October 1595,
when the King and Council adopted the remarkable
policy of dismissing Herries and making the
victorious laird of Johnstone Warden in his place.
It was not a successful experiment, for in 1599 both
Herries and Johnstone were imprisoned, and the
West and Middle Marches were in hopeless disorder, every laird's hand against his neighbour.
The veteran Sir John Carmichael, having no kin
among the Border clan, was recognised as the only
man to restore order. Re-appointed Warden in
1601, he was riding to hold a court at Lochmaben,
when the Armstrongs waylaid him and did this
fearless old gentleman to death. Orders were issued
for the arrest of 'Thomas Armstrang, sone to
Sandeis Ringane,[1] the said Ringane, Thomas's fader,
Lancie, Hew, Archie, and Watt Armstrangies, Sym
of the Syde, Lancie of the Syde, Rob Sandie, Rob
Scott, Thome Tailzeour, William Forrester, Williame
Grahame of the Braid, and divers vtheris'; but the
only one who had the bad luck to be caught at the
time was the first-named, Thomas, who was sentenced, first, to have his right hand struck off; second,
to be hanged; and third, that his body be taken to
the gallows on the Burgh Moor 'to be hangit vp in

---

[1] The old form of naming men from their parentage survived long
in Liddesdale and the Debatable Land. 'Sandeis Ringane' means
Ninian, the son of Alexander.

irne cheinis '—the first example in Scottish criminal procedure of hanging a convict in chains. Thomas, sad to say, was a brother of far-famed Kinmont Willie.

Only one other seems to have been brought to justice for the murder of the Warden, namely, Sandie Armstrong of Rowanburn, who five years later, in 1606, was hanged, as no doubt he richly deserved; nevertheless, ruffian as he was, one cannot refuse a place to the pathetic lines said to have been composed by him when awaiting his doom.—

ARMSTRONG'S GOOD-NIGHT

This night is my departing night,
  For here nae langer maun I stay ;
There's neither friend nor foe o' mine
  But wishes me away.

What I hae done through lack o' wit
  I never, never can recal ;
I hope ye're a' my friends as yet,
  Good-night, and joy be wi' ye all ! '

After Jed Water has descended a thousand feet from its lofty cradle in the Cheviots its banks acquire a sylvan glory with which the embarrassed trout-fisher might willingly dispense, but which imparts exceeding loveliness to the landscape.

Edgerstone Castle, the ancient stronghold of the Rutherfurds, has disappeared, although the lands remain in possession of that family. Among the 'exployts don upon the Scotts' by Hertford in 1544, the capture of Edgerstone is reported as having been accomplished 'by pollicie' with Scots in English pay.

A couple of miles below Edgerstone, on the west bank of the water, is the reputed site of old Jeddart or Jedworth, one of two churches which Bishop Ecgfred of Lindisfarne founded in the ninth century. About the year 1093 Bishop Walcher was slain by a band led by Eadulf Rus, who was himself killed by a woman shortly after, and buried in this place.

Again, two miles further down the stream, on the east bank, stands the castle of Fernihirst, a place of much renown in Border warfare, although the present beautiful house dates no further back than 1598.

The former castle, on the same site, was built by Sir Thomas Ker a hundred years earlier, and, standing as it did beside the usual route of English invasion, had but a brief and troubled existence. When the Earl of Surrey laid waste Teviotdale in 1523, he found that Fernihirst ' stode marvelous strongly within a grete woode ; ' yet he managed to take it by storm after ' long skirmyshing and moche difficultie, ' and thoroughly dismantled it. The redoubtable Dand Ker, laird of Graden, a famous rider in these wars, was taken prisoner on this occasion, but managed to make good his escape shortly after. Sir Andrew Ker of Fernihist died in 1545, and was succeeded by his son John, who, with most of his clan and many other gentlemen of the Border, made unwilling submission to Protector Somerset, seeing no other chance of existence in the distracted condition of the realm. But in June 1549 the arrival of 6000 French, German, and Italian auxiliaries under André de Montalembert, Sieur d'Essé, put another colour on the situation. The ' assured ' Scottish nobles and gentlemen scrupled not to throw over their allegiance to England ; the tide of victory turned, and the Scots, aided by their foreign friends, began to indemnify themselves with excessive ferocity for the massacre of Pinkie and the wrongs inflicted during the English occupation. The two nations had been at war, almost without intermission, for more than two centuries ; nor had they spared each other ; but no period can compare with this for barbarous cruelty.

It may be urged in palliation of the share of the Scots in these horrors that the ogre King of England, Henry VIII., had issued orders through his Privy Council to the Earl of Hertford in 1544 that he should give no quarter, 'putting man, woman, and child to fire and sword, without exception, when any resistance shall be made against you'—orders which were only too faithfully fulfilled. Yet it is to be hoped that the high-water mark in brutality was marked by the proceedings which took place when the laird of Fernihirst came to his own again. Shrewsbury, when he marched back to England in 1548, left a garrison in Fernihirst, and these English soldiers—officers and men—had made themselves peculiarly odious by committing frequent outrages, especially upon women. Sir John Ker having collected his men, made a combined assault with a French column upon his own castle, and stormed the outworks. The garrison retreated into the keep, but the besiegers breached the thick wall by a mine. The English commander crept out of the hole, and surrendered to a French officer, De la Mothe-rouge, claiming protection as his prisoner ; but one of the Scots, recognising in the Englishman the ravisher of his wife, rushed upon him and struck off his head at one blow before the French gentleman could interfere. The rest of the prisoners were put to horrible torments before they were slain. 'I myself,' says M. Beaugé, a French officer serving with the allies, 'sold them a prisoner for a small horse. They laid him on the ground, galloped over him with their lances in rest, wounding him as they passed. When slain, they cut his body in pieces, and bore the mangled gobbets in triumph on the points of their spears. I cannot greatly praise the Scots for this practice ; but the truth is, the English tyrannised over the Borders in a most barbarous manner, and I think it was but fair to repay them, as the saying goes, in their own coin.'

Thus Sir John Ker recovered his paternal tower, though he did not keep it very long. In 1570 the Earl of Sussex took advantage of the miserable state of Scotland after the assassination of the Regent Moray, and once more Teviotdale and the Merse were laid waste. The English claimed to have destroyed in this expedition three hundred farm-towns and cast down fifty castles, Fernihirst being one. Ker was a foremost partisan of Queen Mary, and was one of those who rode with Buccleuch, Huntly, and Lord Claud Hamilton in that spirited raid upon Stirling, 3rd September 1571, when the Earls of Morton and Argyll, with seven other lords, were captured for a time, and the Regent Lennox died by Captain Calder's bullet. The cause of Queen Mary was on the brink of triumph, but the Border men turned to looting, Mar rescued the prisoners with a party of soldiers, and so the affair miscarried.

The walls of Fernihirst remained roofless till Sir John Ker and his son Sir Thomas had both passed

14

away, to whom Andrew Ker succeeded in 1586.[1]
He took in hand to build the present house, 'a
charming example,' says that excellent authority the
late Mr. David M'Gibbon, 'of a Scottish mansion of
the period.'[2] It is sad to see it so dilapidated.
Part of it is still inhabited by work-people, who, it
may be feared, have found the panelling of the
unoccupied rooms very convenient for firewood. In
the circular library is a fine wooden ceiling in a
deplorable state of decay. 'Although but a small
apartment, it has been fitted up with the most fastidious taste and care.'[3] The chapel, with its ornate
doorway, now serves the purpose of a stable. Thus
has the glory departed from Fernihirst, once reckoned
among the principal fortresses of the Middle Marches ; and although the chief of this branch still
challenges the claim of the Duke of Roxburghe, as
Ker of Cessford, to the chieftainship, and as Marquess of Lothian quarters the sun in splendour in
an azure field with the paternal chevron of Ker,
Monteviot and Newbottle have supplanted in his
esteem the ancient house of his fathers.

[1] He was created Lord Jedburgh in 1622.
[2] *Castellated and Domestic Architecture of Scotland.* 5 vols.
[3] *Ibid.*

CHAPTER IX

JEDBURGH

FAMOUS in Scottish history is a place bearing the musical name of Lintalee, nearly opposite Fernihirst on Jed Water, for here Sir James Douglas formed a camp of observation after the rule of King Robert had been firmly established by the great victory at Bannockburn.

In the autumn of 1316 matters were pretty peaceable on the Border, for Edward II. was as usual engaged in fierce disputes with his barons. The King of Scots had sailed for Ireland to help his brother Edward in the conquest of that realm, leaving his own kingdom in the joint-guardianship of Douglas and Walter the Steward. Douglas was employing the slack time in building for himself a castle at Lintalee overlooking the camp. King Edward of England had summoned his forces to assemble at Newcastle on a day in October for the invasion of Scotland, but failed to put in an appearance himself, so the army was disbanded. The Earl of Arundel, however, hearing by his spies that a raid upon the Scottish border might be made profitably at this time, marched a column through the Cheviots down the Jed Water. Barbour probably over-estimates his force at ten thousand men, but is most likely correct in stating that the English

were armed with felling-axes for the destruction of
Jedworth Forest, because it gave such convenient
harbour to raiding Scots.   Douglas, having received
timely warning of Arundel's approach, laid an am-
buscade of bowmen in one of the narrow wooded
gorges of the Jed through which one of the English
columns had to pass.   The day of barbed-wire
entanglement was not yet, but Douglas, a practised
soldier, made use of the material at hand' to effect
the purpose of hindrance to troops under a hot fire.
He caused his men to bend down a lot of young
birches, and weave their tops together across the
paths.   The English advanced guard entered the
defile without hesitation ; when they came to the
obstruction, the cliffs rang to the cry, ' A Douglas !
a Douglas ! ' the bowmen poured in a sleet of
arrows, and Douglas led a charge upon the rear of
the column.   The English had neither time nor
room to form for defence ; they were shot and hewn
down by scores, Sir Thomas de Richmond, a knight
of Yorkshire, falling by Douglas's own hand.

Meanwhile another column of the English, moving
by a different route, had occupied the new house of
Lintalee without opposition, and were making free
with such victuals and drink as they could find
therein.   Douglas, having routed the main body,
returned sharply to his camp, surprised the party in
the house, and put most of them to the sword.

They may be lightly told now, these stirring
exploits of the days of chivalry ; but who shall reckon
the misery of countless households, whose bread-
winners were liable at any moment to be summoned
at the will of their lords to run the chances of hand-
to-hand battle ?

A short distance to the north of Lintalee stood the tower of Hundalee, belonging to the Rutherfurds, but it was demolished in the eighteenth century, and the site is occupied by a modern country house.

We have now come to war-worn Jedburgh, travelling by the same route as was followed of yore by countless English expeditions, treading the ground that has been soaked times without number with the blood of both nations, and moving among fields and houses the very names of which are associated with memories of rapine and violence. Jed Water murmurs as sweetly as ever among her leafy bowers; sombre Carter Fell and Catcleuch Shin to the south, Windygate and the Cheviot to the east, still mark the frontier which it was the chief duty of the burgesses of Jedburgh to guard; but Surrey and Hertford, could they stand again on Dunion Hill and overlook the town which, in 1523 and 1544, they successively committed to the flames, would scarcely recognise the scene of their destructive industry. The castle had already disappeared in their day, for when, in the year 1409, the men of Teviotdale rose and wrested it from the English, who had been in possession since Edward Baliol ceded it in 1356, the castle was demolished, lest the fortune of war should place it again in the hands of the enemy. It was a building of such exceeding strength that the national council held at Perth decreed that every householder in Jedburgh should pay a tax of twopence towards the expenses of its destruction; but the Regent Albany put his veto on the decree, declaring that no tax had been or should be imposed during his regency, and the cost was defrayed out of the royal customs. There remained, however, six bastile towers, which did not protect the town from being burnt by Sir Robert Umfraville in 1410, the year after the castle had been destroyed. Six years later the same knight returned and gave the town to the flames, and in 1464 the Earl of Warwick once more laid it in ashes.

Then came the Earl of Surrey in 1523, and we have his own account of how he served Jedburgh:—

'Whiche towne is soo surely brent that no garnysons [garrisons] ner none other shal bee lodged there unto the time it bee newe buylded. The towne was much better than I went [weened] it had been, for there was twoo tymes moo [more] houses therein than in Berwicke, and well buylded, with many honest and fair houses therein sufficiente to have lodged a thousand horsemen in garnyson, and six good towres therein, which towne and towres be clenely destroyed, brent and throwen down.'

Proximity to the Border, as was explained in a former chapter, was fatal to the town of Roxburgh. After the destruction of its castle it vanished from the face of the earth. Not so Jedburgh. 'Jethart's here!' cried its stout burghers after each successive desolation, and set to work to rebuild their streets with a patience as pathetic as that of villagers on a volcano. When Hertford thundered at its gates in 1544 the six bastile towers were no more, but there stood plenty of new houses ready for the torch. And if any man wish to know how Jedburgh was served by this indefatigable commander, let him read the narrative of one who marched with Hertford and described what he saw in *The Late Expedicion into Scotlande.* His account of the burning of Dunbar, which preceded that of Jedburgh, may serve as a fair example. The work was not reckoned satisfactory unless the inhabitants were burnt as well as their houses :—

'That nyght [16th May 1544] they looked for us to have burnt the towne of Dunbar, which we differred tyll the morning at the dislodgynge of our campe, which we executed by five hundred of our hackbutters [musketeers] beyng backed with five hundred horsemen. And by reason we took them in the mornynge, who, having wautched all night for our comynge, and perceyvynge our army to dislodge and depart, thoughte themselves safe of us, were newly gone to theyr beddes ; and in theyr fyrste slepes closed in with fyer, men, women, and children were suffocated and burnt. . . . In these victories, who is to be moste highest lauded but God ?'

They did not scamp their work, these English lords, yet one grand feature in the landscape resisted all their attempts to destroy it. Upon a commanding height over the river the hoary tower of St. Mary's Abbey of Jedburgh still stands 'four-square to all the winds,' and though the noble nave be roofless and the choir ruined, the church remains more entire than any other on the Border. It is a splendid example of Norman and transitional building. The west end stands entire, with a circular window in the gable and a fine doorway in the richest style of late Norman ornament ; while the nave and clerestory of the choir are pointed work. The south side of the choir shows the only remaining example in Scotland of a treatment occurring occasionally in England. The main piers—huge, simple cylinders—have been carried up to the full height of the arches over the triforium supporting

the clerestory, the effect being exceedingly 'majestic.'
The arches of the nave are in the first pointed style
with bold mouldings : it is doubtful whether this
part of the church was ever built in the Norman
style, the square plinths upon which the clustered
piers are based are characteristic of transitional work.
So much of the choir as remains is late Norman
work, but the east end, which has been destroyed,
was probably transitional, like the nave. The
Norman north transept is well preserved, with a
fifteenth-century chapel thrown out beyond it, now
used as a mortuary chapel for the Lothian Kerrs.

The year 1118 is given by Barbour as the date of
the foundation of a monastery at Jedburgh by Earl
David, afterwards King of Scots. At first a priory,
Jedburgh was erected into an abbey before the death
of its founder, and richly endowed by the 'sair sanct
for the Crown.' Like the other religious houses on
the border, the Augustinian canons of Jedburgh
swore fealty to Edward I. in 1296, a precaution
which failed to protect them from loss in the war
that broke out the following year, for their fine
church and monastic buildings were plundered and
burnt, and the lead stripped off the roofs, while the
canons themselves were fain to accept shelter from
Edward himself until their property should be
repaired. Curiously enough, although the abbey
was restored to wealth and prosperity in the reign of
Robert I., hardly anything is known of its subsequent history until 1523, when the Earl of Surrey
stormed the church and took it, after fifteen hundred
burgesses had maintained a stubborn defence from
sunrise till nightfall. In 1544 Lord Evers pillaged
and burnt it, and in the following year Lord Hert-

ford completed its destruction, so far as lay in his power. The stains of fire still remain broad and dark on the fine ashlar work which defied the flames. The noble tower remained erect above the devastation, and although the priests and monks were set adrift to return no more, and litanies and singing were hushed for ever, the spirit of the Jeddart men could not be crushed, and they laboured hard to repair it, so valuable was it as a lookout. So in 1575 they used the beams of the refectory roof for strengthening the tower, of which the crown arch fell in 1743. After the Reformation 'the western half of the nave, fitted up in the modern style,'[1] (too well we may understand what is conveyed in that phrase !), was made to serve as the Presbyterian parish church, the south aisle, with its groined arches, being removed in 1793, and 'a wall built between the pillars to make the church more comfortable.'[2] The violence of Surrey and Hertford pale almost to insignificance beside such cold-blooded defacement. Since 1875, however, the faithful of Jedburgh have paid their vows in a brand new kirk, erected by Schomberg Henry, ninth Marquess of Lothian, at a cost of £11,000 ; the abbey church has been restored to its dignified desolation, and is well cared for by Kerr of Fernihirst, better known now as tenth Marquess. Built into a staircase of the abbey church is a stone which bears an inscription commemorating the presence in Teviotdale of a body of Roman troops. It is part of a Roman altar, and the inscription runs as follows :—

---

[1] *Origines Parochiales*, i. 371.
[2] MacGibbon and Ross's *Ecclesiastical Architecture*, i. 416.

I O M V E X I
LLATIO RETO
R U M G A E S A
Q . C . A . I V L
S E V E R T R I B

which may be extended thus, says Dr. Collingwood Bruce :—

Jovi optimo maximo : vexillatio Rœtorum Gœsatorum quorum curam agit Julius Severinus tribunus,

and translated :—

'To Jupiter the best and greatest : the vexillation [detachment] of Rhætian spearmen whom the tribune Julius Severinus commands.'

Rhætia, it may be noted, the home of these foreign soldiers, is now the canton of Grisons, in the east of Switzerland.   These Rhætian troops, who were armed with a peculiar *gæsum* or javelin, have left their memorials also at Risingham in Northumberland ; and from an inscription on a Roman altar at that place we get the tribune's full name Julius Severinus, otherwise it would have been natural to interpret the abbreviated IVL SEVER as Julius Severus.

Mediæval orthography has run even more than usual riot in spelling the name Jedburgh or Jedworth, as this ancient town was alternatively called.   In compiling the *Origines Parochiales* (O for some competent hand to carry that invaluable work to fitting completion !) Mr. Cosmo Innes recorded no fewer than eighty-one different forms taken from early manuscripts—Geddeworde, Jeddeworth, Geddkirch,

Jeddewod, Jethart, Jeddart, and so forth. The burgh has been reckoned a royal one from times anterior to any written record, claiming, with less reason than the departed Roxburgh, to be one of the four towns constituting the original burghal Parliament of Scotland. It was certainly a favourite resort of the early kings, and continued long to be a place of muster for the army and a seat of royal justice. King Malcolm the Maiden died there in 1165; in 1285 it was the scene of Alexander III.'s wedding with Yolande, daughter of the Comte de Dreux, whose loveliness fired the sober Fordun into unwonted superlatives. *Speciosissima domina* he calls her, and says that Jedburgh was fixed as the place of her nuptials because of its great natural beauty.

Queen Victoria visited the town in 1869, but Mary Queen of Scots was the last monarch to hold a court there, which she did in the autumn of 1566, in order to quell the chronic disorder among the broken clans of the Marches. There was much need in that district for a royal 'justice air,' but that did not shield the Queen from being discredited with a different motive by her watchful and relentless enemies. Readers must form their own opinion upon the facts; as in the sixteenth, so in the twentieth century, there is little chance of agreement among them.

James Hepburn, Earl of Bothwell, was Warden of the Middle and West Marches, having been so appointed in 1558; in which capacity it was his duty to attend the queen's court at Jedburgh. But it was also his duty to bring in certain freebooters to make their peace with the Queen or to be judicially dealt with at her 'justice air.' While vigorously discharging this task, Bothwell, on the very day that the Queen rode out from Edinburgh on her progress to Jedburgh, came upon one of the worst of the Border thieves, John Elliot of the Park, commonly known as Little Jock Elliot,[1] and arrested him. Jock, as he rode beside the Warden, asked whether his life would be spared. 'The said Erle Bothwill said, gif ane assyiss [assize] wald mak him clene, he was hertlie contentit, bot he behuvit to [must] pas to the Quenis grace.'[2] Jock, with many crimes on his conscience, slipped from his horse and made a bolt of it; whereupon Bothwell put a pistol-shot into him, lighted to catch him, but stumbled and fell. 'The saide Johne, persaveand [perceiving] himself schot and the erle fallin, he geid [went] to him quhair [where] he lay and gaif him thrie woundis —ane in the bodie, ane in the heid, and ane in the hand; and my lord gaif him twa straikis with ane quhingar [short sword] at the paip [breast] and the said theif depairtit; and my lord lay in a swoun quhill [until] his servantis come and caryit him to the Hermitage.' Jock was picked up dead of his

---

[1] He is immortalised in Sir Robert Maitland of Lethington's well-known metrical picture of the Borders at this period :—

> ' Thai spulzie puir men of their packs,
> Thai leave them nocht on bed or backs ;
>   Both hen and cock,
>   With reel and rock [distaff],
>   The Laird's Jock
>   All with him takes.

> Thai leave not spindle, spoon nor spit,
> Bed, bolster, blanket, shirt nor sheet ;
>   John o' the Park
>   Rypis [bursts open] chest and ark ;
>   For all such wark
>   He is right meet.'

[2] *Diurnal of Occurrents*, p. 100.

wounds within a mile of the scene of the encounter,[1] while Bothwell lay in his castle very weak for many days, and it was commonly reported that he was dead. On the face of it, there was nothing but an act of gracious sympathy in the Queen riding over to inquire for her wounded Warden on the first day when she was clear of official duties ; but see how Buchanan, Mary's inveterate slanderer, garbles dates to suit his purpose. He represents her as ' flinging away in haste like a mad woman by great journeys in post in the sharp time of winter,' to visit her lover. Her lover! alas, that is no term for Bothwell, who loved only himself and his own ambition ; but Mary's wayward heart had gone out to this strong man, and she was never circumspect. ' She must,' continues Buchanan, ' betray her outrageous lust, and, in an inconvenient time of year, despising all discommodities of the way and weather, and all danger of thieves, she betook herself headlong to the journey with such a company as no man of any honest degree would have adventured his life and goods among them.' Then he describes how she returned to Jedburgh, made all things ready for Bothwell, and received him there, when ' their company and familiar haunt together was such as was smally agreeing with both their honours.' There was food for scandal—was not this Maria Verticordia ?—but mark how Buchanan, in his eagerness to drive it home, has given away his case and cast a slur upon the head of his own party. Queen Mary arrived at Jedburgh on 9th October, not in ' the sharp time of winter,' and opened her circuit court, which sat for six days and was closed

[1] *Diurnal of Occurrents*, p. 100.

on the 14th. On the 10th and 11th she presided at meetings of the Privy Council ; on the 15th she received the French Ambassador le Croc; on the 16th, her first leisure day, she rode over to Hermitage to inquire for her sick Warden, and *returned to Jedburgh the same night.* It was wicked weather, it is true, slashing rain and furious wind, but Mary was a huntress, rode a slapping pace, and cared not for storm or shine. As for the disreputable company in which Buchanan alleges she rode, his own idol, the Earl of Moray, afterwards his 'Good Regent,' was one, the Earl of Huntly was another, brother of the Countess of Bothwell, and Secretary Lethington a third !

The whole party was drenched long before it arrived at Hermitage, but the Queen would not change her clothes. In the few hours she spent in the castle (which, after all, was a royal one, and not a private house of Bothwell's) she signed the appointment of one George Sinclair to a certain office in Edinburgh,[1] and made arrangements for victualling the garrison. Then she set out in the storm on her return journey. At the head of the Braidlee Burn, on the divide between Liddesdale and Teviotdale, is a place still called the Queen's Mire, where her white palfrey got bogged, and her people nearly lost her in the darkness. But she finished the journey, went to bed, and was seized with violent fever and pains, the consequence of fatigue and exposure, for she had ridden between fifty and sixty miles. She lay at the point of death till 25th, prayer being made for her in all the churches, all men hourly expecting her end. On that day they

[1] Privy Seal Register, dated 'at Armitage, 16th. October 1566.'

thought she was actually dead—'eene closit, mouth fast, and feit and arms stiff and cauld.' As to Buchanan's poisonous innuendo about her intercourse with Bothwell at this time, 'smally agreeing with both their honours,' judge whether either of these persons were in a state to carry on dalliance. It is true that Bothwell came to Jedburgh during the Queen's illness. Bishop Leslie writing on 27th October mentions that 'my Lord Boythwell is heir, quha convalescis weill of his woundis,'[1] but this was scant occasion for tender passages. Poor Lady! she has enough to answer for without being called to account for the prurient exaggerations of a malignant pedant. 'Would that I had died at Jedburgh!' she is reported to have sighed in later years, and none may say that it had not been better for her fame and happiness that fate had so decreed. She had another and more plangent weird to dree.

Mary was so far recovered as to be able to leave Jedburgh on 8th November, after paying Lady Fernihirst £40 in the way of rent for the house she had occupied during these thirty days. There it stands, that grim old building, still inhabited ; its dark thatched roof and sombre walls striking a strange far-off note among the snug shops and spruce villas on the banks of Jed Water. It is three stories high, with the arms of Kerr and Home over the arched doorway, which is now built up. At the end of the eighteenth century it was owned and occupied by Dr. Lindsay, father of Burn's 'sweet Isabella Lindsay.' In 1881 it belonged to Colonel Armstrong of St. Petersburg.

The people of Jedburgh turned against their

---

[1] Keith's Church History, ii. 134.

Queen in the hour of her trouble, and in 1571 stood an assault by the lairds of Buccleuch and Fernihirst, who were beaten off eventually on the arrival of some of Regent Morton's troops under Lord Ruthven.

In the last Scottish invasion of England, that of 1745, Prince Charlie led part of his Highlanders through Jedburgh, and lay the night at No 9 Castle Gate.

Mention has been made of the effective part borne by the men of Jedburgh in the Raid of the Reidswire. Their favourite weapon was ever the 'Jethart staff,' about the precise nature of which antiquaries are not agreed. Some describe it as a pole seven or eight feet long, with a broad, keen axe-blade, and a sharp hook ; but Major, a contemporary authority, says it was a stout staff with a steel head four feet long ! Did he mean that the staff or the head measured four feet ? In 1516 the Scottish Government forbade the use of this weapon, and directed that ' speris, axis, halbertis, bowis and culweringis ' should be used instead ; [1] but not only was the order rescinded, but in 1552 the merchants of Edinburgh were ordered by the Town Council always to have ' long valpynnis ' (weapons) in their houses, ' sic es hand-ex, Jedburgh staif, hawart (Halbert), jawalyng, with Knaipschawis (steel caps) and jakkis, and that they cum thairwith to the Hie-gait incontinent efter the commoun bell ryngyng, or that thay se ony cummaris (disturbance) of slauchteris tulzies or appearance thereof. ' etc. etc.

'Jethart justice,' a proverbial expression for hanging a man first and then trying him, is said to have originated in the summary procedure of a court held

[1] Pitcairn's Criminal Trials, i. 262.

here by Lord Home in 1606, when a number of lawless fellows were dealt with sans ceremony. But Crawford in his Memoirs takes it back to 1574, when the Regent Morton held a bloody assize in Jedburgh, and had no time to listen to evidence.

Largely as violence and oppression, slaughter and arson, figured in the annals of Jedburgh, they prevailed not to purge these light-hearted Borderers of their mirth. The annual Roodmass fair, with its games on the Dunion, was a fair rival to Peebles at the Play, and many a maiden's pulses quickened as the day drew near :—

> ' Ye'll be kissed and I'll be kissed,
> We'll a' be kissed the morn.
> The braw lads o' Jethart
> Will kiss us a' the morn.'

There is circumstantial, if not conclusive, evidence to support the assertion that this practice has survived the cessation of Border war.

The whole of the parishes of Jedworth, Old Jedworth, and Upper Crailing so far as they lay outside the burgh boundaries, were comprised in Jed Forest, which was more than a merely nominal woodland; it was a dense primeval growth of oak and pine, through which roamed herds of red deer of great size.

Originally part of the kingdom of Northumberland, the market town and forest were probably brought into possession of the Scottish kings by David, Earl of Northumberland, and in 1221 Alexander II. settled them upon his queen, Johanna, as part of her dower. In the halcyon reign of Alexander III, the question of English claims to this desirable territory was never raised ; but with the death of that king and his granddaughter, the Maid of Norway, peace spread her wings and took flight from the Borders for many a day. Jedburgh, town and forest, were often in English occupation during the fourteenth century ; although in 1320, and again by the famous Emerald Charter in 1325, King Robert made them over to good Sir James of Douglas. On the fall of the Black Douglas in 1455 these possessions passed to his victorious rival Angus. Differences arose between the Red Douglas and Ker of Fernihirst, who claimed the right of holding courts in the forest as hereditary bailiff of the abbey. The Red Douglas at that time was the formidable fifth Earl of Angus—'Bell-the-Cat'—who could well afford to disregard the feelings of the laird of Fernihirst ; but the position of his grandson, the sixth earl, was not so well assured. The factions of Douglas and Hamilton were very evenly balanced in their contest for power, and in April 1520 Arran and Archbishop Beaton very nearly succeeded in capturing Angus when he was in Edinburgh with a following of only fourscore. It had been more ; but Fernihirst and the Kers, out of revenge for the insult offered them in the matter of the forest courts, deserted to the Hamiltons. However, Angus got timely warning from his uncle, Bishop Gavin Douglas, who had attempted to reconcile the parties. He made the best of the little force at his disposal. Aided by the townsfolk, with whom he was popular, he caused all the wynds leading into the High Street to be barricaded, and posted his men at the head of Blackfriar's Wynd to receive an attack. Presently the Hamilton's came swinging along from the Dominicans' church in greatly superior force, supported by the Kers, and led by Sir Patrick Hamilton. Finding their passage blocked by Angus — 'Cleanse the causeway!' cried Sir Patrick. 'Cleanse the causeway!' shouted his men, and charged furiously. But Angus had posted his little force so wisely that the assailants were repulsed, Sir Patrick Hamilton being slain by the hand of Angus himself. The mellay was still raging, when the old cry of 'A Douglas! a Douglas' sounded from another quarter. William Douglas, Abbot of Hollyrood, and Home of Wedderburn had forced the Hamilton guard at the city gate, and arrived on the scene with a strong reinforcement for their kinsman. The Hamiltons broke and fled. It was now the turn of the Douglases to cry 'Cleanse the causeway!' The Master of Eglinton and about seventy of Arran's men were killed; even Archbishop Beaton only saved himself by seeking sanctuary at the Altar of the Dominicans, where Bishop Gavin interceded for him. Arran and his son, Sir John Hamilton, escaped together on the back of a cart-horse, riding through the Nor' Loch to the open country, and Angus remained in possession of the capital.

The Kers, though badly worsted in the 'Cleanse-the-Causeway' raid as it was called, by no means abandoned their ancient claim. The eleventh Earl of Angus having summoned a court in Jedburgh Forest for 21st. May 1612, Fernihirst issued summons for his court to assemble on the same day. Thereupon the Earl's younger brother, James Douglas, Provost of Abernethy (the Earl himself was only twenty-one), challenged Fernihirst's son to single combat. The Privy Council interfered. James

Douglas was imprisoned in Blackness Castle for having 'undewtifullie behavit'; Fernihirst and his son were ordered into Ward in Edinburgh Castle under penalty of £10,000. Angus, who had brought his kinsman the Earl of Morton with a strong following to defend his rights, was reprimanded for such a display of force; but received confirmation of his rights to hold courts in the forest, while the Kers were forbidden to interferre with him under penalty of 20,000 merks. And so this obstinate dispute was brought to a settlement.

Although Jed Forest itself has long since disappeared, the aspect of the land is far from bare, for plantations have been raised round all the numerous country houses in the neighbourhood. Two trees of note, reputed survivals of the old forest, still remain, or at least were flourishing twenty years ago. One of these, known as the Capon Tree, a little to the south of the town, is a short-stemmed, spreading oak, with a circumference in 1880 of 24 feet 3 inches at the base. It is said to have been a mustering-place for the Kers in time of war, but its name doubtless indicates that under its branches the chief or his representative sat at the receipt of custom, capons being an important item in the payment of rent by 'kind.' A capon, also, was often the 'reddendo,' exacted by a feudal superior for the land held by a vassal.

Another and finer oak stands near Fernihirst Castle and is called not undeservedly, the 'King of the Forest,' for it has a bole of 43 feet, and in 1880 measured 17 feet in circumference four feet above the ground.[1]

[1] Transactions of the Highland & Agricultural Society, 1881 p. 206.

And so we pass from Jedburgh, not without reluctance, for one may travel far before coming to another resting-place so sweet and pretty as this venerable little burgh with its modest-industry and three thousand inhabitants. 'Jethart's here!' and owes its preservation to the stout hearts and ready hands of its burgesses, who brought it through troubles in the past that must have whelmed far wealthier communities poorer in spirit. Long may it flourish, rich in memories of an honourable past!

In the couple of long miles between the town and Jedfoot bridge, where Jed Water joins the Teviot, there is nothing of superior interest to what one is likely to find in the next of Teviot's tributaries, the Oxnam Water, or Ousenham, as the natives call it, faithful to the pronunciation current when patient old Timothy Pont made his wonderful maps towards the close of the sixteenth century. Therefore, instead of following Jed Water in its northward course, we may cross the river, strike eastward across the ridge, leaving Hartrigge woods on the left, and so arrive in three miles or so at the parish church and village of Oxnam.

At its south-eastern corner this parish seems to have pinched some acres of hill pasture from England, for the march crosses the watershed, and is formed for nearly a mile by the head-water of the English Coquet.

Watling Street, the great Roman road between Yorkshire and Lothian, runs for seven miles along the eastern side of the parish, but cannot be pronounced in a state of repair for wheel traffic. If you are tempted to trace it, you will be led upon the head-water of the Kale, which the Watling Street crosses at a point only a mile distant from Oxnam Water at the foot of Woden Law, where there is a circular camp, and nearly opposite on Pennymuir are remains of a rectangular one, probably Roman, commanding the ford.

From immemorial time these steep green sides of Cheviot have been far famed for the breed of sheep reared on them ; and nowhere is the pasture sweeter or richer than upon the uplands of Kale.

‘ O the sheep-herding’s lightsome amang the green braes,
Where Kale wimples clear ’neath the white-blossomed slaes;
Where the wild thyme and meadow-queen scent the saft gale,
And the cushat croods leesomely doon in the dale.
There the lintwhite and mavis sing sweet frae the thorn,
And blithe lilts the laverock aboon the green corn ;
And a’ things rejoice in the summer’s glad prime—
But my heart’s wi’ my love in the far foreign clime.’ [1]

We are in Howman parish here, which suffered no less than its neighbours from the English armies. In 1544 Lord Hertford detached Robert Collingwood with his Irish levies to this sequestered vale, where they ‘ brent the tounes and stedes of Shapely (Sharplaw), Hownomkirk, Hounom town, Hevesyde, Hownome Grange, etc., and brought away certain prisoners, with 280 nolt (cattle), 200 shepe, and 40 horse. ’

Hownam kirk, whereof John the son of Orm [2] was patron in 1185, stood in the form of a cross at the junction of the Capehope Burn with Kale Water ; but the present structure does not invite inspection.

[1] Joanna Baillie.
[2] Orm’s name is preserved in Ormiston on the Teviot, where once stood a pele tower.

The fancy which has dubbed a semicircle of great stones to the east of the village the Eleven Shearers, and the tradition which explains them as so many workers changed into stone for reaping on the Lord's day, bear upon the face of them the stamp of the Calvinist Reformation.

Place-names do not always bear their meaning so plainly that all may read it ; on the contrary, they often receive a spelling which suggests something totally different, whereby snares are spread for the amateur etymologist. Two such examples occur on opposite sides of Kale Water two or three miles below Hownam kirk. One of these is a hill called Grubbit Law, which, in plain Scots of to-day, signifies a hill whence tree-roots had been grubbed. What can be plainer ? This fine green hill was once rough forest, reclaimed by a thrifty peasantry. Possibly, but the name contains no reference to that industry, but comes from a mill at its foot, which so far back as 1170 the aforesaid John the son of Orm, in making over the land of Huneden or Hownam to the Monks of Melrose, referred to as the land of Grubheued or Grubbeheued.[1] The owner of this land was not less pious than his neighbour, for in 1181 Huctred of Grubheued and Symon his son, in presence of Joceline, Bishop of Glasgow, granted some of his land to the same monks, in consideration of receiving 'their fraternity, their prayers, and a participation in all the privileges of their Church'[2]—benefits to which, as a good Christian, he surely was entitled without such solid consideration. But it was by mundane bargains such as this that the Church made sure her

[1] Liber de Melrose, pp. 119-122.
[2] Ibid. I. 110.

foundations. Deeds of gift to monks, and manuscripts referring to their squabbles about possession,
form by far the largest surviving part of the material
for early Scottish history. Simple laymen, conscious,
no doubt, of much in their private conduct that
would not bear analysis, compounded by liberal
gifts to the Church ; but seldom does one find one
so simple as a landowner in this valley of the Kale,
who presented the monks of Kelso with seven acres
of land to grow corn for holy bread ! Seven acres
of good corn land was liberal reckoning for such a
purpose.

The other name mentioned as deceptive is that of
the parish in which the land of Grubbit lies—Morebattle, to wit. Surely here we have direct reference
to some conflict upon this much contested soil.
Not a bit. The parish was written Merebotele and
Merbotyl in the Liber de Melros and Glasgow
Register of the twelfth century, and does not appear
as Morbottle till the end of the sixteenth. ' Battle '
is a very modern corruption of the Anglo-Saxon
botl, a dwelling ; mere botl means the dwelling of
the lake. [1]

The Church of Morebattle was dedicated to
St. Laurence, whose name seldom occurs in connection with Scottish ecclesiastical foundations. The
old building is gone ; the present one dates from
that unpromising period 1757 ; when the New
Statistical Account was being compiled in 1844 it
was undergoing alterations which, we are assured
' will render it more comfortable and handsome.'
To its comfort the present deponent cannot testify ;

---

[1] Cf. Buittle, John Baliol's castle in Galloway, Newbottle Abbey,
Bootle in Lancashire, etc.

upon its comeliness let any impartial traveller pronounce judgment. The well below the churchyard
retains memories of a pious past in its name—
Laurie's Well.

A little more than two miles to the west of
Morebattle village stands a ruined castle of more
than common note, being Cessford, the strength of
the Kers of that line, rivals of the house of Fernihirst. The keep is believed to be the same as stood
here in the fourteenth century; and none but a
building of extraordinary strength could have survived the vicissitudes through which this one has
passed. The Walls vary from 12 feet to 13 feet
6 inches thick. Surrey besieged it in 1523, in the
absence of its owner, Sir Andrew Ker (the same who
fell three years later in the affair with the Scotts at
Melrose)[1] who was attending elsewhere to his duties
as Warden. Let the English earl tell the story of
his good luck in his own words to Henry VIII,
which are instructive as to the manner of siege
operations in the sixteenth century.—

'We went to Sesford and layed our ordynance too the
same about VII of the clok in the morning, which was
esteemed to be the strongest place of Scotland, save Dunbar
and Fas castell. I had with me one very good cortowte,[2]
one very good colveryne, one demy colveryne, four lizards
and four fawcons. The sayd fortress was vawmewred with
erth of the best sorte that I have sen, and had a barbican,
with another false barbican within the same, to defend the
gate of the dongeon, and dyvers pecis of iron gonnyis (guns)
within.

[1] See p. 76, ante.
[2] Cortowtes and culverines were heavy pieces drawn by oxen; the
others were field-guns.

'Our battery began at the vawemeure, which did little prevayle or, in maner, did small hurt thereunto. After that I causid to shote the best pecis at the place of the dongeon (keep) that was thought most weke, whereof none effecte ensewed; for within fewe shottis the cortowtis exile tre (axle-tree) brake, and being of newe mountid with anothir exeltre, was within three shotis soo crased in the seid exiltre that I durste noon suffre her to be shot, having noo newe to bring her home withall. In the mean tyme, divers of your graces servaunts, as the Lord Leonard, Sir Arthure Darcy, Sir William Parre, Harvy and others, took scaling ladders and entered the barmkyn[1] right daungerfully, where many that entered with them were hurte, as well with caste of stonys as with shot of ordynaunce. They took very long ladders purposely made for that entent, and sett theme to the dongeon too have scaled the same; and the ordynaunce with archers shoting continually at the vamewre and lapes; but all that wold not prevaile ... which perceived, remooved the two colverynes to another syde of the dongeon and shot at an old wyndowe, about six fote fro the ground, and the same being mewred [built up], was opened and something enlarged, and then the gonners, for a reward of me promised, undertooke to throwe in the same four barrellis of powdre with shovellis, whiche right herdily they accomplished. The Scotts, perceiving the same, threwe fire into the hous where our men had throwen in the powder, bifore they had all accomplished their busynes, with the which three of our gonners were marvelously brente, but, thanked be God, not slayne, and the said poudre spent, to our knowledge, without doing hurte to the fortresse, which was nothing plesant to us your Graces servaunts, trusting verely by means therof to have thrown a parte of the dongeon.

'Notwithstanding within a while after, the warden of the marches of Scotlande, owner of the same [Sir Andrew Ker], being within a myle, fearing his men to be gotten with

[1] The outer garth.

assaulte and so slayne,[1] sente too me offring me the place, his men having licence to depart with bag and bagage ; which, after requysicion made unto me by all the Lords openly for a color,[2] I condissended unto, and was very glad of the said appointement ; for in manner I sawe not howe it would have been won ; it was tenable for twenty four hours against three of your Graces best curtowts, the wall being no less than fowrteen fote thick.

'I next threw down Whitton, now six o'clock at night, all day rayning and the coldeste wether, men tired, horses without mete, returned to England, your Graces subjects be the most joyful people I ever saw, more rejoicd than if Edinburgh had been taken.'

The reader may well weary at these interminable annals of arson and slaughter, but he cannot understand this Border land unless he has in mind the ordeal through which it has passed.

On the north side of the Kale Water, opposite Morebattle, lies the parish of Linton, a name which, strange as it may seem, bears exactly the same interpretation as Morebattle, being the *lin tun*, or dwelling beside the lake. The loch, which lay to the southeast of the parish church, has been drained away— *stat nominis umbra.* The said church deserves more respectful attention than most of its neighbours in this valley. It is very ancient : Blahan was the name of its priest in 1127, and Sir Richard Comyn presented it to the monks of Kelso for the salvation of the soul of Henry, King David's first-born, who

1 The rules of war justified the slaughter of the garrison of any place taken by storm after being summoned. Instances of such a penalty being inflicted by British commanders occurred during the Indian wars of the Marquess Wellesley.

2 That is, he caused his officers to ask him to grant the terms in order to 'save his face' before the Warden.

died in 1152. Albeit the structure has suffered severely from alteration and restoration, the walls are of Norman work, and there is a piece of sculpture in the tympanum of the porch embodying a very ancient tradition of the district. The porch, be it observed, is a recent addition, the sculpture having been removed from the old doorway in 1858. To the secular mind the subject suggested is the encounter of St. George with the dragon ; but to the eye of faith (in local lore) it represents the exploits of William the son of Roger de Somerville, who dwelt at Linton Tower, now demolished, in the twelfth century. Roger was lord of Whichenour, in Staffordshire, but having taken part in the rebellion against King John, put the Border between him and the tyrant, and died in 1214, at the age of ninety-four, ' at his sones house of Lintoune tour, and was laid in the quier of Lintoune church.' [1] It seems that this part of Roxburghshire was infested by a destructive monster of the nature of a dragon, which harboured in a place still called the Worm's Hole, and defied all pursuit, until young Somerville tackled it and drove his spear down its throat. All doubts about the veracity of this tale must be dispelled by a single glance at the armorial bearings of the Somervilles at this day. Their crest is a golden wheel, and upon it a dragon vert, spouting out fire before and behind—truly a dreadful beast—and who so sceptical as to require more conclusive proof than that ? If more were demanded by any doubting Thomas, it is no longer forthcoming, but it is

---

[1] *Memorie of the Somervilles*, p. 34, quoted in *Origines Parochiales*, i. 432.

said to have existed at one time in the shape of some lines carved under the sculpture on the church.

> 'The wode[1] laird of Lariston
> Slew the Worm of Wormes glen
> And wan all Lintoun parochin.'

The Somervilles of Linton made a considerable figure in history during several centuries, Sir Thomas having been created Lord Somerville before the year 1430, when he was Justiciary of Scotland south of the Forth. In the time of Hugh, fifth Lord Somerville, came the end of Linton Tower. First in 1522 the English Warden entered Teviotdale with two thousand men, 'and went to Leynton tour and set upon it with spere and shield, and in conclusion, or it past none [before it passed noon], wann it and brant it clene down to the bare stane walles. Notwithstanding all the men that were within, which was xvi, were saved by reason of a gable of the house that was of stone, and the wind that was their friend, for betwix the said gable and the batialing, they lay unto the huse rofe was fallen, where we left them, all except one Robyn Carre, whiche cam down in a rope when the huse was first fired.' Next year came Lord Surrey to complete the work, and he enumerates Linton among the two hundred and eighty-seven 'fortresses, abbeys, frere-houses, market townes, villages, towres and places brent, raced and cast downe' in that expedition. The land had passed into the possession of the Kers before 1538, and the Somervilles settled upon their property of Carnwath, in Lanarkshire. The fifth lord had been

[1] Mad.

a Reformer ; not so his son James, sixth Lord Somerville, for he, the Earl of Atholl, and Lord Borthwick were the only three who voted against the ratification of the Confession of Faith in 1560. Gilbert, eighth Lord Somerville, made sad havoc of his fortune. He entertained James VI. with such splendour in his castle of Cowthally as gave his Majesty the chance of making a better joke than usual. He said the place ought to be called Cow-daily, because he noticed that a cow and ten sheep were killed there every day. The family never recovered from Gilbert's extravagance ; the estates were sold, and the nineteenth and last Lord Somerville died in 1870.

The lower reaches of the Kale Water are exceedingly lovely, and before debouching in the Teviot the stream plunges into a deep ravine, where Covenanters used to hold conventicles in the killing time. Near the junction of the waters, on the north side of Teviot, there stood 'the fayre tower called Ormeston,' as Lord Dacre called it in reporting to the Earl of Surrey his 'exployts don upon the Scotts' in 1523. This tower he 'kist down,' but the site thereof deserves passing notice, as having been the dwelling-place of an important family who took their name from it. John the son of Orme has been mentioned above as the patron of Hownam church in 1185. Ormiston, no doubt, was the paternal home, for which John de Ormiston did fealty in 1296 to Edward I. He may have been descended from the original Orme, but it may be noted once for all that many lands had changed owners in the interval, and that during the thirteenth and fourteenth centuries, when surnames were first becoming universal, men assumed the

names of their estates, often quite irrespectively to
their lineage.

James, the Black Laird of Ormiston, and his
brother Hob, figure darkly in the tragedy of Kirk-
o'-Field. They worked with Hepburn of Bowton,
young Hay of Talla, the valet Dalgleish and the
porter Powrie, under Bothwell's personal direction,
in carrying the gunpowder in two travelling-trunks
into the grounds of the house where Darnley lay.
Then on Sunday, 9th February 1567, while Queen
Mary was paying a last visit to her consort, they
brought the powder into the house. Six years later,
in 1573, the Black Laird was brought to trial for
complicity in the affair with Bothwell, Archibald
Douglas, and others. Ormiston and some of the
meaner ruffians paid for their share with their lives ;
but Archibald knew too much. His servant,
Thomas Binning, was hanged, but it was not until
26th May 1586, nineteen years after the crime, that
Archibald was submitted to a shamelessly collusive
trial for the ' crewall, horribill, abhominabill and
tressonabill murthour of vmquhile Henrie King of
Scottis of gud memorie. ' Archibald had flourished
like a green bay-tree in the interval. Morton had
made him Parson of Glasgow and raised him to the
bench. And now Archibald's brother, William of
Whittingehame, sat on the bench to try the case ;
Morton's dying deposition and Binning's evidence,
both deeply implicating Archibald, were withheld
from the jury, which included George Home of
Spott, who in 1582 had been tried for complicity in
the very same crime. The only part of the proceedings that does not stink is that ten Scottish gentleman paid forfeit of £40 each rather than serve as

jurymen in this demoniac travesty of justice. Archibald was acquitted, of course. As for the Black Laird of Ormiston, his dying speech on the scaffold somewhat touches compassion. ' It is not merveill, ' quoth he, ' that I have been wickit, for the wickit companie that ever I have been in ; bot speciallie within this seaven yeiris by-past, quhilk I never saw twa guid men or ane guid deed. ' A study of Scottish history at this period inclines one to perceive no exaggeration in this confession.

That seems to have been practically the end of the line of Ormiston, for in the following century the lands were possessed by the Kers of Cessford. The laird of Ormiston, indeed, does make a last appearance when the Scottish Solomon, James VI., was exerting himself, not without success, to stanch the feud between Cessford and Buccleuch, and endeavoured to settle other *vendettas* at the same time. It is recorded in the draft contract that ' thair is particularlie deidlie feid [feud] and actionis betuix the said Walter Ker of Cesfurde, knycht, and the said James Ormstoun of that ilk,' who had stolen some of Cessford's lands and killed one of his servants. The commissioners are directed to settle the affair on equitable terms.

Yet there is one more mournful reminder of this ancient line. The Rev. A. Milne, minister of Melrose, writing in 1743, mentions that ' George Ormiston, late hangman in Edinburgh, was a cadet of this family, if not the representative of it—a memorandum to old families not to be puffed up with pride on account of their antiquity, for they know not what mean offices they or theirs may be obliged to stoop to.'

Ph :

JEDBURGH ABBEY.

T. & R. Annan & Sons

CHAPTER X

FROM Kalemouth we travel due north through scenes of ever-increasing loveliness to rejoin the Tweed.—

'Bosom'd in woods where mighty rivers run,
Kelso's fair vale expands before the sun ;
Its rising downs in vernal beauty swell,
And, fringed with hazel, winds each flowery dell.
Green spangled plains to dimpling lawns succeed,
And Temple rises on the banks of Tweed.
Blue o'er the river Kelso's shadow lies
And copse-like isles amid the waters rise.'

Not a flattering sample this of Leyden's verse ; he could do, and did, better than that, though he was ever prone to eke out his decasyllables with too many epithets. We passed his birthplace at Denholm a while ago, and now recall him to memory amid those scenes which he was so busy interpreting to his countrymen when Scott eclipsed him with more dazzling flame. Born in 1775, John Leyden was already collecting and adding to Border lore when Scott, only four years his senior, made his acquaintance, and enlisted him as chief contributor to the *Minstrelsy*. In 1803, the year after the first two volumes of that work were published, Leyden went out to Madras as assistant surgeon. In India

16

he found the Elliot as powerful and as ready to befriend a vassal as he had been in Teviotdale. Leyden's writings in prose and verse had not escaped notice from the Governor-General, Lord Minto, who made him assay-master of the Calcutta mint, and took Leyden with him to Java in 1811, where the poet died at the age of six-and-thirty. The Ettrick Shepherd's elegy was more generous, and also more just, than bards are wont to bestow upon their contemporaries.——

> ' Sweet rung the harp to Logan's hand ;
> Then Leyden came from Border-land,
> With dauntless heart and ardour high,
> And wild impatience in his eye.
> Though false at times his tones might be,
> Though wild notes marred the symphony,
> Between the flowing measure stole
> That spoke the bard's inspired soul. '

We have seen how grandiloquently Leyden described the confluence of Tweed and Teviot, bestowing on them the epithet 'mighty,' which, had he known, he would have kept in reserve until after beholding the union of Ganges with Jumna. Less dignified, but not less descriptive, is the metaphor applied by Sir Thomas Dick Lauder to illustrate the effect of Teviot upon the dominant river.——

' Like a gentleman of large fortune, who has just received a great accession to it, the Tweed, having been joined by the Teviot, leaves Kelso with a magnitude and air of importance that it has nowhere hitherto assumed during its course, and which it will be found to maintain until it is ultimately swallowed up by that grave of all rivers—the sea.'[1]

Scottish Rivers, chap. xvi.

This is true enough. The river, which is about to become first half then wholly English, seems anxious to assume an appearance in keeping with the more affluent southern nationality. No more crepuscular dalliance with drooping boughs at Dawick Bank, nor irresponsible brawling at Caddonfoot; no more headlong frolics at the Gateheugh, Craigover, or the Trows of Makerstoun. Henceforward we sweep in stately curves, broad—bosomed as Trent or Thames, slumbering occasionally in lakelike 'dubs' —long reaches of still water at Sprouston, Birgham, Carham, and the like. Our landscape opens into ampler lines; what we lose in wilder beauty we gain in opulence and space.

The highroad on the right bank of Tweed runs through a fine and fertile champaign to the village of Sprouston, hallowed in memory of many an honest angler as the abode of Jamie Wright, than whom none could busk a bonnier fly, and none knew how to display it to greater advantage in the sight of salmon. Bordered by the English march, the rich crops and fat cattle of this fine tract offered of old a standing temptation to marauding bands. Hadden Stank and Redden Burn were often fixed as meeting-places for the English and Scottish commissioners to settle disputes and determine boundaries; and Hadden Rig was the scene of a brisk encounter in 1542 between the Earl of Huntly's Scots and three thousand English cavalry under Captain Robert Bowes. Lord Home came up with four hundred spears in the nick of time to save the day for the Scots. The English were routed, and six hundred of them taken prisoners, with many officers. Not long after, in the same year, the Duke of Norfolk passed that way in force, and burnt the villages of Sprouston, Hadden, and Redden.

If in leaving Kelso we follow the highway down the left bank of Tweed, it leads in a north-easterly direction, scarcely clearing the flowery suburbs of Kelso before it plunges into Sir R. Waldie Griffiths' leafy woods of Hendersyde. Then it runs close along the low cliff bordering Sprouston Dub, famed by salmon-fishers, and so across a stream called by a name that has vexed the souls of generations of antiquaries and etymologists. The Eden—such the simple name, borne by rivers of Fife and Cumberland, as well as by this one of Roxburghshire, yet no man can read the riddle of its meaning—*Eadann*, suggests Mr. J. B. Johnston,[1] the Gaelic for a hill face, but does not explain why one stream should be called a hill face more than another, especially in a country where level ground is the exception. One must be content to add the meaning of Eden to the long list of things that are past finding out ; though it may be noted that it is a name of hoar antiquity, the village of Ednam—Eden ham—having been so called as far back as the reign of King Edgar, who died in 1107. That monarch restored the monastery of Coldingham, which had been destroyed by the Danes, and in one of the few charters remaining of that time Thor informs his lord, Earl David (afterwards King David I.) that King Edgar had given him Ednaham wilderness ; that he had inhabited it, built a church there dedicated to St. Cuthbert, and endowed it with one plough.[2]

Ednam has shared the common fate of so many

---

[1] *Place Names of Scotland, sub voce* Eden.
[2] Skene's *Celtic Scotland*, ii. 368.

Border villages. The last time the English burnt it
was in 1558 ; of the old church no vestige remains ;
cold and grim on its site stands its successor erected
in 1800. James Thomson, the poet of *The Seasons*,
was born here in 1700, a fact duly commemorated
by an obelisk fifty-two feet high, set up in 1820 ;
but he drew his inspiration from other scenes, for,
ten days after his birth, his father moved to the
manse of Southdean, on Jed Water. Few people
read Thomson now ; still fewer remember, if they
ever knew, that he was an ardent fly-fisher, with a
becoming contempt for those who pollute their
fingers with bait.——

> ' Now, when the first foul torrent of the brooks,
> Swell'd with the vernal rains, is ebb'd away ;
> And whitening down their mossy-tinctured stream
> Descends the billowy foam, now is the time,
> While yet the dark-brown water aids the guile,
> To tempt the trout. The well-dissembled fly—
> The rod, fine-tapering with elastic spring—
> Snatch'd from the hoary steed the floating line—
> And all thy slender watery stores prepare.
> But let not on thy hook the tortured worm
> Convulsive twist in agonising folds,
> Which, by rapacious hunger swallowed deep,
> Gives, as you tear it from the bleeding breast
> Of the weak, helpless, uncomplaining wretch,
> Harsh pain and horror to the tender hand. '

A trifle turgid, perhaps, but the principles are un-
exceptionable.

Eden Water has its source far back in Legerwood
parish, on the very verge of Lauderdale, close to
the ruined pele of Corsbie. This was of old Gordon
territory ; it is matter for dispute whether the family

of Gordon gave it the title which they had brought
from a place of that name in France, or whether
they took their name from this Berwickshire parish.
Adam de Gordon was one of the prisoners taken by
Sir James Douglas on that night when he made the
notable capture of Thomas Randolph and Stewart
of Bonkill on the Water of Lyne.[1]   Gordon made
his escape, and two years later received from
Edward II. a grant of the lands of Stichill, further
down Eden Water, which Thomas Randolph had
forfeited by his adherence to the Bruce.   However,
the sun soon crossed to the other side of the hedge;
the crown of Scotland was firm on Bruce's brow,
the coronet of Moray on that of Randolph, before
the whelming victory of Bannockburn (1314), by
which time Gordon had changed his allegiance, and
Stichill remained in possession of his descendants,
the Gordons of Lochinvar, till 1628, when John
Gordon, afterwards Viscount Kenmure, sold it ·to
Robert Pringle.

Just as the original Gordon probably named his
Berwickshire estate from his paternal home in
France, so, when the family became chiefs in Strath-
bogie, did they import with them the name Huntly
from the vale of Eden, and bestow it upon the
Aberdeenshire town and parish, which bear it at
this day.

At Mellerstain the Eden Water spreads into an
ornamental lake.   This property came into possession of the Earls of Haddington by the marriage of
Rachel Baillie, the heiress, with Lord Binning,
eldest son of the sixth earl, in consequence of which
the family name has since been Baillie-Hamilton.

. [1] See p. 27. *ante.*

The connection has honourable associations, for Rachel's mother was Lady Grizell Baillie, the poetess, remembered for her chivalrous enterprise in 1684, when she was but nineteen years of age. She was the daughter of Sir Patrick Home, afterwards first Earl of Marchmont, the close friend of Robert Baillie of Jerviswood and Mellerstain. Baillie, who had been imprisoned and fined in 1676 for contumacy, was arrested in London on a charge of complicity in the Rye House plot, tried in Edinburgh, and condemned to be hanged. Home, urgently desiring to communicate with Baillie, intrusted his daughter with a letter, which she was to find means to deliver to him in prison. She rode alone through the Merse in the night, passed through the city gate in the morning, beneath the grinning heads of those who had laid down their lives in the cause of spiritual liberty, for which Baillie and Home were equally ready to suffer. She fulfilled her mission, bringing back word from the condemned man to her father ; but she left her heart behind her. George Baillie's son, Robert, won it from her during that brief interview in the prison, and gave her his own in exchange. After that the Homes had to go into exile in Holland. Then came the Revolution, and they were free to return to Scotland. Queen Mary would have taken Grizell into her court in London as maid of honour ; but the girl declined, for she longed for the sweet hill air of the Borders. Her father's property was restored to him, and thither she went, to wait until Robert Baillie came to claim his bride. Perhaps it was during these years of waiting that she wrote the tender lines :—

'Oh the ewe-buchtin's bonnie, baith e'ening and morn,
When our blythe shepherd lads play on the bog-reed and horn;
While we're milkin', they're liltin', baith pleasant and clear,
But my heart's like to break when I think o' my dear.

Oh the shepherds take pleasure to blow on the horn
To raise up their flocks o' sheep soon i' the morn ;
On the bonnie green banks they feed pleasant and free,
But alas ! my dear heart, all my sighing 's for thee.'

Here we have two out of the three principal
industries on the Border of old, one or all of which
furnished the theme of every lyric—war, shepherd-
ing, and love-making.   War has ceased in that land,
whose people

'hang the trumpet in the hall
And study war no more ;'

modern sheep-farming has parted with much of its
Arcadian simplicity ; shepherd lads pipe no more,
nor summon their flocks with the horn ; but the old
business of love-making runs its accustomed course.

Nenthorn, founded as a parish in the thirteenth
century under the name of Naithansthirn, which may
give a clue to its meaning, was once a manor of the
puissant de Morvilles, Hereditary Constables of
Scotland, until they threw in their lot with John
Baliol and Edward I.—the losing side.   Now their
very name is lost to remembrance in the district
where they held such sway.

East of Nenthorn, Eden Water enters the pretty
demesne of Newton Don, to which it contributes
the chief ornament in the cascade called Stichill Lynn.
A stream of more innocent appearance could hardly

be imagined, yet it has claimed its victims in a tragedy unsung. Newton Don, now the residence of Captain Charles Balfour, M.P., was in 1795 the seat of Sir Alexander Don, who married a sister of the fifteenth and last Earl of Glencairn. She bore him two lovely daughters. They had just been brought out in Edinburgh by their mother, Lady Harriet, and were walking one summer evening with a friend, Miss Ramsay, on the opposite side of the stream to the mansion-house. Hearing the dinner bell, they ran down to some stepping-stones, which gave easy passage to the slenderest soles. Above the stepping-stones there was at that time a mill, which, by the operation of its sluices, caused sudden rising or fall of the current. Just as the three girls were in mid-stream, down came a foaming torrent and swept them away. Miss Ramsay managed to catch hold of a branch and saved herself, but her two fair companions were drowned.

A long mile to the north of Stichill House looms a massive pile, far seen across the verdant Merse, crowning a rocky height. This is Hume Castle, once the chief place of the fiery clan which now puzzles the southerner by writing its name Home. They pronounce it Hume, however, though neither spelling represents, according to modern notation, the original sound which rhymed with ' room, ' and came to be written 'Home' for the same reason that old-fashioned people in the last century spoke of ' Room ' for ' Rome. ' They sprang from a grandson of the third Earl of Dunbar, who acquired the lands of Home by marriage, early in the thirteenth century, and adopted from them his surname. Here Mary of Gueldres lodged in 1400, while her husband,

James II., was busy bombarding Roxburgh Castle with the intense diligence that cost him his life.

The fourth Lord Home lost his life in a skirmish on the day before the disastrous battle of Pinkie. His widow held the castle gallantly against Protector Somerset ; but the English artillery prevailed, and she had to haul down her ensign—the white lion on the green flag. Two years later her son, fifth Lord Home, recaptured the castle, and put every English-man in it to the sword. In 1569 Hume Castle was held by a garrison of two hundred and forty of Lord Home's men. The Earl of Sussex, marching from Wark in overwhelming force, with siege-guns batt-ered the place for twelve hours, when it capitulated once more, and the Homes were allowed to march out in hose and doublets.

Even after the union of the Crowns there was no peace for Hume Castle. Colonel Fenwick sum-moned it in 1650 in name of Protector Cromwell. Thomas Cockburn, the governor, returned a defiant answer in prose and verse.—

'Right Honourable,' ran the first, 'I have received a trumpeter of yours, as he tells me, without a pass, to surrender Home Castle to the Lord General Cromwell. Please you, I never saw your general. As for Home Castle, it stands upon a rock.—Given at Home Castle, this day before 7 o'clock. So resteth, without prejudice to my native cowntry,

Your most humble servant,
T. Cockburn.'

The doggerel reply was as follows :—

'I, Willie Wastle,
Stand firm in my castle ;

And a' the dogs o' your town
Will no' pull Willie Wastle doun.'

Alas, behind all this bravado lay no stomach for English lead and iron! Fenwick's artillery had delivered but a few rounds when Cockburn beat the chamade, and the castle was razed. About the time of the union of Parliaments, Home, Earl of Marchmont, representing a junior branch of the family, owned the estate; and it is to him that the landscape owes the imposing pile which now stands upon this ancient site. It is but a *gazebo*—a mock fortress to please the eye; erected on the old foundations out of the old materials, it serves as a memorial of the stormy past.

In the fifteenth century the Scottish Parliament constituted Hume Castle the centre of the system of beacon warnings on the Border.—

'Item : it is sene spedfull [expedient] that thar be cost maide at the est passage betwix Roxburghe and berwik, and that it be waukyt [watched] at certane furds the quhilk, gif myster be [if there is a muster], sall mak takynis [tokens] be balys [bale-fires] birnyng and fyre. In the first, a baill to be maide be the waukers of the furds quhar it may be sene at hvme [Hume Castle]. A baile is warnyng of ther cumyng quhat power whatever thai be of. Twa bailes togedder at anis [once] thai cuming in deide. Four balis, ilk ane besyde vther and all at anys as four candills, sal be suthfast knawlege that thai ar of gret power and menys. Als far as hadingtowne, dunbar, dalkeithe, or tharby. Thir samyn takynis to be watchyt and maide at Eggerhope Castell ande mak takyn in lik maner. And than may all lothiane be warnyt, and in especiall the Castell of Edinburgh. And thai four fyris to be maide in lyk maner that thai in fyf [Fife] and fra strivelling [Stirling] est, and in the est part

of louthiane and to dunbar, all may se thaim and come to
the defence of the lande.   And thai will not be sleuthfull
thairin to be warnyt of thir [these] fyris thai sall wit thar
cumyng over Tweide.   And than, considering thar fer
[fair] passage, we sall, God willing, be als sone redy as thai.
And all pepill drawe that are in the west half of Edinburgh
thereto.   And all fra Edinburgh est to hadingtone.   And
al merchaundys of Burowys to presentlie hoiste quhar it
passes.   And at Dunpenderlaw and North Berwyklawe
balys to be brynt for warnyng of the cost syde of the see
[sea-coast] in forme befor writyn.' [1]

This picturesque system of beacon warnings continued in force till the invention of the electric
telegraph.   The last occasion when it was put in
action was during the winter of 1803-4, when Napoleon lay at Boulogne with one hundred thousand men,
and a flat-bottomed flotilla was being prepared to
ferry them over the Channel.   No man knew when
the descent might be made, but all was ready.   Parliament, before it was prorogued, had decreed a levy
en masse of all able-bodied citizens, but that measure
never took effect.   Before the next session four
hundred thousand volunteers had been enrolled, and
were busy drilling over the length and breadth of the
realm.   In no part of it did enthusiasm run higher
than in the Border district.   The Sheriff of Selkirk
—Walter Scott, no less—was the very soul of the
movement ; neither Wicked Wat of Branksome nor
Auld Wat o' Harden would have busied himself
more heartily in preparing for war.   The old watch-
knowes were manned ; beacons were piled as of yore ;
the first kindling was to warn the Border that the
French were on the sea, when every man should

[1] *Acts of Scots Parliament*, ii. 44.

hasten to the muster-well. On the last night of January the watch at Hume Castle saw a blaze in the direction of Berwick. 'They're coming!' was the cry. A torch was thrust into the pile; the signal was taken up instantly, and crag after crag flared forth its summons, just as in the old times of English war. Scott himself was at Gilsland; but he covered the distance of one hundred miles which lay between that place and the rendezvous of his troop at Dalkeith within four-and-twenty hours. There was a good deal of banter, and some natural irritation, when these brave fellows found that they had been hoaxed unintentionally; but Scott was delighted with the alacrity displayed.[1] At Dalkeith the yeomanry were hospitably feasted by the Duke of Buccleuch. Lord Home called in vain upon the Selkirk men for the old song—

> 'Up wi' the Souters o' Selkirk,
> And doun wi' the Earl o' Home'—

so he sang it himself, and was rapturously hailed and enrolled as a Souter.

A mile below Edenmouth the Tweed swerves suddenly from its north-easterly course, turns south-east, meets English soil at Carham, and becomes the boundary between the two countries. Opposite Carham, on the Scottish bank, lies the hamlet of Birgham among its green fields; to the eye—one of those tranquil scenes where the concern of men seems wrapped up in the favour or unkindness of the seasons, the rise and fall of agricultural markets, and the incidence of rent: to the understanding—a spot whereon the Muse of History has set her seal. For

[1] See the notes to *The Antiquary* on the subject.

it was out of an event at Birgham that the long-drawn
dispute between England and Scotland took its rise,
so that men say to this day, ' Go to Birgham and buy
bickers ! '   It was here that the treaty was struck in
the summer of 1290 which, if envious fate had not
interposed, should have knit together two nations
which ought never to have been sundered.—

> ' Quhen Alysandyr oure Kyng was dede
> That Scotland led in love and lé,
> Away wes sons of Ale and Brede,
> Of wyne and war, of gamyn and glé,
> Our gold wes changyd into lede.
> Chryst, born into Virgynité,
> Succour Scotland, and remede !
> That stad is in perplexité. ' [1]

Alexander, last of the Kings of Peace, was dead.
He had won the love of his subjects and the fear of
his barons ; the kindly heart, the wise head, the firm
hand, were cold in death, and the governance of the
realm had passed to his grandchild, the Maid of
Norway, who now became, in right of her mother,
Margaret, Queen of Scots.   Not undisputed Queen,
for the land was like to be rent in the interests of
other claimants, and wavered on the brink of anarchy
for two years, until King Edward opened negotiations
for the marriage of his son, afterwards Edward II.,
with the child Queen.   The Pope granted the
necessary dispensation for cousins-german ; and on
18th July 1290 the marriage-treaty was concluded at
Birgham.   Everybody knows how that fair and
statesmanlike project miscarried through the untime-

---

[1] *Cantus*, quoted by Wyntoun, *Chronicle*, vii. 3619-3626.

ly death of the young Queen of Scots,[1] how Edward's claim to be Lord-Paramount of Scotland was laid before the conference at Norham on 10th May 1291, and accepted by the eight competitors for the succession at the adjourned conference of Upsettlington on 2nd June, and how King Edward gave his final award in favour of John Baliol at the final conference at Berwick on 17th November 1292. All this, and many incidents in the three centuries of war which it entailed, take rank among the best-known parts of the Scottish chronicle ; reference to them would be superfluous, even impertinent, were it not that we are passing among the very scenes where these foundations of national history were laid. As the eye travels over the peaceful landscape, with its teeming fields, sloping woods, and gliding river, it is good to recall what fierce passions here were raised, what manful battle was done for either cause, and how happily all these wasteful disputes have been laid to rest.

Opposite Birgham stands the parish church of Carham, on a bold bluff jutting over one of the surest salmon casts in Tweed. Opposite—in a sense more than merely topographic, for Carham Burn marks the march between England and Scotland, and from Carham downwards the right bank of Tweed is English soil.

In the eleventh century Scotland, as we know it, was still in the making, Malcolm II., King of Scots in Alba, being one of the chief makers thereof. It

---

[1] It was natural that men should demur in their belief that a life so precious had come to a natural end. Stories of foul play flew about, and in 1301 a woman was burned in Norway for claiming to be Margaret, Queen of Scots, and alleging that she had been kidnapped and sold by Ingebiorg, wife of Thor Hakonsson (*Proceedings of the Scottish Antiquaries*, x. 403-416).

was at Carham in the year 1018 that he won a great victory over Edulf Cudal, Danish Earl of Northumberland, whereby he obtained cession of the territory of Lothian, hitherto part of the kingdom or earldom of Northumbria. A crucial point this in Scottish history, for upon it hinged the whole claim of the suzerainty of English kings over the northern realm. The Anglo-Norman chroniclers averred that Lothian was bestowed upon Malcolm's father, Kenneth II., by King Eadgar of England, who received Kenneth's homage for the same ; but there is little room for doubt that Lothian became Malcolm's in right of conquest—the consequence of the battle of Carham.

Hitherto our concern has been with fortresses on Scottish soil erected and held as a protection against English invasion, but from Carham downwards Tweed herself marks the frontier, and a mile below Carham Hall, on the English side, stood the great castle of Wark, which has disappeared almost as completely as that of Roxburgh.

Three times in the first year of Stephen's reign (1135-1154) did David I., King of Scots, lay siege to this stronghold. Twice he was repulsed ; the third time the garrison, in the last extremity of hunger, capitulated on terms ; the keep was dismantled and the outworks razed. In the following February, Stephen and David made up their quarrel for the nonce, Wark, among other Northumbrian castles, being handed over by the Scots to the English. It was repaired by Henry II. in 1158-61, William de Vesci accounting for large sums spent in building during those years, and it was garrisoned as a royal keep ; but in 1212 it had become the

' honour ' or manor of de Ros of Hamelak, [1] although
various kings of England continued to borrow it
from its owners at times of national emergency.

In 1252 King Henry granted de Ros a weekly
fair and market to be held at Wark, and also an
annual fair, ' on the vigil, the day and the morrow
of Pentecost, and the two following days. ' Sir
Robert de Ros of Wark-on-Tweed joined Wallace
in arms in 1302, and among other exploits plundered
and burnt Wark-on-Tyne ; but his brother William,
Lord of Hamelak, remained faithful to his English
allegiance, and received the castle and manor of
Wark as his reward from King Edward I. William
left no heirs, so in 1367 Margaret, daughter and
heir of Sir Robert, sought and obtained from
Edward III. pardon for herself, reversal of her
father's forfeiture, and reinstatement as lady of the
manor. [2]

Previously to that, in 1343 or thereabouts, Bruce's
late-born son, David II., in returning from a successful foray in Durham, passed near Wark Castle,
which was then in possession of the Earl of Salisbury.
His countess was in residence, with Sir William de
Montagu in command of the garrison. They beheld
the clouds of dust raised by the Scots' columns and
the herds of cattle which they were driving off ;
they waited till the main body had passed ; then out
sallied Montagu with forty horse and fell upon the
rearguard. The Scots, encumbered with booty,

[1] De Vesci and de Ros, being descended from two illegitimate
daughters of William the Lion, both put in claims as competitors for
the Crown in 1291.
[2] I do not trouble readers with references for all these details Much
information may be found in the collections of Palgrave, Raine and
Bain.

17

made a poor defence ; many of them were slain, and the English captain made good his retreat to the castle with one hundred and sixty laden horses which he had taken.   Young David turned for vengeance, assaulted the place, was repulsed, and proceeded to invest it.   Edward III. was marching in force towards the Border.   It was imperative that he should be warned of the plight of Wark, so Montagu himself rode out under cloud of a stormy night, passed through the Scottish lines, and found his way to King Edward's headquarters.   On the approach of the English army David hurriedly raised the siege, and drew off into Scotland.   King Edward was received at Wark with great rejoicing ; the Countess of Salisbury was a charming hostess ; she dropped her garter when dancing with the King, who gallantly bound it under his royal knee, a proceeding of which Queen Philippa did not wholly approve ; so Edward restored the garter to its lovely owner with the chivalrous disclaimer, *Honi soit qui mal y pense !* Such, at least, is one account of the origin of the Most Noble Order of the Garter, although other versions of the story alter the date to 1346 and the scene to Windsor Castle.

In 1399 the Scots took the castle from Sir Thomas Gray, ' put his people and children to ransom at £1000, burned his houses, and beat down the castle walls' ; for which misadventure Sir Thomas received pardon from Henry IV. on 24th May 1400.   Rebuilt once more, Wark was stormed again in 1419 by William Haliburton of Fast Castle, who caused the whole garrison to be put to the sword ; the compliment being returned by the English a few weeks later, when they obtained access through a sewer leading from the kitchen to the Tweed. About this time the redoubtable Border family of Grey became possessed of Wark-on-Tweed in succession to that of de Ros ; and in 1695 Lady Mary Grey, daughter and heir of Grey, Earl of Tankerville, married Charles Bennet, second Lord Ossulston, and brought the property of Wark into that family, the earldom of her father being bestowed upon her husband in 1714.

Again the Scots captured Wark Castle in the reign of Henry VI., and demolished the fortifications; and yet again, after the Earl of Surrey had rebuilt them, in 1513, on their march to Flodden. In 1523 the Duke of Albany lay upon the Scottish side of the Tweed, and sent Andrew Ker of Fernihirst with four thousand Scots and French to assault the place. They stormed the outworks and breached the inner wall ; but the garrison, under good Sir John Lisle, made good their defence till nightfall. It was raining heavily ; Tweed was waxing ; the coming spate threatened to cut off Ker's column from the main body, and Surrey was not far off with a powerful army. So Ker beat his retreat across the Tweed, and the English possession of Wark has never been challenged since.

Just above Coldstream Tweed receives from the Scottish side the waters of a curious little stream called the Leet, which, though of insignificant volume, runs a course of fourteen miles through the heart of the Merse. Ditchlike in dimensions though it be, its trout would put to shame those of many waters of greater pretension ; in fact, Tom Stoddart accounted them the best of any tributary of the Tweed above Coldstream. He says that one day in April

1841 he took with fly six-and-twenty of these trout, which weighed 29 lb.

The Leet rises in Whitsome parish, a richly cultivated vale, wherein the Templars once had property, and passes into Swinton parish, the lands of which gave the name to the family which still possesses them, claiming descent from Edulf de Swinton, who held under a charter from Malcolm Ceannmor (1058-1093.)

Fifth in descent from Edulf came Sir Alan de Swinton, a knight of gigantic frame who died about the year 1200, and whose sepulchral effigy, one of the oldest sculptured tombs in Scotland, is built into the wall of the parish church. It is very rudely carved ; on a slab behind the figure are represented the three boars' heads erased, which, with a chevron, are still the arms of the family. The chained boar above the arms is the crest of the Swintons, and indicates a later date than that assigned to the recumbent figure, seeing that crests did not come into fashion till the middle of the fourteenth century. The inscription runs :

HIC JACET
ALANVS SVINTONUS
MILES DE EODEM.

Under this monument was a vault, which, when opened, was found to contain a stone coffin and three skulls, one of which was of immense size, and was supposed to be that of Sir Alan. A cast of it was taken for Sir Walter Scott, and remains at Abbotsford beside a similar one taken from the skull of King Robert the Bruce.

In the lower part of its course the Leet traverses the finely wooded park of the Hirsel, a country seat of the Earl of Home, representative in the female line of the once all-puissant house of Douglas. The name Hirsel is the old Scots for a sheepfold, agreeably significant of the pacific change in the condition of society, enabling a Border baron to dispense with a fortified dwelling-place. Three miles or so east of the Hirsel is the little village and parish church of Eccles, indicating by its name—*ecclesia*, a church—the site of an ancient religious foundation. The village has never recovered from Lord Hertford's destructive raid in 1545, when St. Mary's Cistercian nunnery, founded in 1155, was burnt to the ground, together with the parish church of St Cuthbert. Half a mile north of Eccles stands a memorial cross of the twelfth century, in honour, say some people, of a Percy—of a de Soulis, maintain others. The place used to be known as Deadriggs, but now goes by the name of Crosshall.

At the embouchure of the little Leet, Tweed makes a stately sweep, south-east, north-east, and finally north-west, recovering herself abruptly, and resuming a general north-easterly direction where the pretty town of Coldstream clusters about the steep banks. By the ford here Edward I. entered Scotland in 1296; and here, in 1650, General Monk formed the corps of Fenwick and Haslerig into the Coldstream Regiment, the ranks being filled chiefly by Border men. After ten years' campaign in Scotland, Monk marched the regiment to London, there to become household troops of Charles II., now known as the Coldstream Guards.

Its position on the Border rendered Coldstream a

powerful rival of Gretna Green in the matter of elopements from England, and here it was that Henry Brougham concluded his runaway match with Mrs. Spalding in 1819. Of the Cistercian Priory, founded in 1143 by Cospatrick, Earl of March, no trace remains aboveground ; but—*litera scripta manet*—its chartulary was published by the Grampian Club in 1879.

There is a left-handed compliment to the maidens of this neighbourhood in the following local jingle:—

> ' Buchtrig and Belchester,
> Hatchetknowe and Darnchester,
>   Leetholm and the Peel ;
> If ye canna get wived in ane o' thae places
>   Ye 'll ne'er dae weel. '

Three miles below Coldstream, on the English bank, is Tilmouth, where Tweed receives the river Till, which, though flowing entirely within English soil, has a closer connection with Scottish history than may be claimed for many a northern stream, seeing that it flows close past the fatal field of Flodden. The Till is formed by the confluence of two streams, the Bowmont and the Breamish, to seek the sources of which one must pass far into the heart of the Cheviots.—

> ' The foot o' Breamish and the head o' Till
> Meet together at Bewick Mill. '

To record a tenth part of the feats of arms wrought in the valleys of these streams—to note one in every score of the churches and castles that stand near their banks—would fill a separate volume. The tide of battle ebbed and flowed across the Border for centuries, and if closer attention has been given in these pages to events on Scottish soil and monuments of Scottish history, it is because the northern nation has always claimed the Tweed as a Scottish river. Nevertheless, out of the crowded memories of these dales, two or three claim notice even in the most succinct survey.

The first of these looms through the mist of five centuries—a memory of disaster on the Scottish arms. It was in harvest-time of 1402 that Archibald, fourth Earl of Douglas, marched with ten thousand men through the most fertile tract of Northumberland, wasting ripe crops and driving off cattle in the approved style as far as the very walls of Newcastle. Henry IV. was busy at the time putting down rebellion in Wales, but the Earl of Northumberland lay at Alnwick, with the fiery Hotspur, burning to take the field. Of all the Scottish nobility none were so uncertain in their allegiance as the house of Dunbar. Now on one side, then on the other, it requires close comparison of dates to determine in which camp they are to be found. At this time their chief, George, Earl of March, was a renegade in the service of the enemies of Scotland, and, being at Alnwick with the Percys, persuaded them, though with difficulty, to lie still till Douglas should pass northward again, encumbered by his spoil. The Earl of Northumberland, then, mustered his forces at Wooler, between the waters of Glen and Breamish.

The Scots columns, returning, bivouacked on low ground at Millfield, where Percy moved to attack them. Douglas refused battle, drawing off to the stronger position of Homildon, where, on a bare upland, he awaited attack in the usual Scottish formation of 'schiltroms' or squares. Hotspur was for charging at once, but March held his rein and bade him behold the fair target offered to his archers by the dense masses of the enemy. March's craft prevailed. The clothyard shafts were sent winging into the throng; the Scots pikemen were falling in scores.

'Better die in open mellay than be shot down like deer,' cried Sir John Swinton, and called for volunteers. Adam Gordon, a knight with whom Swinton was at mortal feud, was the first to respond. He fell on his knees, craved Swinton's pardon, and was dubbed knight-banneret on the spot. Together they rode down the hill, followed only by some fivescore spears. Douglas, hesitating, gave them no support, and the whole party were allowed to perish in full sight of their comrades. Then, when it was too late, Douglas sounded the charge, and led it. He fell, a prisoner, blinded of an eye and with five arrow wounds; Murdoch, Angus, Moray, and many others were taken also; Lindsays, Livingstones, Ramsays, St. Clairs—all the best blood of Scotland were among the slain. 'What need of more!' exclaims the chronicler Bower in winding up this dreary chapter, 'the flower of Scottish chivalry, as it were, was taken and held to ransom.'[1] Among the slain were four Scottish earls, and many barons, bannerets, knights, and esquires; and King Henry gave Nicolas Merbury, Esquire, a present of £40, so delighted was he on perusing the despatches brought to him by the said Nicolas.[2] Otterburn was avenged, but now the

[1] Bower, xiv. c. 14.
[2] Bain's *Calendar*, ix. 129.

blood of Homildon cried in its turn for vengeance, which the Scots, rent by internal feud, were in no plight to seek promptly. Requital had to wait till 1421, when, on French soil, it was exacted in full by the Earl of Buchan in his victory over the Duke of Clarence at Beaugé. 'An accursed breed, these Scots,' quoth Henry V. when he heard of his brother's defeat and death; 'let me go where I will, I find them in my beard!'[1] and died a few months afterwards, as the pious chronicler of Pluscardine declares, because he had plundered the shrine of St. Fiacre, son of a king of Scots.

The Breamish heads eastward at first, as if to break an independent way to the North Sea; but the high ground about Eglingham sets it upon a northerly course, and, after passing under the crags of Chillingham, famous for its white wild cattle, it turns sharp to the left at Chatton, and meeting Bowmont Water below Wooler, these two bright streams between them form the sullen Till.

About five miles from Wooler the conspicuous cone of Yeavering Bell (1172 feet) attracts attention from eyes accustomed to the tame outlines and gentle slopes of the Cheviots. Here Bishop Paulinus made his headquarters in the year 625, when he brought Æthelburh, sister of Eadbald, King of Kent, to wed with Eadwine, King of Northumberland, having first made a Christian of him. And not of Eadwine only, for during the thirty-six days that Paulinus remained here, the country people thronged round him, and he baptized them in the Glen Water that winds round the back of Yeavering Bell. The summit of this hill, bleak and gusty as

[1] *Liber Pluscardensis*, x. 27.

it is, was once populous, the plateau on the top being still surrounded by a thick wall, containing the foundations of a large village. The name of the missionary, who afterwards became Archbishop of York, is preserved in that of Pallinsburn, the seat of the Askew family.

Before running its devious course of twelve miles from the Scottish border, Bowmont Water passes between the villages of Town Yetholm on its left bank and Kirk Yetholm on its right bank. Practically these form but a single village, many miles from everywhere, with a combined population of less than seven hundred and fifty inhabitants. Of venerable antiquity, Yetholm has a sorely chequered reputation—a place with a past, in short, rather sensitive under close scrutiny. From the seventeenth century onwards it was the metropolis of the Gipsies, and in the eighteenth century was deeply implicated in the smuggling of strong drink across the Border. When Will Faa, the Gipsy King, died at Coldingham about 1783, his subjects, mounted on three hundred asses, escorted his corpse to Kirk Yetholm for burial; but in 1817 the Gipsy population of this place was reckoned at no more than one hundred and nine. The royal line of Faa was extinguished in 1883 in the person of Esther Faa Blythe, who lived to deplore the faded glory of her court, for, to quote her own words, 'Kirk Yetholm had turned sae mingle-mangle that ane micht think it was either built on a dark nicht or sawn on a windy ane—the folks maist a' Irish noo, and nane o' my seed, breed or generation.'

A strange history, that of the Gipsies. Appearing first in Scotland during the fifteenth century, speaking a strange tongue, governed by their own laws and claiming rank and precedence among themselves, these nomads 'professed to be Christian fugitives from Saracen oppressors, and seem to have been taken at their own valuation by that most pious prince James IV. Jurisdiction over their own people was granted them by James V. in 1540, by a writ in favour of ' Johnne Faa, Lord and Erle of Littil Egipt,' directing the sheriffs of Edinburgh, Haddington, and other counties to support him in the exercise of his authority, ' conform to the lawis of Egipt.' They soon fell out of credit: in 1603 the Scottish Parliament decreed their banishment on pain of death, which caused them to gravitate towards the Border, across which they might slip as often as the laws of either realm were enforced against them. In 1624 Capitane Johnne Faa with seven other Gipsies were put upon their trial and executed as ' vagaboundis, sorneris, common thevis callit, knawn, repute, and halden Egiptianis.' Next Helen Faa, the captain's widow, and eleven other Gipsy women were sentenced to be drowned, but this doom was commuted by the King to one of banishment. And now there is no distinct Gipsy community ; their race has been merged in the general population. The Romany speech is heard no more, neither does any bear the name of Faa ; although that of Marshall, representing a Gipsy sept, remains common enough ; and George Romney, the painter, belonged to a family said to derive their surname from Romany.

Pass we now to that ridge of mournful memory near which a sudden bend in the Till gives a name to the hamlet of Crookham ; for here in the last days of August 1513 the King of Scots entrenched his army, containing all that was best and bravest of his realm, and awaited the approach of English Surrey. Wark and Eital strengths had surrendered to him ; Norham also, wellnigh impregnable, had yielded after five days' siege ; the game was surely in the Scottish King's hands.   So at least thought Surrey, for while the Scots were well provisioned and their communications sure, the English were on short commons, with no beer, and weary with marching and counter-marching in the rain.   But Surrey was a fine tactician, and King James was negligent in scouting.   He allowed his enemy to manœuvre behind Barmoor, full seven miles to the east of the camp at Flodden ; took no precaution to ascertain his subsequent movements ; and the first he knew was that Surrey, on the afternoon of 9th September, was marching upon him from the north, having recrossed the Till at Twizel Bridge, passing his columns over the picturesque arch which still spans the stream. Still James had but to hold his ground, for he was splendidly posted, and might have lain on the ridge well provisioned till hunger should compel the English to move elsewhere.   But chivalrous tradition vitiated the Scottish King's strategy.   What followed is written in history as the battle of Flodden.   Had it been so, victory must infallibly have remained with the Scots.   It was James's demon that made it the Battle of Branxton.   Forming line of battle in five divisions, the King took command of the central one himself.   'Forward, banners ! ' was the order, and the whole array descended from the commanding position of Flodden to meet the enemy on the lower ground of Branxton.

What followed is known to all men. If the King of Scots had blundered, he and his soldiers, gentle and simple, showed how brave men should take their punishment. Next morning, when the English were collecting their spoil, they found King James lying stark, in the middle of a bodyguard of twelve dead earls, fourteen lords, an archbishop, a bishop, and a pair of abbots; while far and wide upon the blood-boltered slopes lay the Flowers o' the Forest in swathes.

A hush seems to lie upon the scene of this awful massacre. The Till has none of the rattling sharpness of other Border streams, but winds silent and profound through the meadows till it merges passively in the greater Tweed. The local rhyme may be threadbare with age and use, but it still carries a fitting strain of dread.—

> 'Says Tweed to Till—
>   "What gars ye rin sae still?"
> Says Till to Tweed—
>   "Though you rin wi' speed,
> And I rin slaw,
> Whaur ye droon ae man,
>   *I droon twa!*"'

It has been a current slander upon Henry VIII. that when Surrey reported his victory and suggested that the body of King James, Henry's brother-in-law and cousin, should receive sepulture in St. Paul's Cathedral, a flat refusal was returned. King Henry has plenty to answer for without adding falsely to his indictment. James had died excommunicate, and so could not receive Christian burial without special sanction from the Pope. King Henry wrote to Pope Leo X. for that sanction, and obtained it; but the King of Scots, it is supposed, had been buried meanwhile in the monastery of Sheen, in Surrey.

CHAPTER XI

HALF-A-DOZEN miles below Coldstream—say eight by the windings of the river—Ladykirk stands in a fine setting of woodland. The kirk itself might attract little notice in any English or French village ; but in Scotland it is remarkable because, despite its hazardous proximity to the Border, it has come unscathed through the terrible raidings of the sixteenth century. Erected in 1500, a debased period, by James IV. out of gratitude for an escape from drowning in the Tweed, it measures 94 feet 6 inches in length, is built in the form of a cross with apsidal ends to the chancel and transepts. The whole is covered with pointed barrel vaulting, roofed over with overlapping stone flags. To resist the pressure of this massive structure the walls are supported by numerous buttresses, each crowned with a short pinnacle.

Ladykirk Bridge was built in 1839 to supersede a dangerous ford—Ubbanford, it is called in ancient writings—which, during the Border wars, often gave passage to armies or marauding bands of both nations. The see of Durham was famous of old for its succession of military prelates, and among them all there was none, not even the dauntless Antony Bek of Edward I.'s reign, more restless as a neighbour, more dangerous as a foe, than Bishop Ranulf Flambard—Rafe the torch-bearer—who was consecrated in 1099. Symeon of Durham has recorded how in 1121 the 'magnificent' Bishop Flambard ordered the erection of a tower upon the height overlooking Ubbanford, to put an end to the incursion of 'robbers and Scots.' Flambard died in 1128: ten years later his new castle of Norham was invested by David I. of Scotland, and, although vigorously defended at first by nine knights, it capitulated and was promptly dismantled. There remain of Flambard's work the whole east side and part of the south side of the keep. In 1154 Hugh de Pudsey, a priest of no more than four-and-twenty years old, became Bishop of Durham, and immediately set his architect, Robertus Ingeniator, to rebuild the fortress of Norham on a superb scale ; and although the outer defences have nearly all disappeared, the great curtain wall described by Camden as connecting the many towers of the outer enceinte having been undermined by the Tweed, the gateway of the bridge across the moat still remains, and the Norman keep still frowns across the Merse, defiant even in the last stages of decay. Second in importance and strength to none of the Border fortresses, fierce and frequent were the conflicts waged for its possession ; many a fine pageant enlivened the brief periods of truce.

In the year 1200, Berwick Bridge having been carried away by a flood, William the Lion, King of Scots, passed this way on his journey to London, where he was to press before King John his claim on Northumberland. The bills of fare for two of the King's meals in Norham have been preserved.

The season being Lent, no meat was allowed, yet the variety was such as to read about it almost suffices to give one heartburn :—

I

Frumentie ryall and mammonie to potage
Lung [ling] in foyle
Cunger p in foyle
Lampreys with galantine
Pyke in latmer sauce
Cunger roasted
Halibut roasted
Salmon in foyle roasted
Carp in sharp sauce
Celes [? seals] rost
Salmon baked
Custard planted
Leche Florentine
Fritter dolphin

II

Jolie ipocras and prune drendge to potage
Sturgeon in foyle with welkes
Turbit
Soles
Bream in sharpe sause
Carps in armine
Tenches flourished
Crevesses [crayfish]
Camprons [?] rost
Roches fried
Lampreys baked
Quince and drendge baked
Tart melior
Leche Florentine
Fritter ammell [? honey fritter]
Fritter pome [apple fritter]
A subtiltie in three stages with towers embatteled

Malwesse—wine of Malvoisie—was provided in liberal measure to wash down all this good cheer withal.

Edward I. was particularly indifferent to splendour in dress, and is known to have set his face against the increasing foppery of both clergy and laity. Yet he seems to have departed from his customary simplicity in attire when he summoned his nobles to meet him at Norham in May 1291, to decide the knotty point of the Scottish succession. It is recorded that he rode in a jupon of scarlet silk, with a tabard or 'coat of arms' over it, embroidered with the lilies of France and the leopards of England. On his head was a golden crown, on his breast a golden brooch, on his shoulders many jewels. If all this was meant to overawe the Scottish magnates with a sense of the superior wealth of England, Edward's suite played up with spirit to the same key. Bishop Antony Bek's mitre was trimmed with pearls ; his crosier was of gold set with jewels ; his very hood sparkled with precious stones, and a heavy sword swung beside his saddle. Following him rode abbots in scarlet and green and long-pointed shoes— monks with furred sleeves and jingling bells on their bridles—friars who seemed 'not poor men in threadbare capes, but apparelled like the Pope himself.' Even Chief-Justice Brabazon and his lawyers made a dazzling show in scarlet shoes, scarlet gowns faced with blue, girt with silk striped of many colours, and wearing white silken coifs.

In the sixteenth year of Edward II.'s disastrous reign, 1323 to wit, Norham Castle was committed to the custody of that fine old soldier Sir Thomas

Gray[1] of Heton, coupled with the sheriffship of Norhamshire and Islandshire. By this time the English government had become so deeply seamed with dissension between the King and his indignant barons that the defence of the Scottish border was left, practically, in the masterly hands of William de Melton, Archbishop of York. But for him and his lieutenants—Sir Thomas Gray on the East Marches and Sir Andrew de Harcla on the West Marches— the northern counties of England must have passed into permanent possession of the King of Scots. Sir Thomas Gray had a son of the same name, who, being taken prisoner in a skirmish on Nesbit Moor in 1355, beguiled his captivity in Edinburgh Castle by compiling the record entitled *Scalacronica*—the Ladder Chronicle—in allusion to the crest adopted by his family—a scaling-ladder. Written in Norman-French, which was still the official language of England in the fourteenth century, this chronicle has never been translated, except in so far as Leland made a brief abstract of it in English.

That portion which deals with the times when Gray and his father were actively engaged is of infinite value to the historian, for Gray is the only historical writer of that period who was not a cleric. We have, therefore, in his narrative a unique example of military affairs under the three first Edwards described by an eye-witness who was a soldier, and thoroughly understood his subject. The passages relating to Norham Castle give such vivid insight into the vicissitudes of life in a Border fortress that I make no apology for translating for

---

[1] The English family of this name now write it 'Grey,' while the Scottish Grays retain the usual orthography of the fourteenth century.

the first time a liberal extract from this work. This
extract begins with events of the year 1318.—

'The King of England [Edward ii.] undertook hardly
anything more against Scotland, so much had he lost by
indolence of what his father had conquered. Gilbert de
Middleton, also, held against him many of the fortresses
within his Marches of England, and raised against much of
Northumberland. In the bishopric of Durham, Gilbert
pillaged two cardinals who had come to consecrate the
bishop, and seized Louis de Beaumont, Bishop of Durham,
and his brother, Henry de Beaumont, because the King had
caused his cousin, Adam de Swinburne, to be arrested, for
having spoken too frankly to him about the condition of the
Marches. This same Gilbert, with support of others on
the Marches, made a raid into Cleveland and committed
other mischief, having nearly the whole of Northumberland
at his command, except the castles of Bamborough, Alnwick,
and Norham. The first two of these were treating with
the enemy—one by hostages, the other by collusion—when
the said Gilbert was taken in the castle of Mitford by
treachery of his own people, [his captors being] William de
Felton, Thomas de Heton, [1] and Robert de Horncliff, and
was hanged and drawn in London.

'In consequence of all this, the Scots had become so bold
that they subdued all the Marches of England and dismantled
the castles of Wark and Harbottle ; so that scarcely did any
English dare to oppose them, and they subdued the whole
of Northumberland by means of the treachery of the
deceitful country-people. Thus they had scarcely anything
more to do in any part of these Marches, except at Norham,
where a knight Sir Thomas Gray' [2] was in garrison with his
relations.

---

[1] This was probably the chronicler himself, for his father, Sir
Thomas Gray of Heton, was constable of Norham Castle at this time,
and most likely had enough to keep him there.
[2] The chronicler's father.

'It would be too lengthy a matter to relate the exploits [1] and the feats of arms, and the suffering for want of food, and the sieges, which he experienced during the eleven years which he spent during the evil and calamitous period for the English. Moreover, several persons have compiled the history of his days in the said castle.

'It was evident that after the town of Berwick was taken out of possession of the English, the Scots had so greatly the upper hand and were so insolent, that they made little account of the English, who could not regain spirit, but allowed it to perish.

'At that time there came a certain page [2] to a great banquet of lords and ladies in Lincolnshire, bringing a war helmet with a curious gilded crest to Sir William Marmion, with a letter from his lady commanding him to repair to the most dangerous place in Great Britain, and there to make this helmet famous. Straightway it was decided by the chevaliers present that he should go to Norham, as the most perilous and adventurous place in the country.

'The said William went off to Norham, whither, within four days of his arrival, Sir Alexander de Mowbray, brother of Sir Philip de Mowbray, formerly constable of Berwick, came before the castle of Norham with the most celebrated chivalry of the March of Scotland, and, with more than eightscore men-at-arms, drew up before the castle at the hour of noon. At that time those within the castle were just sitting down to dine. The constable, Thomas de Gray, drew up his garrison before the barriers, saw the enemy formed up in array close in front, and, looking back, beheld the said Sir William Marmion coming on foot, all glittering with gold and silver, splendidly attired, and with the helmet on his head. The said Thomas, well knowing the cause of his having come, cried aloud to him : "Sir Knight, you have come here as knight errant to make that helmet famous, and it is a far more becoming thing that

Lez punyes.
[2] *Vn damoisel faye.*

deeds of chivalry be wrought on horseback than on foot, where that is possible. Mount your horse ; behold the enemy ; spur forward and charge among them. I will deny my God if I rescue not your body alive or dead, else shall I die myself ! ''

'The knight mounted a beautiful charger, spurred forward, and charged into the midst of the enemy, who struck him down, made shipwreck of his countenance,[1] and dragged him from the saddle to the ground.

' At this moment the said Thomas came up with his whole garrison, with lances lowered. They struck the horses in the bowels, so that they threw their riders, drove back the enemy's cavalry, raised the fallen knight, replaced him on his horse, and pursued the enemy, of whom many were left dead in the first encounter, and fifty valuable horses were taken. The women in the castle brought horses out to their men, who mounted, gave chase, and cut down all whom they could overtake.

' Thomas de Gray caused to be slain at the Yarford one Cryn, a Fleming, a sea admiral and brigand, who was in high command under Robert de Brus ; the other fugitives were chased as far as the nunnery of Berwick.

' Another time Adam de Gordon, a Scottish baron, having collected more than eightscore men-at-arms, came before the said castle of Norham, thinking to seize the cattle which were grazing outside the said castle. Some young fellows of the garrison ran rashly to the extreme end of the town, which at the time lay waste and in ruins, and began skirmishing. The hostile Scots surrounded them. The said sortie party established themselves behind some old walls and defended themselves stoutly. At this moment the said constable, Thomas de Gray, issued from the castle with his garrison, and, perceiving his people in so much danger from the enemy, said to his lieutenant :—

' '' I put you in charge of this castle, although in truth it is my duty to guard it in the King's service, so that I may

[1] *Ly naufrerent hu visage.*

drink the same cup that my people yonder have to drink."

'So off he started at high speed, having with him of common people and others not more than sixty all told. When the enemy saw him approaching in this fashion, they left the skirmishers among the old walls, and drew out into the open fields. The men who were within the ditches, seeing their chieftain coming in this manner, leapt the ditches and ran out into the field upon the said enemy, who spurred upon them and drove them back. Thereupon, up came the said Thomas with his people, when the horses fell into confusion; the men of foot, crouching on the ground, killed the horses and rallied to the said Thomas, charged the enemy and chased them from the field across the water of Tweed. Many were taken and many slain; many horses lay dead; so that had they [the English] been mounted, hardly one [of the Scots] would have escaped.

'The said Thomas de Gray was twice besieged in the said castle—once for nearly a year, and another time for seven months. The enemy erected fortifications against him one at Upsettlington, another at Norham church. Twice he was revictualled by the lords Percy and Nevill, greatly to the relief of the said castle. These [lords] became wise, noble and rich, and did good service on the Marches.

'On one occasion during de Gray's time the outer ward of the said castle was betrayed on the eve of St. Catherine by one of his people, who killed the porter and admitted the enemy, who were concealed in a house outside the gate. The inner ward and the donjon were safely held. The enemy did not remain there beyond three days; but, fearing the coming of the said Thomas, who presently returned from the south, where he had been at the time, they evacuated the outer ward and burnt it, after failing in an attempt to mine it.

'Many fine feats of arms happened to the said Thomas which are not recorded here.'[1]

---

[1] *Scalacronica*, fol. 209ᵇ, 210, 210ᵇ, 211; pp. 144-147 of the edition printed for the Maitland Club in 1836.

Four times in its history Norham Castle was taken by the Scots—by David I. in 1138, by Robert I. in 1326, by Douglas and Moray in 1327, and by James IV. on his way to Flodden in 1513—but the captors were never able to hold it for more than a month.

Opposite Norham, on the Scottish side, lies the parish of Ladykirk, containing the hamlet of Upsettlington, where, on 2nd June 1291, the conference between Edward I. and the Scottish magnates, adjourned from Norham on 11th May, reassembled to receive his award. Eight out of the nine competitors for the Crown appeared before the English King : the ninth, John de Baliol, mistook the day but turned up on the morrow. On 4th June all present surrendered the kingdom of Scotland into the hands of King Edward, agreeing to accept his decision as Lord-Paramount as to who was to be King of Scots. Again the conference met at Berwick on 2nd August, by which time four fresh competitors had put in claims, making thirteen in all ; and on 15th October a parliament was summoned at Berwick to receive Edward's final award. He delivered judgment in favour of John de Baliol on 17th November.

One may look dispassionately upon these proceedings in the perspective of centuries. Lord Hales has denounced Norham and Upsettlington as disgraceful chapters in Scottish history ; but they record the acts of the whole Scottish nation so far as the existing constitution admitted of any act being national. The bitterness which Scotsmen still bear (some of them) to the memory of Edward I.—the greatest ruler England had ever owned up to that time—had no existence at the time of these conferences. In their

perplexity the Guardians of Scotland had recourse to
his arbitration as the most likely means of protecting
the realm from the unspeakable miseries of a disputed succession.   He gave his award deliberately and
fearlessly to the best of his judgment, and as ruler of
England he was justified in exacting the best security
he could devise against the evils which he had sought
by contracting his heir, the Prince of Wales, in marriage with the Queen of Scots.

Below Ladykirk the river winds in a series of
majestic reaches till it passes under the Union
Bridge at Paxton.   This was the first suspension-
bridge in Great Britain, erected in 1820 to the design
of Captain Sir Samuel Brown, R.N., at a cost of
£7500.   Paxton House, a fine example of the work
of the architect Robert Adam (1728-1792), is the
mansion of an estate abutting upon the ancient
boundary of the liberties of Berwick-on-Tweed.

The last of Tweed's tributaries deserving notice
before that river merges with the North Sea is the
Whitadder, which forms its junction two long miles
above Berwick-on-Tweed.   For the last time, then,
the reader is invited to quit the rich Merse, and,
passing to the bleak summits of the Lammermuirs,
survey the course of Whitadder, some thirty-four
miles in length, and take note of its principal feeders.
On the flank of Clint's Dod, which rears itself to the
respectable height of 1307 feet in Whittinghame
parish, Haddingtonshire, Whitadder takes her rise,
and speeds in a south-easterly course between Spart-
leton Edge and Redstone Rig—crests of the Lammermuir range.   Of Gamelshiel Tower, on the east
bank, only one end of a small keep remains ; it was
probably a strength of the Hepburns.   Of Penshiel,

on the west bank, once a fortalice of the monks of Melrose, some of the vaulting still stands, perhaps part of the original building mentioned in a grant by the Earl of Dunbar to the monks of the Isle of May in the year 1200.

Below the junction with Bothwell Water is Cranshaws parish church, and beside it the well-preserved castle of Cranshaws, dating from the sixteenth century, an ancient possession of the Earls of Morton, still remaining with that branch of the Douglas. The lord of this barony used to enjoy the services of a ' brownie '—one of those invisible household spirits so helpful while kept in good humour, so spiteful when slighted. The brownie of Cranshaws undertook all the work of ' inning ' the corn, threshing it, and ' mowing ' it—that is, heaping it in the barn. One day the said lord rudely criticised the brownie's work, complaining that he had ' mowed ' it like a sloven; which his supernatural ally resented so deeply that next morning all the corn was found to have been thrown over the Raven's Craig, a mile further down the Whitadder ; and this must be the reason, of course, why the Douglas family no longer enjoy the advantage of the brownie's help !

Inside the church, which, dating only from 1739, contains no other feature of interest, is a stone panel, carved with the royal arms of Scotland, as they were before the union of the Crowns in 1603, with a pair of unicorns supporting. People tell (and believe) a quaint story about this stone—how that James VI. attending divine service in Cranshaws kirk was scandalised by the minister's omission to pray for the royal family, and sent the stone to be set up opposite the pulpit as a perpetual reminder.

A little below Cranshaws, Whitadder is doubled in volume by the inflow of the Dye Water, a most troutful stream, rising between Lowran's Law (1681 feet) and Willie's Law (1628 feet) in the western Lammermuirs.   Near Byrecleugh, a quaint old shooting-box of the Duke of Roxburghe's, there is a mighty cairn known as the Mutiny Stones, 240 feet long, 75 feet broad, and 18 feet high.   It is said to commemorate a fight which took place here in 1402 between the men of Hepburn of Hailes and those of the Earl of Dunbar ; but in all probability it marks a prehistoric place of sepulture. [1]

About three miles further down the Dye Water, on the north bank, is a hill of 1194 feet, written Wrink Law, but locally called Runklie, where is a remarkable fortification of the kind usually termed British.   Next, the stream leads to Longformacus, an early religious site, as testified by the prefix ' Long,' which has no business to appear in that form.   It is the creation of the Ordnance Survey ; for the name Langformacus seemed to the English mapmakers to be Scottish dialect—' lang ' for ' long ' —whereas it represents the Welsh *lann*, a church. The parish church is still here, and a hamlet containing less than four hundred inhabitants.

Below the junction of Dye Water with Whitadder is Ellam Inn, much frequented by trout fishers, and three miles further on Whitadder turns north to meet the Monynut Water at Abbey St. Bathans, a name that raises expectation of ecclesiastical remains. It is supposed to represent a dedication to Batheine, Columba's cousin, who succeeded him as Abbot of

---

[1] I hazard this statement purely *ex hypothesi*, for I have not seen the stones.

Hy (Iona), and died A.D. 600. In the twelfth century
Ada, Countess of Dunbar, founded here a nunnery;
part of which, or the church belonging to it, is incorporated in the present ill-favoured parish church.
The only traces of ancient art remaining are an east
window of two lights surmounted by a quatrefoil, and
the recumbent figure of a prioress within the church.
The name Godscroft, half a mile up the Monynut
Water, seems to indicate land attached to the
religious house, but owes its origin to a different
source. It was the dwelling-place of David Hume
(1560-1630), the devoted chronicler of the house of
Douglas.[1] Like Sir Walter Scott, David had an
ear for euphony, and, not relishing the suggestion
contained in the original name of his lairdship, he
altered it from Gowkscroft to Godscroft. But in
his day, and for many a day after, the land was
traversed by a privileged class, the gaberlunzies,
licensed mendicants, who picked up sustenance from
the doors of kindly housewives, and recorded their
experience in rhyme for the benefit of their kind.
Here is some of their doggerel describing the cheer to
be expected at places in this neighbourhood, in which
David Hume's mansion retains its ancient title :—

> 'Gowkscroft and Barnside,
> Windy wallets fu' o' pride ;
> Monynut and Laikieshiel,
> Plenty milk, plenty meal.
> Straphunton Mill and Bankend,
> Green cheese as teugh as bend ;
> Shannabank and Blackerstane
> Pike the flesh to the bane.'

[1] Hume's history exists in MS. at Hamilton Palace, containing
much that was suppressed in the published editions. It is greatly to
be desired that it should be put into the hands of a competent editor.

Another historian, of the same surname as him of Gŏdscroft, but of wider renown, David Hume (1711-1776) lived much in this neighbourhood and composed his *Essays Moral and Political* at Ninewells, near Edrom.

Upon entering the parish of Duns, Whitadder describes three parts of a circle round Cockburn Law, a conical mass of granite rising to the height of 1065 feet through the prevailing Silurian beds. The summit of this hill, like so many others in this warworn region, retains traces of an encampment or fortified village, while on the north-eastern slope may be recognised the remains of a prehistoric 'broch,' or circular tower with chambered walls. Only two other specimens of this primitive style of architecture are known to have survived through the Middle Ages in southern Scotland, though plenty of them remain north of the Highland line. This one was destroyed during those years of agricultural enterprise which set in towards the close of the eighteenth century, the materials having been quarried for building dikes and filling drains. According to the old *Statistical Account* the tower was eighty-six feet in diameter, and the chambered walls were about sixteen feet in thickness. The adjacent ground has been worked into heavy entrenchments. The building goes by the name of Edinshall, perhaps commemorating Edwin, King of Northumbria (A.D. 616-633), or some other individual bearing this frequent name. Edington and Ednam, both in this neighbourhood, and even Edinburgh or Dunedin, are suggestive of a similar origin.

People have returned to the custom of men of

old : 'their inward thought is that their houses shall continue for ever, and their dwelling-places to all generations ; they call their lands after their own names.' There was an intermediate stage in the thirteenth and fourteenth centuries, when men took their surnames from their lands, and this custom still lingers in North Britain, where lairds and tenants alike are best known locally by the names of their estates or farms.

The sudden sweep described by Whitadder round Cockburn Law and Edinshall is appropriately named Elbick or 'Elbow,' but the farmhouse within the crook appears on the ordnance map under the misleading title of Elba.

Duns Law (713 feet) is another boss of igneous rock, greenstone, not granite, about four miles SSE. of Cockburn Law,[1] and upon its flank once stood the ancient town of Duns. The English destroyed this in 1545, and the present pretty little town of two thousand two hundred inhabitants was begun about forty years later upon lower ground. 'Duns dings a'' is its proud motto, that is, surpasses everything ; 'but in what respect,' dryly observed Robert Chambers, 'it would be difficult to imagine.'

On the broad, tabular summit of the Law is a block of Old Red Sandstone, much altered by volcanic heat, known as the Covenanters' Stone. Here in the early summer of 1639 General Leslie was encamped with his whole force, while King Charles remained irresolute at Berwick, spying his enemy's position through a telescope. Montrose was not royalist yet ; far otherwise, he was Covenanter-Gen-

[1] Not to be confused with Dunse Law or Down Law (665 feet) at the hilly end of Roxburgh parish.

eral in the north of Scotland. Had he been the
King's man, it would have been easy to scatter
Leslie's forces, for they were in sore straits for
sustenance, and prayers proved but a depressing
substitute for rations. Ministers went about en-
couraging the troops, says Baillie, 'by their good
sermons and prayers, morning and even, under the
roof of heaven, to which drums did call them for
bells.' The precious time slipped away ; Leslie
brought up his supplies, and the King was first to
open the negotiations which ended in the hollow
Pacification of Berwick on 18th June. Of ancient
buildings Duns can boast none. Its Norman church
was superseded in 1790 by the sort of edifice that
experience teaches us to expect from builders of that
date. This was burnt down in 1879, but has been
rebuilt ; and now, thrice happy Duns ! the *Ordnance
Gazetteer* is able to record that it 'contains 920 sit-
tings of pitch-pine, stained and varnished.' Pitch-
pine, you know, is something, though perhaps not
exclusively devotional in its suggestion ; but when
you come to stain and varnish it—Sathanas avaunt !
   It is well that the present writer knows not the
name of the incumbent in 1874, else he might be
tempted to proclaim it as that of the doer of a
barbarous deed ; for it is on record that he caused
the original chancel, which had survived as a burial
vault, to be removed 'under the pretext of improving the churchyard.' And so another relic of
Norman building was effaced from the Merse.
   The environs of Duns were boggy once, but that
has been put all right by skilful draining, and what
was once merely the Hen Poo' is now a pretty sheet
of ornamental water in the well-timbered demesne

of Duns Castle. The original tower, with walls eight feet thick, is supposed to have been built about 1320 by Randolph, Earl of Moray, to whom King Robert granted the lands ; but it is doubtful whether any part of it remains, for we read how, when Lord Hertford crossed the Tweed in 1545, he 'birnd and destrued the nonery cald Coldstreme, so to Fogga, and thair campeit that nyght, and many a town [farmstead] birnd that day, and a Monday Downes [Duns] tower and towne awaretrown [overthrown] and birnd all the pares wch is l. [the parish which has fifty] towns and willaiges bylongeing [belonging] to the said Downes ; and the nexht day to West Nysbed, w^o was birnd and owaiertrown the castell, and many mor.'[1] A list is added of fifty-two places burnt in the parish and 'the towre of Dunce raced [razed].' The ancient tower with walls 8 feet thick now forms part of the present house ; but the whole has been so masked by modern building in the castellated style that it requires careful scrutiny to distinguish Randolph's work. Hay of Drummelzier obtained the estate at the close of the seventeenth century, in whose family it still remains. General Leslie made the castle his head-quarters in 1639.

Duns parish is divided by the Whitadder from the parish of Bunkle, which contains several places of interest, notably the site of Bunkle Castle, which became the possession and chief residence of Sir Alexander the Steward in 1288 by his marriage with the daughter and heiress of Sir Alexander de Bonkyll. The barony passed by descent to Stewart, Earl of

[1] *Proceedings of the Society of Antiquaries of Scotland*, 1851-4, pp. 275, 278.

Angus (1329-1377), thence to the Douglas Earls of Angus (1389-1633), and finally to the Hon. Lucy Montagu, Countess of the eleventh Earl of Home, whose son, the present earl, owns it now. The seal of Sir Thomas de Bonkyll, a cleric of the thirteenth century, is preserved in the Record Office, showing three buckles—a somewhat feeble pun on the name Bonkyll ; and the Stewarts of Physgill in Wigtown-shire bear a buckle in the sinister point of their shield, indicating descent from this line, with the motto—*Suffibulatus majores sequor*—'I follow my ancestors with a buckle.' Bunkle Castle was des-troyed in Hertford's raid of 1544, together with the towers of Blanerne and Billie.

Irreparable outrage, worse than Hertford's, as having been perpetrated in cold blood, was the destruction in 1820 of the ancient parish church, which dated, probably, from the eleventh century. Such is the evidence of the only fragment remaining —a semicircular apse, with the choir arch and a semi-domed roof, like that of St. Margaret's Chapel in Edinburgh Castle. The material of this priceless relic of early times was ruthlessly quarried and hewn to build the present parish church, in which may be seen some of the old ornamental carving rammed into the rubble walls.

Of Blanerne, the house of the Lumsdaines since the days of Robert the Bruce, a ruined keep remains, and what is called the guardhouse, now fitted up as a dairy to supply the modern mansion alongside. The site of Billie Castle—a dry knoll in the middle of a marsh—is marked only by a few grassy mounds. Originally the property of the Dunbars, it passed successively to the Earls of Angus, the Homes of

Wedderburn, and the Rentons, representing the ancient foresters of Coldingham. Sir Thomas Lauder tells a grisly story about an old lady of the family of Home who lived alone here, collected her own rents, and hoarded her money within her own bedchamber. The door of this room was secured by a heavy cylinder of brass, which the old dame by means of a cord used to let fall into a slot after she had gone to bed. Her solitary manservant, well knowing where the cash was concealed, made his plans to secure it. He filled the slot of the lock with cherry-stones, so that the bolt would not act, entered his mistress's room at midnight, cut her throat and ransacked her store. He might have walked downstairs and out of the front door without risk of meeting anybody, but he chose instead to escape through a window on the second floor, and in so doing broke his leg. He was found concealed in the shrubbery next day, and was put to a fitting end on the gallows.

Old people repeat a rhyming prophecy of unknown antiquity about these three castles:—

> ' Bunkle, Billie and Blanerne,
> Three castles strong as airn,
> Built when Davy was a bairn ;
> They'll a' gang doon
> Wi' Scotland's croon,
> And ilka ain shall be a cairn. '

At Broomhouse, where once stood a castle, there is, or was lately, a cairn marking the grave of Sir Anthony Darcy, Sieur de la Bastie, a French knight whom the Regent Albany appointed Warden of the Marches in place of Alexander, third Lord Home,

19

who, with his brother William, was executed on a charge of treason in October 1516. As it was believed that de la Bastie had brought this about, David Home of Wedderburn attacked him near Langton on 12th October 1517, routed his party, pursued him over the moor of Duns, where the French knight's horse got bogged. De la Bastie tried to escape on foot, but Home was too quick for him ; he rode him down, cut off his head, bore it in triumph through the streets of Duns, and fastened it aloft on the battlements of Hume Castle.

At Edrom may still be seen a beautiful Norman doorway, with three richly carved orders, sole remainder of the original parish church, preserved as the entrance to a burial vault at the west end of the present building. Of a more recent aisle, founded in 1499 by Robert Blackadder, Bishop of Glasgow, the two angle buttresses remain, with canopied niches for figures of saints, which have gone the way of most of the ecclesiastical art of Scotland. Berwickshire once was rich in Norman churches. The walls of one remain at Chirnside, only three miles from Edrom; but the western tower was demolished in 1750, and the only architectural feature preserved is the south doorway, consisting of an outer order with mouldings, and an inner one enriched with the chevron ornament.

Next to Chirnside comes Allanton, built at the junction of Whitadder, with its chief tributary, the Blackadder, a fine trout stream flowing from the upland parish of Westruther on the confines of Lauderdale. At its source is a hill called the Twinlaw Cairns (1466 feet), connected in misty legend with the fate of twin brothers of the family of Edgar, who, having taken opposite sides in some warfare, and ignorant of their mutual relationship, stood forth as champions of their respective armies and perished in single combat by each other's hand. Sir Thomas Dick Lauder quotes at length a ballad describing the combat; but, as he justly remarks, it has lost all trace of the antiquity which is claimed for it.

The family of Edgar possessed land in this parish as early as the fourteenth century; their old keep of Wedderlie has been incorporated with a larger mansion in 1680, and although much decayed, remains a fascinating example of a Scottish country-house of that period. The lands of Wedderlie were bought by Lord Blantyre in 1733. Evelaw Tower is not far off, at the foot of the hill of that name, a Border keep of the usual type; but there remain no records of its history.

The junction of Faugrist Burn with Blackadder has been heavily fortified, and the place is called the Blackcastle Rings. Greenlaw, which used to divide with Duns the dignity of the county town of Berwick, cannot claim importance in proportion to its antiquity, for it contains but twelve hundred inhabitants. It grew up under the shelter of a castle of the Earls of Dunbar, but the 'green law'[1] or conical height on which it originally stood is a full mile to the south-east of the present village. The church is modern, but in dignified accord with the fifteenth-century tower and its corbelled out-parapet.

At Greenlaw the Blackadder abandons its south-easterly course, striking sharply north-east, past

[1] The Anglo-Saxon 'law' is by far the commonest name for a hill in this district, just as 'fell' prevails in the Cheviots and on the western Border, where the Scandinavian influence predominated.

Marchmont House, a stately pile designed by Robert Adam, built in 1754, when Bedbraes Castle, which stood here, was deemed inadequate to the dignity and wealth of the third and last Earl of Marchmont. The first earl was that Sir Patrick Home of Polwarth, father of that Lady Grizel Baillie whose adventures have been sketched in an earlier chapter.[1]   He rebuilt the parish church of Polwarth in 1703, no improvement, as may be safely affirmed, upon the former structure which dated from 1378.   He had good cause, too, to respect the old kirk, for in the days of his adversity, after he had already suffered five years' imprisonment and was 'wanted' again for his part in Argyll's rising, he lay hid for many weeks in the family burial-place under the church, his daughter bringing food to him under cloud of night.

Opposite Marchmont House the site of a Roman camp bears the name of Chesters, a common modification of the Latin *castrum*.   Nisbet House, a couple of miles further down the water, has been identified as the scene of that most dismal of ballads *Edom o' Gordon*, but Aytoun showed that the true House o' the Rodes was Towie Castle in Aberdeenshire, that 'Edom' was Adam Gordon of Auchindoun, and that the subject of the ballad was an incident in the war of anarchy which followed the dethronement of Mary Queen of Scots.   The landscape between this point and the meeting of waters at Allanton is enriched with the wooded parks of Kimmerghame, Wedderburn, Kelloe, and Blackadder House, whence the Whitadder winds through fine alluvial land to Hutton, where Edward encamped on that night in March 1296 before his memorable sack of Berwick.

[1] See p. 247, *ante*.

NORHAM CASTLE

Wedderburn, by the bye, is one of the oldest possessions of the Home family. Sir David Home, slain at Flodden, left seven sons by his wife Isabel Pringle of Gala—the Seven Spears of Wedderburn.[1]

High on the right bank of the stream stands picturesque Hutton Hall, a keep of the fifteenth century, with rambling additions of later date. The second Lord Home, who died in 1506, obtained the lands by his marriage with the daughter of George Ker of Samuelton in 1467, and probably built the original tower, which was dismantled in Surrey's retaliatory raid in 1497.

A nameless bard has summed the characteristics of Hutton parish with brevity, if not with wit :—

> ' Hutton for auld wives,
> Broadmeadows for swine ;
> Paxton for drucken wives
> And salmon sae fine.
> Crossrig for lint and woo',
> Spittal for kail ;
> Sunwick for cakes and cheese
> And lasses for sale.'

Edrington Castle, opposite Paxton, once a place of great strength and importance, has been quarried away to near the ground level. Mordington may be noticed, where Cromwell held his headquarters after crossing the Tweed in July 1650 ; and so the Whitadder enters the bounds of Berwick-on-Tweed, joining the river just before it broadens into the estuary.

[1] *Lay of the Last Minstrel*, canto v. 6.

CHAPTER XII

THE 'Berwick Bounds' enclose an area of about eight square miles—defining the whole extent of territory which the English succeeded in wresting from their northern neighbours by dint of three centuries of war. An exiguous gain—was it worth the price? These few thousand acres of cornland, windswept from the North Sea, were surely scant counterpoise for sunny Aquitaine and Guienne, opulent Bordeaux and the Pas de Calais—all lost to the Crown of England in the Hundred Years' War. Such was the result of forcing the Scottish nation into alliance with the kings of France—such was part of the price paid for the lesson that Scotsmen may never be coerced.

Berwick-on-Tweed became a Scottish town when Malcolm II. wrested Lothian from Northumbria by his victory at Carham in 1018. David I. made it one of the Four Burghs of Scotland, established Flemish craftsmen there, founded the Cistercian Nunnery of St. Leonard, and probably caused the original castle to be built. All went well with the thriving seaport till William the Lion attempted to enforce his hereditary right to the whole ancient earldom of Northumberland. During his great raid in 1172, Richard de Lucy and Humphrey de Bohun retaliated by crossing the Tweed and laying Berwick in ashes—the first in a long series of calamities to come. King William himself was captured at Alnwick, and when he regained his liberty in 1174 under the treaty of Falaise, it was at the price of doing homage for his kingdom to Henry II. and of surrendering the five principal Scottish castles, whereof Berwick was one. It remained in English hands for fifteen years, during which it was greatly strengthened; and then reckless, impecunious Richard Cœur de Lion remitted the homage and restored the castles to William in consideration of a cash payment of ten thousand marks.

In 1216 Berwick again underwent ordeal by fire. Alexander II. of Scotland besieged Norham Castle, assisted by a number of King John's rebellious barons, but was forced by John's approach to raise the siege and retire across the Border. On 15th January 1216 King John stormed the town and castle of Berwick, and, according to the Melrose Chronicle, inflicted inhuman torments upon both men and women. He then pushed forward as far as Haddington, plundered Coldingham, returned to Berwick, and in quitting it gave it to the flames, thrusting a torch with his own hand into the thatch of the house where he had lodged the night, *contra morem regum indecenter*—'scandalously contrary to kingly etiquette.'[1]

After John's death in 1216 peace reigned on the Borders for a while, and Berwick became a busy trade-port ; so that in 1266 the Franciscan monk of Carlisle, writing what we call the *Chronicle of Lanercost*, compared the town with Alexandria (which

[1] *Chronicon de Mailros*, 122.

it is not likely he ever saw) as having the sea for the source of its wealth and the water for its walls. All commerce at that time had to run the gauntlet of Norse pirates, but despite the dread which these sea-wolves had inspired on all our coasts, they found their match in the men of Berwick. Erlend, Jarl of Orkney,[1] having captured a ship belonging to a certain merchant of Berwick called Cnut the Rich and carried off Cnut's wife, who was on board returning from a pilgrimage, Cnut paid a hundred silver marks for the hire of fourteen vessels well manned, and set off in pursuit. Unluckily Torfæus, who tells us this much, does not say how Cnut's gallant enterprise ended.

The wealth of Berwick and its citizens in the thirteenth century is well attested by their liberality to the Church. 'There was scarcely an abbey in Scotland,' says Mr. John Scott, 'that had not property in Berwick.'[2] In 1286, the last year of that excellent monarch Alexander III., Berwick paid £2190 into the Scottish exchequer to account of customs derived chiefly from export duties on wool and hides—a sum equal to one-fourth of the whole customs revenue of England. Had not the fair project of marriage between the heir of England and the Queen of Scotland been marred by the untimely death of the bride in 1290, there is no saying to what greatness Berwick might not have grown. Her position as a seaport at the junction of two nations united under one Crown must have ensured her importance; but as matters turned out, it was that very advantage which brought about her undoing.

[1] Orkney was Norwegian territory in the thirteenth century.
[2] *Berwick-upon-Tweed*, by John Scott, p. 14.

Her citizens must have felt an agreeable sense of the importance of their burgh during the summer and autumn of 1292, for the King of England held his court there and assembled his Parliament to hear him give momentous award in favour of John de Baliol against Robert de Brus. All the Scottish magnates were there also, of course ; the streets were thronged with prelates and earls, barons and knights, with their innumerable retinues : conceive how brisk trade must have been and what a competition for lodgings. Alas ! it was but the splendour of sunset. King Edward departed, and presently began to exercise his suzerainty in a manner very distasteful to the Scots. The trouble first took shape out of a dispute between two citizens of Berwick. Marjory Moigne, a widow, having sued Master Roger Bertlemew for a debt, won her plea under the law of the Four Burghs. Roger appealed to the English court sitting at Newcastle ; King John [Baliol] was prompted to forbid the appeal as contrary to the provisions of the treaty of Birgham, which expressly debarred Scottish suitors being summoned before an English court. King Edward snapped his fingers at this interpretation of the treaty, ordered the case to be heard, and the Scottish judgment was reversed. In another case, Macduff, the Earl of Fife's son, failing to sustain a claim before the Scots Estates, appealed to the English Parliament. King John was summoned to attend as an English peer—refused—hesitated—finally obeyed. Before judgment was delivered Edward himself was summoned to France to do homage for his possessions there to King Philip, and no sooner was his back turned than Scottish indignation broke forth.

The malcontents negotiated a treaty offensive and defensive with King Philip, expressly directed against the King of England, and in this document the Mayor of Berwick's signature stood first among the representatives of Scottish burghs. At the same time King John sent an expedition under Comyn, Earl of Buchan, to harry the northern counties of England—an expedition which, if the English chroniclers are to be credited, exceeded in savage cruelty all that had gone before. But these partisan writers are studiously careless of chronology. In making out a case against the Scots, they do not explain that the massacre of Corbridge was by way of reprisal for the horrors of Berwick. Briefly the sequence of events was thus :—

King Edward, hearing of the Scoto-French treaty while he was still in France, took immediate measures for instant and signal punishment. He summoned a powerful army to meet him at Newcastle on 25th March 1296, and ordered Osbert de Spaldington to co-operate with a fleet of a hundred sail. Meanwhile Buchan's army invaded Cumberland on 26th March, invested Carlisle on the 28th, which town was held for the King of England by Robert de Brus, son of ' the competitor ' and father of the future King of Scots. Repulsed from Carlisle, Buchan turned eastward, and, according to a notarial instrument drawn up on King Edward's behalf some months later (August 1296), burnt Hexham and Corbridge, committing ' Herodian ' barbarities on pregnant women, and burning two hundred ' little clerks ' (schoolboys) at Corbridge. [1] Yes ; but assuming this to be literally true, it took place on

[1] Bain's *Hist. Doc. Scot.*, ii. 217.

8th April, and what meanwhile had been the course of events on the eastern Border ? It were easy to fill pages with description of the portents and apparitions which had heralded them, conscientiously recorded *ex post facto*—of the huge ball of fire seen by 'a simple burgess of Haddington' descending upon the doomed city ; of the bloody Christ which terrified some school-children in Berwick before Christmas ; of the man robed in white, with wings on his shoulders and a drawn sword, who visited the house of the veracious chronicler of Lanercost (in Carlisle, probably), and whom he 'conceived to be an angel.' Taken together, these phenomena betokened something unpleasant in store for busy Berwick ; taken separately, one fears the evidence in their support would not stand scrutiny by the Society for Psychical Research.

King Edward led his army across the Tweed at Coldstream on 28th March, when Antony Bek, Bishop of Durham, joined him with a contingent of fifteen hundred horse and foot, and on the 30th he appeared before the walls of Berwick. Sir William Douglas, 'le Hardi,' father of the 'Good Sir James,' was in command of the castle and town, with a body of knights of Fife and their supporters. The townspeople, secure as they thought within their walls, rashly taunted the English in gibberish which, for reasons beyond our understanding, proved peculiarly irritating to King Edward. The Latin chronicler of Lanercost has preserved them in the vernacular :—

'Kyng Edward, wanne thou havest Berwic,
    Pike thee !

> Wanne thou havest getten,
>> Dike thee !'

In another version the personal sting is perhaps less obscure :—

> 'What wende the Kyng Edward
>> For his langge shanks,
> For to wynne Berewyke
>> All our unthankes.
> Go pike it him !
> And when he have it won,
> Go dike it him !'

The first assault was delivered by the fleet, which sailed up on the flood tide ; but on a landing being attempted, the townspeople, women and all, flocked down to the wharves, piled combustiles on board several of the ships, and so burnt them ; the rest of the squadron escaping on the ebb.   Edward attacked by land on Good Friday.   There was no city wall, only a ditch and stockade, which were easily carried ; but Richard, the Earl of Cornwall's brother, and cousin to the King, raising his visor to get a better view, was struck dead by a bolt in the forehead, which did so greatly enrage Edward that he gave the order—'No quarter !'   Then began a horrible butchery lasting nearly throughout two days.   Wyntoun says that it was brought to an end when King Edward saw a woman in the act of childbirth being put to the sword.—

> 'Thus thai slayand ware sa fast
> All the day, qwhill [1] at the last
> This Kyng Edward saw in that tyde
> A woman slayne, and off her syde

[1] Until.

A barne,[1] he saw fall out, sprewland[2]
Besyd that woman slayne lyand.
Lasses, Lasses![3] than cryid he ;
Leve off, leve off ! that word suld be.[4]

The Flemish merchants defended their *Aula Rubra*
or Red Hall right gallantly, holding out after the
town had been taken till evensong, when the hall was
fired, and thirty of them perished in the flames.

Accounts vary of the number massacred. Wyntoun, on the Scottish side, makes the lowest estimate,
putting the death-roll at seven thousand five hundred.
The Lanercost chronicler, from the English point of
view, complacently reckons it at fifteen thousand,
adding that ' this most merciful prince showed that
humanity to the dead which he had offered to the
living. I myself saw large parties of men told off to
bury the dead, and all of them were entitled to the
reward of a penny from the King's treasury, although
they began work only at the eleventh hour.' The
butchery was done without regard to age or sex ;
any women or children that were spared were sent
into perpetual exile, and the good town was ruined
for ever. It never recovered its trade ; from being
the greatest merchant city in Scotland it sank to the
grade of a fishing-port and garrison town.

No act of the first Edward has left such a dark
stain upon his fine character as this sack of Berwick.
Taking place a whole week before the atrocities of
Hexham and Corbridge, no palliation can be found
for him in respect of Buchan's outrages. At the

[1] A babe.
[2] Sprawling.
[3] *Laissez, laissez !*
[4] Wyntoun's *Cronykil*, VIII. c. xi. ll. 1831-1838.

same time, it should not be forgotten that the immemorial custom of war sanctioned the sack of any place, and the massacre of its garrison and citizens, which, having been duly summoned, should be taken by storm. The common assent of civilised nations has brought about a change in this, favourable both to soldiers and non-combatants; but that change is a very recent one. Down to the very end of the Napoleonic wars the old rules held good, as British troops gave proof at Seringapatam, Badajos, and Ciudad Rodrigo.

The one spark of leniency shown by King Edward in this affair was the permission he gave to the garrison of Berwick to go free, after swearing that they never again would bear arms against England; but their commander, Douglas 'le Hardi,' was kept a prisoner. Edward's policy of terror proved a signal failure—he lived not to learn how complete, but he left the lesson to his successors. Torrents of blood were to flow—tons of treasure to be squandered—before English statesmen could be got to understand that Scotsmen may be easily led, but that they are the last people in the world to be driven. For the moment it seemed as if King Edward had accomplished his purpose. The Scots had not yet found a leader whom they could follow. Warenne's victory at Dunbar on 28th April shattered the cause of King John: on 13th May James the Steward surrendered Roxburgh Castle, swearing on the Holy Gospels to aid the King of England against 'John de Baliol, late King of Scotland,' then, after spending three weeks personally laying out new defences for Berwick, Edward went on a progress through Scotland, exacting fealty from nobles and

knights and their renunciation both of Baliol and
the French alliance. Returning to Berwick in
August, he held a Parliament there, and established
an Exchequer, to be managed under Hugh de
Cressingham, in all respects the same as his West-
minster Exchequer.

Next, in 1297, followed the rising which aborted
in the capitulation of Irvine, brought about by the
refusal of such mighty personages as the Bishop of
Glasgow, the Earl of Carrick, and Sir William
Douglas to serve under command of William Wallace
the Landless. These proud chevaliers, therefore,
once more made hollow submission to King Edward,
leaving Wallace, who had nothing but his life at stake
and the cause of his distressed country at heart, to
withdraw into Selkirk Forest and wage guerrilla warfare against the English. Douglas having failed
to produce the hostages required of him, was imprisoned at Berwick when Chancellor Cressingham
wrote to King Edward on 24th July as follows :—

' Cher sire, forasmuch as Sir William Douglas has not kept
the convenants which he made with Sir Henry de Percy, he
is in your castle of Berwick, in my keeping, still very savage
and very abusive (uncore mout sauvage e mont araillez) ;
but I will keep him in suchwise that, please God, he shall not
get out. And the church of Douglas is vacant, well worth
200 marks, as I have heard ; and if it please you to give it to
your Treasurer of Scotland (Cressingham himself) I believe
that you will have bestowed it well, for by the faith, which
I owe you he does not grow slack in your service, but takes
the greatest pains to make things go right.' [1]

In another letter of the same date Cressingham

[1] Preserved in Public Record Office. Printed in Stevenson's
Documents illustrating the History of Scotland, ii. 204.

says that Douglas is kept in irons (en ferres e en sauve garde, Deu mercy), and begs the king not 'to let him be liberated on any account of profit or influence.' Douglas was removed to the Tower of London in October, where he died some time before the beginning of 1299.

Wallace, though deserted by his wealthy colleagues, managed by his indomitable energy and confidence to assemble a considerable force of Clydesdale pikemen, Ettrick bowmen, and Highland swordsmen. Warenne, Earl of Surrey, leaving his command at Berwick, marched north to quell the rising, and was totally defeated at Stirling Bridge (10th September 1297), where Treasurer Cressingham met his death. Warenne left this fatal field and galloped back to Berwick at such speed that his horse fell dead as soon as his rider quitted the saddle. Then he pressed on to the south, leaving the English garrison in the castle to look after themselves. When Wallace returned from his raid upon Northumberland in the winter of 1297-98, he found the Scots in possession of the town, but the garrison still holding out. In the following summer, 1299, the English reoccupied the town, and Patrick, Earl of Dunbar, was given command thereof, while King Edward went forward to overthrow Wallace at Falkirk. Dunbar was succeeded as governor in 1302 by a knight of great renown Sir John de Segrave, who was wounded almost to death at the battle of Rosslyn in the following February.

When Wallace was taken in 1305, tried, executed, and cut into quarters as a traitor (which he certainly was not, never having acknowledged King Edward), his left arm was sent to Berwick to be exposed there.

A year later when the Countess of Buchan who crowned Bruce at Scone, was taken at Kildrummie, the King ordered his lieutenant at Berwick to place her in a cage of strong lattice-work. Two English-women were to be found in Berwick to serve her, and she was to be so guarded that no Scot of either sex should hold communication with her. The Countess remained four years in this cage.

In 1310 she was handed over to the custody of the Friars of Mount Carmel in Berwick, who guarded her till 1313.

Down to that year the English government made use of Berwick as their principal depot of supplies for the desultory Scottish War. King Robert's successes by this time had become so alarming that Edward II. determined once more upon a supreme effort to reduce Scotland to submission, and assembled an immense host at Wark in June 1314 for the relief of Stirling Castle. It had been ever King Robert's strategy to avoid pitched battles with the power of England; repeatedly he had impressed his captains with the importance of retiring and laying bare the country before the enemy, allowing the invaders to march and countermarch till they were forced to beat a retreat for want of provender ; time after time the wisdom of this course had been proved to the hilt. But now Edward Bruce, with excess of chivalry, had given his royal brother away. Since Lent he had been closely besieging Stirling Castle. The English governor, Sir Philip de Mowbray, proposed a sus-pension of arms, pledging himself to surrender the castle if it was not relieved within a year from mid-summer 1313. Edward rashly agreed to this com-pact; the King was very angry, but holding his

20

brother's knightly honour as dear as his own, accepted the challenge, though with much misgiving. Both nations having a full year to prepare for a pitched battle, victory seemed a foregone conclusion for the wealthier and more powerful.   Moreover, the occasion was just what was needed to put the whole chivalry of England on their mettle and, Piers Gaveston having expiated his offences on the scaffold, to induce the barons to compose those grievances and disputes which hitherto had so sorely crippled the power of their monarch.   All of them except the Earl of Lancaster and his adherents—Warwick, Warenne, and Arundel—responded heartily to the summons.

It has been commonly stated that the English army which assembled on the 11th June at Wark amounted to one hundred thousand of all arms, but there is nothing in the Patent Rolls to show that the total exceeded fifty thousand troops.   Nevertheless, in equipment, in splendour of display, and probably in numbers, it was superior to any force that ever crossed the Scottish border.

Edward marched by way of Berwick, so as to keep in touch with his supplies from the fleet.   Barbour describes the magnificence of the sight when the army marched north from that town :—

> ' Quhen the Kyng apon this kyn wyss
> Hadordanyt as ik her duiuss,
> His bataillis and his stering,
> He raiss arly in a morning,
> And fra Berwick he tuk the way.
> Baith hillis and walis helyt (shone) thai,
> As the bataillis (columns) that war braid
> Departyt our the feldis raid
> The sone (sun) wes brycht and schynand cler,

And armouris that burnyst wer
Swa blomyt (bloomed) with the sonnys beme
That all the land was in a leme (flame)
Baneris rycht fayrly flawmand (flaming)
And penselys[1] to the wynd wawand (waving) '

A brave sight it must have been, for war has never been so pictorially perfect as it was at this period—the very noontide of chivalry. A few days later, behold King Edward landing at Berwick, a broken fugitive, having made his escape from Dunbar in a fishing boat. Of all his superb army, thousands had laid down their arms to the King of Scots ; thousands more lay stark in the bogs of Bannockburn, the rest were being hunted like vermin by the peasantry as they sought to escape to the Border. It must have been a bitter ordeal for the King of England to issue from Berwick on 27th June a proclamation announcing the loss of his signet, and warning all men against obeying orders issued thereunder. However, it had fallen into honest hands. Roger de Northburgh, Keeper of the Signet, had been taken prisoner at Bannockburn with his two clerks, and King Robert sent the seal to Edward, on condition that it should not be used in Scotland.

Stirling Castle was surrendered according to compact on the morrow of Bannockburn ; Bothwell Castle capitulated to Edward Bruce a little later ; and now the only Scottish fortress which still displayed the red cross of St. George was Berwick. On the night of 10th January 1316 King Robert and Sir James Douglas attempted to surprise it by escalade ; but the moon was bright ; the attack was

---

[1] Pensils, the pointed or forked ensigns of knights.

repulsed, and Douglas only escaped capture by means of a small boat. A few weeks later Sir Maurice de Berkeley, Governor of Berwick, wrote to King Edward declaring that his men were actually dying of starvation, and that the place must be lost unless relief were sent speedily. He said that whenever a horse died, the men-at-arms boiled and ate it, refusing to give the foot-soldiers a single mouthful till they themselves had eaten all they could. On 14th February the garrison mutinied, and a party of Gascons rode out to foray. Sir James Douglas, being informed of this, set out to intercept them at Scaithmoor as they were driving in some cattle. Barbour, whose account is amply confirmed by contemporary letters in the Tower collection, says that Douglas, had with him but a small clump of spears, but charged so furiously that twenty men-at-arms and sixty footsoldiers were slain. He adds that this was the hardest encounter Douglas ever had to put through, which is likely enough, seeing that the starving Frenchmen would fight fiercely for their beef. Their Captain, Raymond de Caillu, King's Sergeant-at-arms, was among the slain.

Hearing of this exploit, Sir Robert de Nevill, the 'Peacock of the North,' declared that he was sick of hearing about the prowess of the Black Douglas, and pledged his knightly word to attack him whenever and wherever he should see his banner displayed. Of course Douglas was told of this, and of course he gave Nevill his opportunity. He rode in the night to Berwick, where Nevill was, and in the morning displayed under the walls his well-known banner, the azure chief and silver stars. To ensure the English chevalier's attention, he fired a few villages in the neighbourhood ; whereupon out pricked the Peacock with a party of his best men-at-arms. Douglas proposed single combat ; Nevill could not but accept, and down he went at the first onset to rise no more. But Douglas was not satisfied : he led his troop in a charge upon the English cavalry, which broke and fled, leaving Nevill's three brothers, Sir Alexander, Ralph, and John among the prisoners, and these gentlemen were held to ransom for two thousand marks each. It was not Napoleon who invented the principle of making the war support the war.

No serious attempt was made upon Berwick until 1318, after King Robert returned from his Irish campaign. He then took up his quarters in Old Cambus woods, employing his men in the construction of siege engines ; but these were never called into play owing to the part played by a certain burgess of Berwick named Sim of Spalding. This man, disgusted by the tyrannous conduct of the English governor, Sir Roger de Horseley, sent secret word to the Earl of March, offering to admit an escalading party on a certain night when he, Spalding, was to be on guard. When March showed Spalding's letter to the King he was told that he had done well not to take it to either Douglas or Moray, so jealous was each of the other in deeds of daring ; but it was arranged that both these knights should share with March in the enterprise. The column of attack mustered on 27th March in Duns Park,[1] where all horses were left. They marched after dark to the city walls, set their ladders at ' the

[1] Not probably Duns Park on Whitadder, but a place of this name, which cannot be identified on Lamberton Moor near Berwick.

Kow' at the appointed hour, and were in possession of the town before the alarm was given. A party of Scots was told off for the indispensable work of plunder, the main body being kept under arms with their officers. But the discipline of these wild fellows was unequal to such a test ; soon the officers were left without any men ; nearly all had gone off after the booty. Day broke on the scene revealing the state of matters to Governor de Horseley; a fine old fire-eater, who had a strong garrison in the Castle. The Scottish leaders also were fully aware of their peril, and sent Sir William Keith of Galston through the streets, driving the men back to their standards. Keith did his work so briskly that a strong sortie from the castle was repulsed. Barbour says that de Horseley surrendered in six days, and later historians have accepted the statement without question ; but official correspondence lately published proves that the stern old knight held out for sixteen weeks—till 20th July, when he was compelled by famine to strike his flag, after losing an eye. [1] He had appealed to his King for relief in vain. Robert de Blackburn, who had lost his brother and 'all his friends' at Bannockburn, [2] swam the Tweed on horseback, leading a string of twenty-one horses, and carrying letters to King Edward.

King Robert appointed his son-in-law Governor of Berwick—young Sir Walter the Steward, future progenitor of the Stuart dynasty, who had received the knightly accolade on the field of Bannockburn. No sinecure this post, as Sir Walter soon found, for in 1319 King Edward, having temporarily composed

[1] Bain's *Hist. Doc. Scot*, iii. 113. 115.
[2] Ibid, 113.

his quarrel with the Earl of Lancaster, and obtained
the Pope's sanction to use some of the funds collected for a projected crusade, assembled an army of
twelve thousand men at Newcastle under such re-
doutable commanders as Aymer de Valence, Earl of
Pembroke, Umfraville Earl of Angus, Sir Hugh de
Lowther, Sir Andrew de Harcla, and Sir Anthony
de Lucy. At the beginning of August this force
invested Berwick by land, while a powerful fleet
blockaded the estuary. A general assault was delivered on 7th September but was repulsed, to be
renewed again on the 13th. The English had con-
structed a huge siege engine which they called the
Sow—a wooden tower moving on wheels, designed
to land stormers on the ramparts, and at the same
time to convey a mining party to the foot of the es-
carp. One John Crab, a Flemish engineer in pay of
the Scots, made a machine to match the Sow—a
powerful crane or catapult, also on wheels, by which
huge stones and fireballs could be discharged.

Early on the morning of the 13th a flourish of
English trumpets announced the advance of the
Sow. As it crawled ponderously forward Crab's
crane rolled along to meet it, Crab having been
warned that if he failed to demolish the Sow instant
death should be his doom. The excitement was
tremendous when the two great engines halted face
to face. Crab caused an enormous stone to be put
in position, and let fly, but his aim was bad.—

> ' In hy he gert draw the cleket, [1]
> And smartly swappit out the stane,
> That even out ower the Sow is gane

[1] Caused the trigger to be drawn.

And behind hir ane litil we [1]
It fell. ' [2]

On came the Sow. Crab's next shot fell short, and
before he could prepare another discharge the Sow
was touching the city wall, and the stormers were
lowering their gangway with loud cheers. He could
not miss this time. The great stone crashed right
into the Sow's belly ; the men inside were thrown out
right and left; ' Your Sow had farrowed ! ' cried the
Scots in derision. Then Crab plied his fireballs, and
the wrecked engine was soon ablaze.

Now came a cry for Crab from another quarter.
An English ship, her fortified tops full of crossbow-
men, drew alongside the river front. Crab's crane
rumbled away at its best speed to meet her. The
engineer had learned his trajectory better by this
time : the first shot brought down the mainmast with
all the sharpshooters, and fireballs did the rest.

One last assault came very near success. It was
reported to Sir Walter that the barricade outside the
Mary Gate had been forced, and that the English
were piling combustibles against the gate itself.
Bringing his reserve down from the castle, Sir Walter
drew the men up behind the gate, which he caused to
be flung open suddenly. Then he charged at their
head through the flames which had already been
kindled—charged with such fury that the assailants
fled pell-mell. Seldom do sorties succeed, but this
one put an end to the operations of that day.

Famine must have accomplished what could not
be done by assault, and none knew this better than
the King of Scots ; so he planned a diversion—that

[1] Way.
[2] Barbour's *Brus*, CXXX. 86.

raid across the West Marches by Douglas and Moray, which ended in the 'Chapter of Myton,' where Archbishop Melton lost all his silver spoons and scores of his clergy. The siege of Berwick was raised on 24th September.

After this Berwick remained a Scottish town for fourteen years. The experience of the last siege has shown how faulty were its defences. The wall erected to the first Edward's plan was so low that, says Barbour, men on the top were within a spear-thrust of those attacking from the outside. King Robert now set this to rights, causing the wall to be raised to a uniform height of ten feet. Some shape-less fragments of the work may still be seen near the Bell Tower. Although the town never regained its former importance in commerce, its citizens turned to best account the years of good government which Scotland enjoyed under Robert I. In 1331, two years after his death, the customs levied on exported goods amounted in Berwick to £570, as compared with £400 in Edinburgh, £484 in Aberdeen, £88 in Perth, and £83 in Dundee. It was still the prin-cipal trading centre of Scotland.[1]

Edward II. died his shameful death at Berkeley Castle in 1327: 'grave, gentle and amiable in con-versation, but indolent in action,' was the lenient judgment passed on him by one who knew him well.[2] The third Edward succeeded as a minor in

---

[1] It may be noted that the fiscal policy of the Scottish government at this time affords the earliest authentic example of free imports. No duty was allowed to be levied on foreign imports, except the *parva costuma* levied by every burgh on all produce, foreign or domestic, coming within its boundary. Revenue was raised solely by duty on exported goods.

[2] 'Il fust sagis, douce et amyable en parole, mais mesoerous en fait.' —Gray's *Scalacronica*.

leading-strings to his mother Isabella and Mortimer, murderers of his father. Truce prevailed at the time between England and Scotland; but it was extremely precarious, and it has been alleged that it was broken by the King of Scots besieging Sir Robert de Manners in Norham Castle on the very day, says the Lanercost chronicler, of young Edward's accession. Against this may be set the original documents whereby Edward III., on 15th February, three weeks after his accession, appointed Percy, Nevill, and other knights as commissioners to maintain the truce made by the late King with 'Robert de Brus and his fautours' (criminals). Anyhow, both nations assembled their forces for war; while the English army was mustering at Newcastle, Moray and Douglas crossed the West Marches and entered upon what became known as the campaign of Weardale. How the two armies manoeuvred and reconnoitred—how the chevaliers of both nations performed heroic exploits before, and even within, each other's lines—and how, in the end, the Scots gave their enemy the slip—may be read with advantage elsewhere, but has no direct relation with the story of Berwick-on-Tweed. It may be noted, in passing to our proper business, that Barbour states that this campaign was notable for two novelties—namely, the display of crests on the helmets of knights and the use in action of 'crakkis of weir'— 'cracks of war'—that is, cannon.

The Lincoln Parliament, held in the autumn of 1327, brings us back to Tweedside, because the outcome of its deliberations was that John de Denoun was sent to make certain proposals to the King of Scots, whom he found busily besieging

Norham Castle. These proposals were as welcome as they were unexpected. They consisted of direct overtures for the marriage of Princess Joan, sister of Edward III., to Prince David, heir of Scotland. Hostilities were suspended at once, for the sole cause of them existed no longer. The independence of Scotland had been acknowledged by the only monarch who had continued to dispute it—King Robert's sovereignty recognised by the only court which called it in question.

The treaty of Northampton carried these overtures into effect, establishing what English writers have termed 'the Shameful Peace.' There was to be perpetual peace between the two kingdoms—the Coronation Stone was to be restored to Scone (which has never been fulfilled to this day)—and the King of England was to use his good offices at the Papal See to obtain remission from excommunication for the King of Scots. The Ragman Roll, being the damning record of all the Scottish gentlemen who had done fealty to Edward I., was to be returned to Scotland, and also that chip of the true cross which the Scots had learned to revere as the Black Rood. In return for the surrender of all claim to suzerainty on the part of England, the Scottish government bound itself to pay £20,000 in three instalments at Tweedmouth.

The royal marriage was fixed to take place at Berwick in the summer of 1328. The battered old town, so long the scene of bloody strife between the nations, was chosen as the theatre of that act which should unite them in lasting amity, and great was the bustle of preparation. Peter the Mechanic (*Petrus machinarum*), a Flemish merchant of Berwick, was

sent to the Continent to lay in stores of furs, rich
cloths, and spices, on which he was allowed to charge
commission at the rate of ten per cent. His
purchases included cloth for the knights' robes, a
gift from the King, costing £173, 9s. 2d., and for
the esquires' £90. Hoods and capes of vair,
miniver, lambskin, etc., were provided in great
abundance; much linen, also, for the household;
twenty tuns of wine, 2200 eels in barrels, 4360lb.
of almonds, 600 lb. of rice, forty loaves of sugar,
180 lb. of pepper, with mace, nutmegs, saffron,
and many other delicacies. Then another trader,
Thomas de Carnock, was despatched to Flanders to
spend £400 for the King in silks, satins, and jewellery; and so high did the reputation of the said
Thomas stand that the King, by a letter under his
own hand, exempted him from submitting his
accounts to audit. The household expenses, apart
from all this money spent abroad, amounted to
£966, 10s. 10d.—a very lavish expenditure in
money of the fourteenth century; but all must
have felt it a relief to commit extravagance in something less grim than preparations for war. The
bridegroom, created Earl of Carrick for the occasion,
was but four years old, the bride no more than six
—Joan of the Tower, as she was called, having been
born in that place of dismal memories. King
Robert's growing infirmities kept him at Cardross,
but he sent those tried brothers-in-arms, Thomas
Randolph, Earl of Moray, and Good Sir James of
Douglas, to receive the bride at Berwick from the
hands of Queen Isabella and the Bishop of Lincoln,
Chancellor of England.

The common folk, burgesses, and country people

of both nations went about their merry-making with
a will; English and Scottish knights, too, paladins of
chivalry, fraternised freely. The style of official
correspondence underwent a sudden change. Hitherto the King of Scots had been referred to invariably as 'our rebel Robert de Brus, lately Earl of
Carrick:' now Edward III. addressed letters (with a
privy grimace, no doubt) to 'the magnificent Prince
Sir Robert, by the grace of God King of Scots, his
dearest friend, greeting and embraces of sincere
affection.'[1]

'Tongue cannot utter,' exclaims the chronicler of
Pluscardine, 'nor pen describe, what pride and joy
prevailed in Scotland after so much hardship. For a
time that country abandoned itself to festivity.'
Ay, for a time only—for three short years. Wise
King Robert died in 1329; peerless James of Douglas in 1330; dauntless Randolph of Moray in 1332,
leaving the King of Scots, a minor of eight years, to
meet the storm with which the fiery Edward was
preparing to devastate the north. He had espoused
the cause of the disinherited lords, and Berwick, as
usual, was to bear the brunt of invasion.[2] Great
oaks were felled at Cawood in Yorkshire and fash-
ioned into siege engines; stones were quarried there,
rounded into balls, and shipped, with the catapults,
at Hull; and on 4th April Berwick woke to find
herself once more beleaguered.

On 16th May 1333 King Edward arrived on the
south bank of the river, and took up his quarters in
Tweedmouth. A memorial of his presence remains

[1] August 9, 1328. Bain's *Hist. Doc. Scot.*, iii. 173.
[2] It had been ceded to the English by the usurper, Edward Baliol,
under the treaty of Roxburgh, but it remained loyal to King David.

in the name of Parliament Street.   Berwick was now
a harder nut to crack than it had been ever before,
so diligently had King Robert improved its defences.
An assault by land and sea had failed before Edward's
arrival.   Sir Alexander Seton was governor of the
town—inflexibly loyal, as became one of that devoted house.   As much cannot be written of the Earl
of March, who commanded in the castle, unworthy
husband of Black Agnes of Dunbar.   The siege resolved itself into a blockade.   Citizens and soldiers
were put on short commons; overtures from the
King of England resulted in a bargain like that made
by Philip de Mowbray at Stirling—the place would
surrender if not relieved within a fixed time.   Sir
Alexander Seton's son Thomas was handed over,
with others, as a hostage.

Before the date arranged for surrender Sir Archibald Douglas, Guardian of Scotland, appeared with
a numerous army, sent Sir William Keith with men
and provisions into the town, crossed the river at the
Yare ford in full view of the enemy, and passed on
to waste and pillage Northumberland in rear of the
English.   This we have on the testimony of Sir
Thomas Gray, who was present.   He distinctly
states that the Scots 'bouterent gentz et vitailes de-
denz la vile,'[1] and this was claimed as relief of the
town within the terms of the agreement.   Young
King Edward scouted the notion.   'Relieved! not
a bit; you are just as you were before; better surrender quietly, or it will go ill with your hostages.'
The besieged protested; the English King met their
arguments by hanging Thomas Seton on a gibbet in
full view of the ramparts.   Wyntoun fills in the

[1] *Scalacronica*, folio 218 b.

picture with some ghastly details. He says that Sir
Alexander Seton had lost two sons already in the
defence of the town, and that now, when he and his
wife beheld a third threatened with a shameful death,
their spirits did not quail.—

> ‘ Than sayd the lady that scho was yhyng [young],
> And hyr lord wes yhowng alsua,
> Off powere till have barnys ma. [1]
> And set [allow] that thai twa dede war thare
> Yhit off thare barnys sum lyvand [living] ware.’ [2]

But King Edward's terrible *argumentum ad hominem*
prevailed. The parents of the other hostages had
not the same Roman fortitude as the Setons. They
beset the governor with entreaties, so that a fresh
bargain was struck. Berwick town and tower would
surrender if the siege was not raised within a fortnight. Messengers were sent, under English safe-
conduct (for Edward III. was the soul of chivalry),
to recall Douglas from his foolish raiding. He
came—he saw—and was pulverised.

Better for Scotland had he never come—had
Berwick fallen quietly—for so closely had disaster
ever dogged the heels of this Douglas that already
he had earned the ominous title of ‘ Tineman ’—
the Loser. [3] He was Archibald, youngest brother
of the Good Sir James, and had been appointed
Guardian of Scotland during the absence of young
David II. in France, where he had been sent for
safety. This Archibald would make Berwick a
second Bannockburn, for had he not an army far

---

[1] Able to have more children.
[2] Wyntoun's *Cronykil*, VIII. c. xxvii. l. 3886.
[3] The name has also been applied, with equal reason, to Archibald,
fourth Earl of Douglas.

stronger and better equipped than had conquered there ?

Ay, but Archibald Douglas was not a second Bruce, and Bruce's warning against pitched battles he flung to the winds. While his columns were recrossing the Tweed and marching into camp at a place then called Duns Park, King Edward took up a strong position on Halidon Hill, that rising ground which one travelling north by rail may see from the train about two miles to the north-west of Berwick. He was not in easy circumstances ; the northern shires had not mustered readily ; supplies were short and deserters numerous. The Tineman, had he possessed the wit, had only to bide his time and wait. But he was 'fey,' as Scotsmen term it ; his doom was that he should never prevail, just as it had been his brother's destiny never to fail.

On 19th July the Scottish line of battle was formed on Lamberton Moor opposite the English on Halidon Hill. Between the two positions, as at Bannockburn, lay a marsh; and, as at Bannockburn, a champion stood forward on either side to test fortune by single combat—the giant chief of the Turnbulls for the Scots, Sir Robert de Venale or Benhale for the English. The issue of that duel— the death of Turnbull—has been told in another chapter. [1] It was but a foretaste of what was to follow. Douglas gave the command for a general attack. In four divisions—respectively under the Earl of Moray (Randolph's son), the Steward of Scotland, Sir Archibald Douglas himself, and the Earl of Ross—the Scottish line advanced and plunged into the morass, where the English archers

[1] See p. 184, *ante*.

wrought terrible slaughter. At the foot of a steep brae on the far side an attempt was made to rally the shattered ranks. Ross with his Highlanders breasted the steep and perished in the charge. One after another the other divisions followed, only to be broken on the English hedge of steel or to be cruelly shot down by those matchless bowmen. The Tineman finished his career of disaster by a soldier's death ; six Scottish earls—Lennox, Ross, Sutherland, Carrick, Menteith, and Atholl—fell with him. William, Lord of Douglas, son and heir of the Good Sir James, three brothers Fraser, and other good knights too many to number, laid down their lives on that crowded field. Moray and the Steward saved themselves in flight. The pursuit was long and bloody.—

> ' There men myhte well see
> Many a Skotte lightly flee,
> And the English after priking
> With sharp swerdes them stiking.
> Then their baners weren found
> Alle displayde on the grounde.
> And layne starkly on blode
> As thei had foughten the floode.' [1]

Mediæval arithmetic was taxed to estimate the Scottish loss. English chroniclers put the slain variously between 14,055 [2] and 56,640, [3] while the victors only reckoned fifteen slain on their side. Let the numbers have been what they may, it was all over, men said, with Scottish independence. Edward Baliol, vassal of English Edward, was secure

[1] Laurence Minot, Edward III.'s Claudian.
[2] Continuation of Hemingford.
[3] Cambridge MS. quoted by Barnes.

in so much kingship as it should please his superior to allow him. Berwick surrendered at once ; the Earl of March, governor of the castle, becoming Edward III.'s 'man' for the nonce. The King of England, in gratitude for these crowning mercies, presented £20 a year for ever to the Cistercian nuns of Halystane, that perpetual thanks might be offered for the victory. An altar was to be placed in their chapel dedicated to St. Margaret, upon whose feast-day the battle had been fought. Nevertheless King Edward, pious though he was, distrusted the Scottish clergy. He scattered the monks of Berwick far and wide among the English monasteries, that 'the occasion of their malignity might cease,' and imported English friars in their place who should disseminate sound political principles.

From this time Berwick became the great military dépôt of the English kings in their Scottish wars. The wool trade—the great source of its revenues—fell away to a serious extent, and the citizens were heavily rated to strengthen and maintain the fortifications. During six months' truce in 1341-2 King Edward spent Easter at Berwick, and great joustings took place during three whole days between English and Scottish knights. One match especially moved Wyntoun's admiration—twelve a side—when two English knights were slain outright, and the Scottish Sir John Hay died of his wounds. Sir William Ramsay, a Scot, was highly applauded for his courage. He was struck through the helmet ; the truncheon of the spear broke off, leaving the point sticking in his skull. All men thought he must die ; a priest shrove him straightway ; the Earl of Derby, standing by, declared it was 'a fayre sycht, no fayrere sycht

ma man se !' and prayed God that when it came to
his turn to die, it might be in as glorious a fashion.
When the shriving was over Ramsay's brother
Alexander tried his hand at a cure, and, marvellous
as it may seem, succeeded. His surgery was of the
heroic kind. He

> ' Gert lay hym down forowtyn lete, [1]
> And on his helme his fute he sete,
> And wyth gret strynth owt can aras [2]
> The trownsown [3] that thare stekand [4] was.
> He [William] rase allane, fra it wes owte, [5]
> And wyth a gud will and a stowte
> He sayd that he wald ayl na thyng.
> Tharoff the Erl [of Derby] had wonderyng,
> And gretly hym commendit then,
> And said—" Lw ! stowt hartis of men. " ' [6]

Rough play this for peace-time ; but rougher was to
come on the morrow ; for Sir Patrick Graham, newly
landed from the Continent, arrived in a terrible
taking lest he should be too late for this splendid
tournament. Sir Richard Talbot, however, took
him on to run three courses : in the first of which
Graham's spear pierced the English knight's corselet
and bore him to the ground. Then it was discovered that Talbot had put on *two* breastplates of the
new Milan fashion, and that the Scotsman's spear
had only entered his breast 'ane inch or mare.' So
they ran the other two courses without further
scathe, and Graham accepted Talbot's invitation to

[1] Made them lay him (William) down without delay.
[2] *Arracher*, drew out.
[3] Truncheon, spear-shaft.
[4] Sticking.
[5] As soon as it was out.
[6] Wyntoun's *Cronykil*, VIII. 5214 *et seq.*

supper. While they were discussing their meal,
entered a nameless chevalier—

> ' A cumly knycht
> That semyt stowt, baith bald and wycht ' [1]—

who challenged Graham to a fresh encounter, bidding
him rise early next morning, hear Mass, get well
shriven, and come out to the barriers. Graham
' made tharoff na gabbing '—never hesitated—accepted the challenge, met his man, and killed him cleanly.

Then came the award of prizes by the heralds, the
chivalrous custom at international tournaments being
that the heralds of each nation should reward the
knight of the other side who had borne himself best.
Accordingly, the Scottish heralds pronounced that
knight winner who had run Ramsay through the
head, and the English heralds gave their prize to
Graham, for the following peculiar reasons, fully
approved by Lord Derby. It was held that Talbot
had not played fair in wearing a double breast-plate;
that technically he was dead, wherefore

> ' He that a knycht yhistyrday
> Slew, and ane othir today, the prys [prize]
> Suld have, Patryk the Grame that is.'

One cannot but marvel at the insatiable love of
fighting that in the brief and rare intervals of truce
found its only solace in these gladiatorial displays.

David II., returning to his kingdom a lad of eighteen in 1342, was taken prisoner four years later at
the battle of Neville's Cross. Nevertheless the
English were losing their hold of Scotland. The
Knight of Liddesdale having recovered Ettrick and

_____
[1] Bold and strong.

Teviotdale for his country, set about feathering his own nest, and ended his days in a quarrel with his godson, as has been shown already. [1] In 1355 a strong French contingent, bringing much needed bullion—forty thousand *moutons d'or*—arrived in Scotland. Edward III. being absent waging war in France, the Scots saw their chance for another dash at Berwick. Patrick, Earl of March, happening to be in patriotic phase at the time, arranged with Stewart, Earl of Angus for an escalade by night. It succeeded well; the town was taken and plundered— not burnt, this time—but the castle held out, strongly garrisoned. This brought King Edward back to the Border in force.—

> 'Till wenge hym [2] on the Scottis men,
> That he cald ill and wykyd then.'

On his approach, in January 1356, the Scots evacuated the town. Edward Baliol, who accompanied that other Edward, now made abject and final surrender of his kingship, delivering his golden crown, with a sod of Scottish soil, to the King of England in exchange for a life-pension of £2000 a year. A cheap bargain for Edward III., had it carried all that it implied, for Baliol was well stricken in years ; but in truth Scotland, with that marvellous recuperative virtue which is the puzzle of historians, was never further from subjection than at this moment. King Edward carried his invasion as far as Edinburgh, the Scots falling back and sweeping away all victual before him. They could not prevent the enemy destroying many fair churches, including

[1] See p. 40, *ante.*
[2] To avenge himself.

the Abbey Church of Haddington—'Lamp of the Lothians,'— but flaming rafters fill no bellies, and the English host was in sore straits before it reached the Border again. Men called this season ' the Burnt Candlemas, ' because of the destruction wrought in this fruitless foray, whereof the remembrance did not serve to sweeten relations between the two countries.

Time and space—probably the reader's patience also—would run short in an attempt to follow all the incidents that chequered the history of Berwick after this—the raids and counter-raids that raged in Richard II's feeble reign. On 27th August 1377 the Scots were lucky enough to capture the governor, Sir Thomas Musgrave, and hold him to ransom for ten thousand marks. On 25th November following the castle itself was taken by a ruse of some enterprising fellows ' of the meaner sort, ' says Bower— ' robbers, ' says Walsingham. The names of six of these adventurers have been preserved : Thomas Hog was one, Jak de Fordun, Leighert, Gray, Artwood, and Hempsede the others. The Constable, Sir Robert Boynton, was slain in the affray, to avenge whom the Earl of Northumberland speedily came on the scene, retook the castle after eight days' siege, and put the whole party, forty-eight in number, to death, save one whose life was spared because he had betrayed the others.

Once more, in December 1384, the Scots got possession of Berwick and burnt the town. It was a time of truce, and the Scottish Warden, Douglas of Dalkeith, wrote to King Richard a long, windy justification of the proceeding, declaring that the English had been the first transgressors :—

' I understand,' said he, ' that giff your hee [high] Excellence war clerly enfourmete of the brennyng, slachter and
takyng of prisoners and Scottis schippis that is done be your
men to Scottysmen within the saide trewis [truce] in devers
places in Scotland before the brynnyng of Berwike, the
quhilk skathis [which injuries] our lege lorde the Kynge
and his liege has pacientlye tholyte [borne] in the kepyng of
the saide trewis, and chargit me til aske and ger be askyte
be my deputy redresse tharof, the quhilk my depute has
askyte at dayis of March, [1] and nane has gottyne, methink
o resoune yhe sulde erar [rather] put blame and punicioun
to the doarys of the saide trespas done agayn trewis in swilke
[such] maner, and callys thai rather brekare of the trew
than me, that has tholyte sa mykylle injur so lang and nane
amends gottyn.'

After burning the town the Scots got the castle
also, it is said by bribing the deputy-governor. But
they had no strength to hold it, and quietly surrendered it to the Warden, the Earl of Northumberland,
who, being like to be called on to pay with his head
for the loss of the fortress, paid a couple of thousand
marks in ransom to the captors.

During the Earl of Northumberland's rebellion
against Henry IV. in 1405, his son, Hotspur Percy,
being deputy-governor of Berwick, admitted the
Scots, who pillaged and burnt the town—every house
in it, says Holinshed, except those of the Friars.

After this, for half a century the battered old
borough seems to have enjoyed comparative immun-
ity from mischief. James II. espoused the Lancas-
trian cause, and helped Henry VI. by raiding the
lands of the Yorkists. When that cause was hopelessly wrecked at the battle of Towton (29th March

1 ' Days of March,' namely, the joint courts held by the Wardens of
the English and Scottish Marches for the redress of grievances.

1461), King Henry fled to Berwick. James II. had been killed at the siege of Roxburgh Castle in the preceding year, but the Queen-mother and young James III. received the royal fugitive so kindly that he made them a free gift of both town and castle, 'to have and holde for ever.'

Once more, then, the tressured lion of Scotland flaunted defiance across the Border from the grey keep, and from Carham to the sea the Tweed divided realm from realm.   So matters continued for twenty-one years, and might have endured for aye ; but just as the Wars of the Roses had weakened the English grasp on this coveted fortress, so it was torn from the Scots when they were demoralised by civil dissension.   Edward of York besieged it in 1481, but was repulsed and driven away.   Next year came the Duke of Gloucester with twenty-two thousand men, having with him the renegade Albany.   It has been shown elsewhere how James III. marched from Edinburgh to the relief of Berwick, and how Douglas 'belled the cat' at Lauder Bridge, paralysing the kingly power.[1]   The English made easy conquest of the town, but Lord Hailes held out stoutly in the castle, never doubting that relief was at hand.   But instead of relief came orders from Edinburgh that the place was to be handed over to King Edward, and so the Bounds of Berwick passed into English keeping : fortress and town were lost to Scotland for ever.

A Border fortress—little more ; for the foreign trade of this modern Alexandria had been scared away, never to return, and of local industries there never had been any except the salmon-fishings.   Of

[1] See p. 109, *ante.*

pageants the old town still had its share. Princess Margaret of England rode this way in passing to her marriage with James IV., King of Scots.—

The xxix day of the sayd monneth [July 1502] the sayd Quene departed from Alnewyk for to go to Barrwyk, and at haff of the way, viz. Belleford, she bayted. For Syr Thomas d'Arcy, Capittayne of the said Barrwyk, had maid rady her dynner at the said place very well and honnestly. . . . Betwyx Alnewyk and Barrwyk cam to the Quene Maister Rawf Wodrynton, having in hys company many gentylmen well apoynted ; his folks arayed in liveray, well horsed, to the nombre of an hundreth horsys.

' At the comyng ny to Barrwyk was shot ordonnounce the wiche was fayr for to here. And ny to the sayd place the Quene drest hyr. And ichon [each one] in fayr aray went the on after the other in fayr order. At the entrynge to the bryge was the said Capittayne well apoynted, and in hys company hys gentlemen and men of armes who receyved the Quene into the said place. At the tother end of the bryge, toward the gatt, was the Maister Marshall compayned of hys company, ichon bearing a staffe in his haund. After him was the college revested with the crosse, the wiche was gyffen hyr to kysse by the archbishop as before. At the gatt of the said towne was the maister porter, with the gard and soyars of the said place in a row well apoynted. Ichon of those had an hallebarde or other staffe in his haund as the others. And upon the said gatt war the mynstryalls of the sayd Capittayne pleynge of their instruments. In the midds of the said towne was the Maister Chamberlayn and the Mayre accompanyed of the bourges and habitaunts of the said place in fayre ordre and well apoynted.' [1]

The Princess stayed two days in the castle, witnessing bear-baiting and other diversions. On 1st August she set out once more, accompanied by

---

[1] Sykes's *Local Records*, quoted in Scott's *History of Berwick*, p. 106.

the Earl of Northumberland, and two thousand gentlemen and others riding three abreast, as far as Lamberton Kirk, where they handed her over to the Scottish commissioners.

A memorable occasion this, for it was in virtue of this marriage that James IV's great-grandson succeeded to the crown of England, and so, at last, the feud between the two nations came to be stanched. A hundred weary years of invasion and raiding were to run before that happy consummation came about; but although many a time the burgesses gathered on the walls to watch the smoke rolling over blazing villages in the Merse, they never again had their own houses burnt about their ears, which was a changed experience for dwellers in that city.

Sir William Bereton, writing in 1635, has recorded his impressions of the place.—

' A stately Bridge over the Tweed, consisting of 15 arches, was built by King James VI., as it is said cost £17,000. This river is infinitely stored with salmon, one or two hundred salmon at one draught. The Haven is a most narrow, shallow-barred haven—the worst I have ever seen. It is a poor town; many indigent persons and beggars therein.'

In 1639, soon after King Charles left Berwick, where he had signed the ' pacification, ' there befell a mysterious event which is gravely recorded in the official correspondence of the day. Sir James Douglas, writing to the Secretary of State, reports as follows :—

' On the 22nd August, not quite a month after the King left Berwick, there was a most violent tempest of wind. At Berwick Bridge, the end next England, there is put up a very strong gate ; at least, there are three, which are shut every night. The Sentinel walking over the Bridge about one o'clock in the night, there came towards him, as he reports, a black cat, which he did push at with his pike, yet could not slay it, but it went to the gate, which, at that instant, was blown up, the hasp breaking that received the bolt of the lock. At 3 o'clock the Governor of Berwick went, and finding it so, examined the soldier, who was in great amazement, and upon the 25th the poor man died with fear. Some report that the fort next Scotland was blown up that same night, but no such certainty for it.'[1]

The castle, which plays such a commanding part in the annals of Berwick, stood on the site now occupied by the North British railway station, between the river and the Mary Gate—that gate through which Johnnie Cope clattered in such haste to announce his own defeat at Prestonpans. It was no longer habitable when King Charles held his court in Berwick. Queen Elizabeth had ordered its demolition, and Lord Grey, the governor, used part of it as material for the new fortifications—that inner wall, still existing, which superseded the wider enceinte of Edward I. This was about 1560 : four years later, Francis Russell, Earl of Bedford, being governor, orders were given that the castle and the Bell Tower should be razed ; but these orders were not carried into effect. The castle, though much defaced, continued to hold a garrison till the year 1603, when it was granted by the Crown to the Earl of Dunbar. He began to reconstruct it as 'a stately, sumptuous, and well-slated house' but did not live to see the work finished. The next owner was the Earl of Suffolk, who sold it in 1641

---

[1] *State Papers*, Charles I., 22nd August 1639.

to the corporation as a quarry for their new church, in which divine service was to be conducted by Mr. Harrison, preacher and lecturer, in consideration of a house and meadow, estimated together at the value of £10 a year, and a salary of £14. The vicar, Mr. Hunt, was an absentee High Churchman, but, it is presumed, drew his salary of £6 from the Guild in addition to £5, 10s. from the Crown.

When the corporation had taken all the material they wanted from the castle, they sold it to Alderman Jackson for £100. About 1770 it became the property of the Askews of Pallinsburn, and so remained till the North British Railway Company bought it in 1843, and blew it up to make room for the present station buildings. There remain now only the foundations of a few towers and part of the western curtain—the White Wall—stretching down to the river. But the Bell Tower still stands firm, and near it are two masses of masonry, representing bastions in the fourteenth-century work of Edward I. Mr. John Scott states that the platform of the railway station is believed to occupy the area of the Great Hall, where King Edward declared his award in favour of John Baliol.

Few contrasts between past and present could be more complete than that presented by the two bridges of Berwick. The bridge begun in the reign of James VI. and I. consists of fifteen arches, is 1164 feet long, and only 17 feet wide between the parapets. It was reckoned a masterpiece of seventeenth-century engineering, and it took three hundred workmen four-and-twenty years to finish it, at a cost of £17,000. The Royal Border Bridge, which carries the railway on twenty-eight arches at a height of 120 feet above the river, is 2000 feet long, employed two thousand workmen for three years in building, and cost £253,000.

Time has dealt harshly in some respects with Berwick-on-Tweed; her churches and religious houses have all vanished or given place to edifices which afford small solace to the eye or interest to the antiquary; she has sunk from her proud eminence as the chief emporium of Scotland to inferior rank among the fishing-stations of England. Yet neither the destructive passions nor the constructive energy of many generations has destroyed the noble landscape, of which you may catch a fleeting glance from the window of a twentieth-century dining-car. There is none of that grime amid which millions of our fellow-countrymen are doomed to grope for a living. River, sea, and sky are as free and pure as they were when Malcolm the son of Kenneth wrenched this fair territory from the grasp of Eadulf Ciudel by the battle of Carham. Cold must be his spirit, slow his imagination, for whom this scene brings no message from the long past. Even the Reform Act of 1885, though it robbed the old borough of its two members of Parliament and swamped it in the Berwick-on-Tweed division of Northumberland with only one member, could not strip it of its historic dignity. This received official recognition of a peculiar kind until quite recent years, by the specific mention 'of our town of Berwick-on-Tweed' in all royal proclamations. Its burgesses claimed civic independence of both the adjacent kingdoms; and if any curious traveller asked explanation of such an anomaly, he was told that it arose during the Temptation on the Mount

334 THE STORY OF THE TWEED

in the following manner. The Evil One, when he showed the Saviour all the kingdoms of the world and the glory of them, kept his thumb upon Berwick-on-Tweed, so greatly did he covet it for his own possession as the most desirable spot on earth !

CHAPTER XIII

TWEEDSIDE ANGLING

ANY reader who is in sympathy with the gentle craft of angling must be wondering by this time how one to whom that mystery remains the only mundane illusion still unshattered has managed to conduct this sinuous narrative thus far, and yet has had no word to say about the fishing. Well, the temptation has been almost irresistible, so crowded are the memories of happy days, never to return, spent upon these streams and 'dubs;' but to yield to it would have been to risk the due proportion of this sketch. It was of set purpose that the subject was avoided until there remained but a single chapter for its admission, and the Procrustean office of the publisher might be trusted as a check alike upon the garrulity of age and the volubility of a salmon fisher. A salmon fisher and no more; for although I have passed shining hours in beguiling, or attempting to beguile, the speckled residents in Tweed and its tributaries, the time so spent has been as one of the smallest of those tributaries to Tweed herself, in proportion to that devoted to pursuit of the migratory tribes. Wherefore, if I have aught to say about trout in these waters, it must be mainly hearsay.

We have heard with our ears, and our fathers have told us, of the prodigious baskets they used to obtain of yore, the like of which may never be had now. We may be tempted to exclaim with a character in one of Dean Ramsay's yarns—'There's surely mair leears in Peebles nor me, minister!' Tom Todd Stoddart, for instance, mentions incidentally having killed with fly in a single day forty-two pounds weight of trout in Meggat Water; and again he records how he and 'Christopher North,' fishing together one day in Jed Water, landed thirty-six dozen—four hundred and thirty-two—pink-fleshed trout. There is not the slightest reason to doubt the truth of these wonderful stories. In those days it was a mere question of moderate skill and industry how many trout one chose to take.

Probably at this day there are as many trout landed each year in the valley of the Tweed as ever there were; but while the area of angling water and spawning-ground has been grievously diminished by the pollution poured in from the mills of Galashiels and Hawick, it is probably no exaggeration to estimate the increase in the number of anglers during the last fifty years at one thousand per cent. It sounds pretty fabulous put in that way; nevertheless, it only means that ten persons cast angle in Tweed nowadays for every one who went forth in the time of our grandsires. See the railway platforms in Edinburgh early on Saturday mornings in spring and summer, and say whether I have exaggerated matters. Not one of these eager fellows with rods and baskets and waders could have spent their week-end on Tweedside before the establishment of cheap railway fares. And there is room and sport for all of them if everybody would play fair. In the whole of the British Isles there is no watershed, unless it

be that of the Shannon, which produces river trout
equal in number, size, and quality to those of
Tweeddale and Teviotdale. The Tay surpasses—
the Spey approaches—the Tweed in drainage area ;
there are good trout in both these rivers, but the
angling in the best of their tributaries is insignificant
compared with that in Biggar Water and the Lyne,
Jed Water and the Kale, Whitadder and the Eden
—to name but half a dozen out of a list that can
scarcely be reckoned for multitude.

Fifty years ago none but a few enthusiasts like
Stoddart, and local pot-hunters, ever gave a thought
to Scottish river trout. In England it was otherwise to some extent. (I am endeavouring to beat
the record by writing a chapter upon fishing without
once citing the authority or even quoting the name
of Iz-k W-lt-n.) It was early in the eighteen
hundreds that Colonel Hawker celebrated the charms
of the Hampshire Test, and before the century had
half run out a few people had thought it worth
while to pay moderate rents for the privilege of
trout-fishing in the southern counties. But in
Scotland the idea of spending money on the preservation of trout, or on the hire of waters to catch
them in, is one of the latest outcomes of civilisation.
Use and wont sanctioned the capture of these fish
by all persons and by any means at all seasons ; any
endeavour to improve private fisheries was resented
as an infringement of public rights ; a good deal of
irritation was roused and a demand for free fishing
was set up.

Still there remained a great deal of free trout-
fishing in Tweed and its affluents ; but the rapid
increase of anglers, combined with and partly caused

22

by the development of travelling facilities, threatened
to prove as fatal to sport in general as a system of
free strawberry-beds would be to the housewife's
prospect of jam-making. Remote glens, once solitary and unfished except at long intervals by some
adventurous tourist or inexpert shepherd lad, were
depleted season after season by holiday-makers from
the towns,—ay, and by foul fishers, too, whom the
railways enabled to send their booty to a profitable
market. These upper streams had been, from immemorial time, the prolific nurseries of the main
rivers. Had every trout been netted out of Tweed
and Teviot one year, the next season had seen these
rivers well stocked again from their natural semina-
ries. Moreover, there were always unscrupulous
individuals who slaughtered trout without ruth at a
season when all useful or harmless animals should
be respected. Many a day in November have I seen
great trout dragged out of Tweed on a line baited
with worms, with the ripe spawn running out of
them. Relief came from the very source which
had seemed to threaten the welfare of the fishery—
from the multiplication of fishers. So long as the
proposal for a statutory close time for trout was
believed to come only from the land-owning class,
successive Governments treated it with indifference;
but when the angling clubs of Tweedside and
Clydesdale, numbering many hundreds of members,
beheld their efforts to restock and protect their
waters rendered futile by the destruction of spawning
fish, they brought such effective pressure to bear
upon their representatives in Parliament that, no
longer ago than 1902, an Act was passed prohibiting
the netting of trout at any season, and the taking of

them by any means between 15th October and
1st March. Now, therefore, one may expect that
the natural fecundity of these waters will restore to
some extent the primæval abundance of these lovely
fish.

Seeing, also, that in the purity and productiveness
of this great water system, not the privileged few
only, but the hard-working myriads in the hives of
industry, possess a direct interest, surely it is not
too much to hope that measures will be taken, if not
to remedy the pollution from mills, at all events to
take stringent measures to prevent it getting any
worse. Commercial and industrial interests are vital
to national prosperity, but the whole nation is
concerned in preserving its fairest scenes—its most
accessible playgrounds. In all nature there is no
more mournful spectacle than a polluted river : the
type of purity becomes the very emblem of defile-
ment : the cradle of innumerable forms of life is
turned into the image of the most loathsome form
of death : the focus of all loveliness in landscape is
made the shame and reproach of the whole valley.
Legitimate haste to grow rich on the part of a few,
culpable indifference on the part of the many, have
permitted the worst of ruin to overspread some of
the fairest scenes in northern England and southern
Scotland. It will be a lasting reproach to the nation
if the mischief be allowed to increase.

It may be affirmed generally that every tributary
of the Tweed, even those upland channels which
score the sides of Ettrick and Eskdalemuir in winter,
dwindling in summer to insignificant rills, are naturally capable of yielding excellent sport to the fly-
fisher. Many of them flow from sequestered lakes

or tarns abounding in trout, which waters, being remote from the ways of men, still retain much of their
pristine promise. The enterprising angler will hunt
out these choice retreats for himself. It may often
be his fortune, as it has been the present writer's,
when making his way to some important stream or
sheet of water of wide renown, to light upon some
secret linn among the rocks of an unsung rivulet, or
some reed-bound pool of trifling extent in the
heather, which others have passed by untried, wherein
great and unexpected reward awaits the explorer.

If he take Tom Tod Stoddart as his guide, sure he
cannot find a trustier one through Tweeddale and
Teviotdale as they were seventy years ago ; but time
has wrought its work upon these waters ; they are
not what they were, and each one must seek his profit
where he may find it. Yet never shall Tom Stoddart fall out of favour. He wrote with such a relish
of his subject, such a passion for the sport, such a
grateful sense of the glory of moorland air, flowing
water, and free winds, that, although he never wastes
his own time or his reader's patience in the laboured
craft of 'word-painting,' no man ever made his
pages more fragrant of the fresh air. To open his
Angler's Companion at any chapter is like throwing
wide a window. You feel the breeze on your cheek
—you hear the wings of summer flies—the sun glints
on the ripple—the flying clouds cast grateful shade
—for here is a man telling you unaffectedly of what
he knew and loved, without a thought about grace
of phrase or pretty writing.

Tom had his flights too. Like so many of the
children of Tweedside, he was always breaking into
song. The son of a retired navy captain, he was

destined by his father for the bar, and in 1825 began
to attend classes at Edinburgh University in preparation for that sober vocation. Fate ruled that his
chief instructor should be one with inclinations far
outside the lecture-room and Parliament House.
Professor John Wilson—the tempestuous Christopher North of the *Noctes*—was perhaps the last preceptor one would have chosen to wean a lad from the
waterside and wed him to the courts. He took him
to his own house, where Tom found himself in
company greatly to his fancy, but, as it turned out,
fatal to his professional future. Aytoun, Terrier and
Gordon, De Quincey, Hartley Coleridge and the
Ettrick Shepherd, 'Delta' and Henry Glassford Bell
—what wonder if this student conceived among them
a taste for lore far different from Balfour's *Practiques*
and Dalrymple's *Decisions* !

In 1826 he visited Yarrow, the cradle of his race,
and two years later found himself in Tibbie Shiels's
'howff' on St. Mary's Loch in the company of
Professor Wilson, Aytoun, and the Ettrick Shepherd.
From that moment it was all over with Tom. Wig
and gown faded from his horizon. Rods, reels,
and rings of rising trout became all his care by day,
and the fashion of a gross age must be reckoned
responsible for much that had better not have gone
on at night. 'There was mony a ane,' Tibbie Shiels
used to say in going over old times,—'There was
mony a ane cam here, gentle and simple, but I aye
likit the Cock o' the North best—that was Professor
Wilson, ye ken. I likit him and Mr. Tom Stoddart
and Hogg. Eh ! but they were the callants for
drinkin' ! Mony's the time, when they were at it,
I've fried a bit o' ham, and took it to them and said

—"Ye'll just tak this bit ham, gentlemen ; maybe it 'll sober ye. " And they wad eat it, and just on to the drinkin' again.' And so it came to pass in after-years, when Sheriff Glassford Bell came across Stoddart again, and asked him what he was doing now : ' Doing ?' cried Tom, ' man, I'm an angler !'

He was something more than that ; he was a poetaster. Stoddart was not twenty-one when Henry Constable published for him *The Deathwake, or Lunacy ; a Necromaunt in three Chimeras*. The title of the dish will deter most people from tasting it ; but Mr. Andrew Lang has done so, and though he declines to pronounce the piece a pearl of great price, he declares that ' it does contain passages of poetry—of poetry very curious, because it is full of the new note—the new melody which young Mr. Tennyson was beginning to waken. It anticipates Beddoes ; it coincides with Gautier and *Les Chimères* of Gérard ; it answers the accents, then unheard in England, of Poe.' One virtue *The Deathwake* possesses of which no critic shall prevail to rob it : it is incalculably scarce. It fell flat upon the public, and nearly the whole edition was returned to the poet in sheets and stowed away in a garret. For forty years to come it served the cook for kindling, and so the whole edition ebbed slowly away. The bibliophile's chance—a slender one—is to come across a stray presentation copy.

In literature Tom was to do something better than *The Deathwake* ; but in law he was hopeless. Admitted to the Faculty of Advocates in 1833, he never passed beyond the threshold ; at least he never held a brief. He managed to make his narrow—very narrow—allowance support him in wandering over the length and breadth of Scotland, casting angle, as one might do in those early days, almost wherever he listed, and collecting materials for his *Art of Angling* and *Angler's Companion*, two treatises which, while they brought him a little useful cash, also tended to curtail the freedom which had given them birth. Not only did they tempt to the riverside many competitors with Tom, but they also opened the eyes of fishery owners to the sporting capabilities of their waters. The time had not arrived, indeed, when leave to fish was to be hard to obtain by wandering strangers ; but the time had gone by when Tom might fish where he pleased without asking anybody's leave. And in a great measure he had himself to thank for it.

The rod and the pen—those were Tom's weapons, and I will rest his claim to rank among the sweet singers on Tweedside upon one song alone—*The Taking of the Salmon.*

'A birr ! a whirr ! a salmon's on,
  A goodly fish, a thumper !
Bring up, bring up the ready gaff,
And if we land him we shall quaff
  Another glorious bumper.
Hark ! 'tis the music of the reel—
  The strong, the quick, the steady ;
The line darts from the active wheel,
  Have all things tight and ready.

A birr ! a whirr ! the salmon's out,
  Far on the rushing river ;
Onward he holds with sullen leap,
Or plunges through the whirlpool deep,
  A desperate endeavour.

Hark to the music of the reel !
    The fitful and the grating ;
It pants along the breathless wheel,
    Now hurried, now abating.

A birr ! a whirr ! the salmon's off !—
    No, no ; we still have got him ;
The wily fish is sullen grown,
And, like a bright, imbedded stone,
    Lies gleaming at the bottom.
Hark to the music of the reel !
    'Tis hushed—it hath forsaken ;
With care we'll guard the magic wheel
    Until its notes awaken.

A birr ! a whirr ! the salmon's up,
    Give line—give line and measure ;
But now he turns—keep down ahead,
And lead him as a child is led,
    And land him at your leisure.
Hark to the music of the reel !
    'Tis welcome, it is glorious ;
It wanders through the winding wheel,
    Returning and victorious.

A birr ! a whirr ! the salmon's in,
    Upon the bank extended ;
The princely fish is gasping slow,
His brilliant colours come and go
    All beautifully blended.
Hark to the music of the reel !
    It murmurs and it closes ;
Silence is on the conquering wheel,
    Its wearied line reposes.

No birr ! no whirr ! the salmon's ours,
    The noble fish—the thumper !

Strike through his gill the ready gaff,
And bending homewards, we shall quaff
Another glorious bumper.
Hark to the music of the reel !
We listen with devotion ;
There's something in that circling wheel
That wakes the heart's emotion.' [1]

'Man, I'm an angler !'—the summing up, it may seem to the worldly-wise, of a wasted life, yet a life whereof the memory still enriches the lovely scenes in which it was led, and of how few lives can as much be said. Untouched by professional ambition, Stoddart earned all the reward he sought in a tight line ; careless of lucre, he won renown as a fisher, the only kind of fame he prized. 'Contented wi' little and canty wi' mair,' it is surely no matter for reproach that he shunned the breathless struggle for wealth which counts with some as the first duty of man. The bar—the bench—may have missed an ornament in Tom, but the world won an original, which is a far rarer creature than a great lawyer.

Tom wanted but one year of threescore and ten when, in June 1879, he was fishing alone in the Teviot, and fell into the swirling Turn Pool, some miles above Kelso. He clambered out with some difficulty ; cramp and chill followed, and it became plain, even to himself, that his rambles were nearly numbered. Yet, frail and broken as he was, it was his lot to feel once more the thrill of hooking a salmon. In September of the same year kindly Mr. Forrest, before whose counter innumerable anglers have been tempted and fallen, got the white-

[1] These verses are printed by kind permission of Messrs. W. Blackwood and Sons.

bearded veteran down to Kelso cauld, where he killed a fish—the last in his long record. He lingered among the flowers in his little garden at Kelso till November 1880, passed quietly away, and was laid in a corner of the cemetery chosen by himself, 'where I can hear the Tweed.'

Well, as aforesaid, there is no better guide to the trouting waters of this valley than Tom Tod Stoddart. They retain their *relative* productiveness, but much fishing has made the trout wary and reduced the average weight. Colonel Thornton, who made his celebrated sporting tour in the north in 1786, would not find his quarry so facile and numerous as in those primitive times. He notes in his journal that he stopped his chaise to fish the Teviot at Mindrum Mill before entering Scotland. But Mindrum is on the Bowmont, not the Teviot, and it was in that dainty stream that he took thirty-nine trout in an hour or two's fishing.

'When fishing the last stream, I hooked a fish which I thought of great magnitude, and took considerable pains to kill him ; but he proved less than I imagined : about three pounds and a half, but in the highest condition, thick to the very fork, and yellow as saffron, as all these trout are.'

Leaving the description of the trout waters to better instructed guides than myself, turn we to consider Tweed as a salmon river. In that respect it has suffered more sorely than any other in the United Kingdom from political reasons. For centuries it was the fiercely contested frontier between two realms ; all the damage that could be done to the fisheries by one nation was hailed as so much detriment to the other. And so it came to pass that Tweed and her tributaries, like Solway on the west, was left outside the general fishery laws of both kingdoms ; each of these frontier watersheds remains to this day under its separate and peculiar Act, and Tweed salmon are exposed to capture for a far longer period in each year than is permitted in other rivers. It took a long time to impair the splendid productiveness of this fine river, but that has been accomplished at last. The modern improvement of netting, the sedulous removal from the channel of every obstacle to the free sweep of the seine, combined with the long stretch of river above the tide which is surrendered to netting, practically have put an end to spring and summer angling, except in the lower reaches. It is hardly worth any man's while to cast a line in the waters above Floors until the nets are removed in September. The proprietors from Innerleithen upwards, chief guardians of the best spawning-grounds, have been robbed of all chance of fair sport until a season when fish are in a condition in which no fair sportsman would care to take them. It is no longer their interest to check poaching, and it is notorious that they have ceased to make any attempt to do so. Hence the early running fish, which naturally run to the upper waters and perpetuate the spring and summer race, are nearly all destroyed by ' black fishers,' and Tweed has become to all intents and purposes an autumn angling stream.

The rod-fishing remains open until 30th November, a full month too late, as all honest anglers would agree, were it not for a peculiarity which distinguishes Tweed salmon from those of every other river in the United Kingdom. Salmon of both sexes as the spawning season draws near usually become discoloured and unsightly, the skin of the females becoming dark and tarnished, that of the males rusty red. But in the Tweed it is otherwise. Gravid fish ascend from the sea in October and November with all the summer lustre on their sides ; anglers are deceived into the flattering belief that they are taking seasonable fish. *Nimium ne crede colori !* These fish are just as far gone—with flesh just as much deteriorated—as the sooty and foxy-hued spawners in other rivers. But what will you have ? The riparian owners having been robbed of their share of spring and summer fish by the nets, it is but natural that they should claim an extra privilege so as to recoup themselves from the autumn run. To curtail their existing rights without corresponding restriction of the netting would be manifestly unfair. There seem to be only two ways of restoring the balance : namely, first and best, to buy up the netting rights above Thomas's Island, which would ensure the admission to the upper waters of such fish as run in during the weekly close time ; and secondly, to modify the weekly close time so as to permit the escape of a proportion of each run of fish. Then, and not before then, it would be fair to curtail the open season for rods by at least a fortnight.

It remains true at the present time, as Stoddart wrote seventy years ago, that, except in unusually wet seasons, the salmon-fishing above Ashiestiel is hardly worth attention. Plenty of fish are taken above that point, but, as he truly said, they are 'in execrable condition.' But from Ashiestiel downwards every reach of the river has its store of sporting chronicle—recalls the presence of some bygone worthy. Take Caddonfoot, for instance.

William Scrope had an ear for Scottish idiom and accent such as is given to few Southrons. An Englishman may tell a Scottish story well enough, yet hardly shall he deceive a north countryman as to his nationality. He may escape detection for a time ; but suddenly the false turn of a phrase, or the misplacement of stress, bewrays him, and he stands revealed. But the following extract from his *Days and Nights of Salmon fishing* is almost faultless, given, as Scrope says, 'as nearly as possible in the words' of the narrator, the famous Tom Purdie.—

'I had risen a sawmon three successive days at the throat of Caddon water-fut, and on the fourth day I was determined to bring him to book ; and, when he rose as usual, I went up to Caddon Wa's, namely, the pool opposite the ruins of Caddon Lee, where there had been a terrace garden facing south ; and, on returning I tried my old friend, when he rose again without touching the heuck ; but I got a glimpse o' him, and saw he was a sawmon o' the biggest sort. I then went down the river to a lower pool, and in half an hour came up again and changed my heuck. I began to suspect that, having raised the fish so often, I had become too anxious, and given him too little law, or jerked the heuck away before he had closed his mouth upon it. And as I had a heavy rod and good line, and the castin' line, which I had gotten frae the Sherra,[1] had three fadom o' pleit gut at the end of it, and the flee was buskit on a three plies of sawmon gut, sae I was na feared for my tackle.

'I had putten a cockle-stane at the side o' the water fornent the place where he raise ; forbye, I kent fu' weel where he was lyin' ; it was at the side o' a muckle blue clint that made a clour in the rough throat, e'en when the Queed was in a brown flood, as she had been for twa days afore. Aweel, I thought I wad try a plan o' auld Juniperbank's

[1] The Sheriff—Sir Walter Scott.

when he had raised a sawmon mair nor ance. I keepit my e'en hard closed when the heuck was comin' owre the place. Peace be here ! I fand as gif I had catched the branch o' an aik tree swingin' and sabbin in a storm o' wind. Ye needna doot I opened my eyne ! An' what think ye was the sawmon aboot ?—turnin' and rowin' [rolling] doon the tap o' the water owre him and owre him, as ye hae seen a hempie o' a callant row doun a green brae-side, at great speed, makin' a fearfu' jumblin' and splashin', and shakin' the tap o' the wand at sic a rate, that, deil hae me, but I thocht he wad hae shaken my airms aff at the shouther joints, tho' I said to mysel' they were gey firm putten on. I never saw a fish do the like, but ane in the Auld Brig pool in the Darnwick water. I jalouse [suspect] they want to unspin the line ; for a fish has far mair cunnin' and wiles aboot him than mony ane wad think. At ony rate, it was a fashious plan this yen fell on ; for or he wan to the fut o' the pool, I was tired o' him and his wark, and sae was he, I'se warrant ye. For when he fand the water turnin' shallow, he wheeled aboot, and I ran up the pool as fast as I could follow him, gien' him a' the line I could at the same time ; and when it was just about a' aff the pirn [reel], and he was comin' into the throat, he wheeled again in a jiffy, and cam straight for my feet as if he had been shot out o' a cannon ! I thocht it was a' owre between us, for I fand naething at the wand as the line was soomin' i' the pool a' the way doon. I was deid sure I had lost him after a' my quirks ; for whan they cast a cantrip o' that kind, it's done to slacken the line to let them draw the heuck out o' their mouths wi' their teethy toung—an' they are amaist sure to do sae. But he was owre weel heuckit, this ane, to wark his purpose in that gyse, as ye sall hear ; for when, by dint o' runnin' back thrae the water as fast's I could and windin' up the line, I had brought a bow on the tap o' the rod, I fand the fish had reistit in the deepest part o' the pool, trying a' that teeth and toung could do to get haud o' the heuck ; and there did he lie for nearly an hour, for I had plenty o' time to look at my watch, and now and then to tak mony a snuff too. But I was certain by this time he was fast heuckit, and I raised him again by cloddin' stanes afore him, as near as I durst for hittin' the line. But when I got him up at last, there was mickle mair to do than I thocht of ; for he ran up the pool and doun the pool I dar' say fifty times, till my feet were sair wi' gangin' sae lang in the channel. Then he gaed owre the stream a'thegither. I was glad to let him change his gait ony way ; and he gaed doun to Glenbenna, that was in Whitebank's water, and I wrocht him lang thair. To mak a lang tale short,' [short ! quotha, honest Tom !] ' before I could get at him wi' the gaff, I was baith hungry and tyrt ; an' after a', he was firm heuckit, in the teuchest part o' the body, at the outside o' the edge o' the wick bane. He was a clean sawmon, an' three an' an twenty meal punds.'

Windy as it is, I have let Tom Purdie tell his story in his own way—the graphic, simple narrative that endeared him so much to his master, the great story-teller. It is the best way to bring before readers a figure, without whom Tweedside would be shorn of one of its most honoured memories. ' I have lost, ' wrote Sir Walter Scott to Cadell, 4th November 1829, ' my old and faithful servant—my factotum—and am so much shocked that I really wish to be quit of the country and safe in town. ' Tom lies close to the wall of Melrose Abbey, of which the burial-ground holds no worthier dust.

Dearly do the fishings of Tweed pay for that woollen industry which has appropriated the name of the river as the designation of its special fabric. Gala Water, especially, discharges an evil-smelling, highly coloured contribution which effectually closes that stream against the ascent of spawning fish, and, when the main river is low, spreads an ugly scum upon its surface and a filthy slime upon its bottom. Nevertheless the Pavilion Water, extending from Gala Water foot to Melrose, contains many excellent casts, and retains much of its well deserved reputation. The Drygrange fishings extend from about Melrose Bridge to Leader Foot ; below that point many an angler has had to chew the bitter cud of hope deferred ; for the Leader Water is easily discoloured in times of flood by the wash from cliffs of red earth and friable sandstone, rendering the main river thick and unfishable for miles below the junction. Gladswood and Old Melrose have pretty reaches of salmon water annexed to them, and then comes bonny Bemersyde, perhaps the best, as it is the most varied, of all the fishings in these parts, or, indeed, in the whole length of Tweed above Makerstoun.

The uppermost cast in Bemersyde Water is from the left bank of the tail of Cromwell, where great numbers of salmon congregate at times. Then comes the Gateheugh ; a wilder piece of fishing-water there is not in the whole river, and one that has to be fished in a peculiar way. The river is very wide and swift here; the salmon lie in little pots and catches in a vast waste of boulders. The boatman, wading to his armpits, picks his way down the very centre of the torrent by secret shallows known only to the expert, holding the boat from which the angler casts his flies right or left according to the position of the various casts. It is a truly sporting bit of water, and the pleasure of fishing it is greatly enhanced by the magnificent cliffs and hanging woods on the left side. The right bank along Cromwell and Gateheugh belongs to Old Melrose.

Below the Gateheugh comes the Haly Weil, or Holy Pool, so called from its former owners, the monks of Melrose. Many and many a famous fishing has been done here ; but perhaps the greatest salmon ever hooked in Tweed came to an ignoble end in this part of the water. Colonel Haig of Bemersyde, fishing here late one evening a few years ago, found himself fast in something heavy at the Cradle Rock. The fish did not show, but, swimming deep and sullen, pushed slowly downstream with resistless force. Down, ever down, past the Woodside and Jock Sure, over the Monk's Ford, and into the Tod Holes in Dryburgh Water full half a mile below where it was hooked. Here the Colonel at last got a pull upon his fish, which he reckoned to be one of moderate size foul-hooked. It was getting dark, and he, rather impatient to be off home, sent his attendant in with the net to finish the performance. Finish it he did, but not in a happy way. The lad had one try at the exhausted fish as it lay glimmering in the gloaming, and cried to his master, ' He's that big I canna get him into the net. ' ' Oh, nonsense ! ' cried the Colonel, ' put it under him ; get his head in ! I can't wait here all night. ' Another effort : the rim of the net struck the line, severing the single gut cast, and the great fish wallowed away across the smooth tail of the pool. The Colonel did not realise the magnitude of his disaster until two or three weeks later, when he happened to be waiting for a train at St. Boswells station. The porter came to him and said :—

' Hae ye ony mind, Colonel, o' yon big fush ye slippit in the Tod Holes yon nicht ? '

' Oh, I mind him well, ' replied the Colonel ; ' a

23

good lump of a fish he was, I believe, but I never saw him rightly.'

'Ay,' said the other dryly, 'yon wad be the biggest sawmon that ever cam oot o' the water o' Tweed, I'm thinking.'

'Why, what do you know about him ?' asked the Colonel.

'Oh, I ken fine aboot the ae half o' him, onyway,' replied the porter. 'Ye see, there was twa lads clappit amang the trees below the Wallace statue forenenst ye, waiting till it was dark to set a cairn net, ye ken. Weel, didna they see ye coming doun the water taigled wi' a fish ? and when ye cam to the Tod Holes they saw ye loss him, and they got a visee o' the water he made coming into the east bank, ye ken. There's a wee bit cairn there, ye ken, wi' a piece lound water ahint it, where they jaloused the fish wad rest himsel' a wee. Weel, they waited till it was mirk night, and then they jist whuppit the net round him, and they sune had him oot. He was that big he wadna gang into the bag they had wi' them ; so they cuttit him in twa halves ; and the tae half they brocht to the station here to gang by rail to Embro '. Weel, if the tither half was as big, yon fish bud to be seeventy pund weight ; for the half o' him I weighed mysel', and it was better nor thirty-five pund. Ay, a gran' kipper ! '

It is a thing not easy to explain why the salmon flies habitually used in Bemersyde Water should be so much smaller than those in favour upon other parts of the river, but so it is. Tweed boatmen are terrible tyrants ; it would take a bolder man than the present writer to act against their prescription, and I have seldom ventured to display at Bemersyde so large a lure as the condition and depth of the water seemed to justify. Once, indeed, when the river was very heavy, after fishing the Haly Weil blank with the usual small flies, I had the temerity to put on a great Highland 'eagle', and immediately hooked and landed a salmon. Never shall I forget the tone of profound disdain with which the boatman observed—'Ay, that would be a fine bait for a pike!'

No man knew that water better than the said boatman, Moodie by name. A fine, handsome, tall, black-bearded fellow he was—is still, I hope ; and a notable exploit he performed one evening in this water about twenty years ago. He was alone, fishing the uncertain cast called Jock Sure, when he hooked a mighty fish. He had to play it dead and tail it out, for the use of the gaff is prohibited in the Tweed after the close of the net season. No mean feat this, for the fish weighed forty-two pounds ; nor is it a mere legend, for the fish is there, stuffed, to testify to Moodie's prowess. Unlike Tom Purdie, Moodie was laconic, and the incidents of the struggle had to be 'howked oot' of him.

Dryburgh Water, upper and lower, comes next below Bemersyde, and there are some picturesque casts in the loops and reaches of the river round the old abbey. The salmon, however, do not seem to rest here so comfortably as in Bemersyde above and in Lord Polwarth's Mertoun Water below. The latter, indeed, is a most delightful stretch of varied pool and stream, containing the rocky 'foss' at Craigover, and the long rippling reach called Willow-bush, where a fifty-pounder was landed to the fly a few years ago, and where, in the autumn of 1903, I had the luck to take twelve fish weighing a hundred

and ninety-five pounds between eleven A.M. and five
P.M.   The average weight was diminished by the
intrusion of a four pound grilse among eleven salmon.

Many a one who has cast angle in this delightful
stretch of water the last thirty years carries with him
kindly reminiscence of the head fisherman, Goodfellow.   Even in the old days, before family names
were fixed, when men were designated according to
their mental or physical qualities, no better appella-
tive could have been devised for this admirable
specimen of his class than the surname bequeathed to
him by his sires.   He is a tyrant, as all Tweed boatmen are, but a benignant one ; his rule is an example
of that wise and good despotism which all men in
their hearts admit to be the only perfect form of
government.   A despot, yet a democrat.   A large and
varied assortment of the titled aristocracy must have
passed through Goodfellow's hands—anglers of every
degree of incompetency and efficiency ; yet he classes
them all alike, never addressing any one by a loftier
title than ' mister ', and assuming, apparently, that
each one is but an apprentice at the craft.   A fish
rises and misses the fly.   ' Dod, mister, but you were
ower quick wi' that ane !   You pulled it clean awa'
from him. '

You cast over a likely bit of water and nothing
moves.

' The fly's too high in the water,' says Goodfellow
reproachfully.   ' Let it doon aboot his heels, mister.
Sink it weel to him ! '

You venture to produce a favourite fly, strange to
Tweed, but with which you have wrought mighty
deeds elsewhere.

' Ay, pit that ane on.   Pit it on and send every

fish in the water scoorin' back to Berwick!' where-upon he will produce some tattered eidolon from the recesses of a dingy pocket-book, and you must be of more than common fortitude if your lustrous confect-ion of silk and tinsel is not replaced in your box with a sigh.

Mertoun Water ends at Littledean Tower, where the Rutherford fishing begins, highly prized by those who know it, of whom I am not one. Next below Rutherford lies classic Makerstoun, to which most anglers will give the palm for beauty and variety over all the fishings in the river. The very names of the different casts revive a host of association, though there be none now living who remember Robert Kerss—Rob o' the Trows—a very prince among Tweed boatmen. The casts in order from the top are Willie's Bank, Hirple Nelly, the Orchard-heads, the Dark Shore, the Clippers, the Laird's Cast, Elshie Stream, the Shot, the Red Stane, the Side Straik, the Doors, the Nethern Heads, Willie's Owerfa', and Killmouth. Between the Red Stane and Killmouth is the only really dangerous water in the whole of the Tweed—dangerous, that is, in regard to the natural advantage it gives to the fish over the fisher. It is one of the few places in this river where one may look for adventure.

The Duke of Roxburghe's fishings begin below Killmouth, and extend, on the right bank at least, as far as Carham Burn, fully nine miles. The Floors Water proper, commanding both banks, reaches to Maxwheel, below Kelso Bridge, and includes the famous casts of the Slates, the Black Stane, Weetles, Huddles, the Shot, Hedge-end, Shirt Stream, the Skelly, the Coach Wynd, Income, Cobby Hole, the

Putt, the Back Bullers (just above the junction with Teviot), and Maxwheel.

Below the junction of the rivers the character of the angling alters, and in the Sprouston Water we encounter the first 'dub.'—a long, still stretch where the river is held back by a 'cauld' or weir. The mode of fishing such water is peculiar to the Tweed. A breeze to ruffle the surface is essential. Starting at the foot of the dub, the boat is paddled very slowly upstream, the fly being cast across the water and allowed to creep round astern, a fresh cast being made after the line lies straight downstream. It is dull work indeed when fish are not moving ; but given a brisk curl on the water, the number and weight of salmon that come to the fly compensate one for the monotony of the toil. It is just the thing for elderly sportsmen who can no longer stand the test of wading and tramping necessary on a Highland river ; but even so, the playing and landing of heavy fish is no light labour. The bones of many a younger man might ache after such a performance as that of the late Hon. and Rev. Robert Liddell, who in the year 1887, being then within a few months of fourscore, and in the last year of his life, killed eighteen fish, including two of over thirty pounds weight, in Birgham Dub, in a single autumn day. I have the assurance of his boatman that the rod never left Mr. Liddell's hand except on two or three occasions when, having landed to kill a salmon, the fish ran faster than the veteran could follow, and he surrendered the rod to his assistant, resuming it again immediately he could overtake him.

This, as aforesaid, was in Birgham Water, where, besides the Dub, there are some famous streams which yield sport when there is no breeze upon the still water, especially the Cradles, the Wheel, Flummie, and the Kirkend, where the fishing merges in that of Carham. Of Wark, Lees, Coldstream, and Till-mouth fishings I may only speak from hearsay, but that they command favour from those who know them may be concluded from the rents which are easily obtained for the angling.

'Were all the rod-fishings on the river disposed of at the rate of value set upon them by anglers, the rent drawn from those alone would, there is no question, approach that which is commanded by the whole of the netting-grounds at the mouth of the river.' Thus wrote Tom Stoddart seventy years ago; were he writing now, instead of 'approach' he would have to say 'far exceed', so greatly has the demand for salmon-angling increased of late years. The day cannot be far distant when the riparian owners of Tweedside will follow the example of those of the Tay, the Dee, and other northern rivers, and indefinitely increase not only the value of their own sporting rights, but the productiveness of the estu-arine nets, by buying up all netting rights above the tide. The regeneration of this fair river—its restoration as a spring and summer angling water—is merely a question of wise co-operation. It has been proved elsewhere, beyond a shadow of doubt, that, by reducing the number of nets and regulating the weekly close time, the supply of fish to the market, so far from being stinted, may be very largely increased.

ENVOI

IN following our river from its Scottish cradle in the shadow of Corsehill to its English bridal with the North Sea, the reader has traversed shrill uplands where no kindly woodland lends shelter from the blast—where every hillside was once fortified against its neighbour, where no manor was secure without its pele tower and barmekin, where green mounds and shapeless walls mark the primitive shrines of dawning faith. He has passed into a softer clime and a richer land, where the monuments of the past are grander in scale and nobler in design—a land humming with industry and closely set with prosperous homes. The stream, which he first beheld as a furtive rill among the heather and rushes, drawing volume from a thousand glens and deans, has become a broad-bosomed river set with towns, and mills, and shining housesteads.

Greatly as the aspect of river and landscape has altered since we first set forth, the change is not greater than that which has come over life upon the Borders—nay, upon the national life as a whole. For just as this majestic river is the product of innumerable rivulets, so the power of Britain has been created by the incorporation and union—first of petty septs and clans; then of provinces and principalities; lastly, after much tumult and chafing, of realms themselves.

The result is Peace—Peace in a land where once the clash of arms was seldom still; and never will he realise the full spirit of this valley who does not care to fathom the passions of the past. It may be an idle dream—surely it is not an ignoble one—to picture the whole world lulled to peace in like manner as this Border land has been. For hundreds of weary years Scots and English conceived it to be their chief mission in life to fly at each other's throats—burn each other's houses and crops—steal each other's goods and cattle. It is vain to hope that it is within the destiny of the human race to bring about in the general community of nations what was once deemed impossible here, yet which has been so thoroughly fulfilled. Here—as a modern singer had turned it :—

'Long years of peace have stilled the battle thunder,
    Wild grasses quiver where the fight was won ;
Masses of blossom, lightly blown asunder,
    Drop down white petals on the silent gun.
For life is kind, and sweet things grow unbidden,
    Turning the scenes of strife to bloomy bowers ;
One only knows what secrets may be hidden
    Beneath His cloud of flowers.

Poor heart ! above thy field of sorrow sighing
    For smitten faith and hope untimely slain,
Leave thou the soil whereon thy dead are lying
    To the soft sunlight and the cleansing rain.
Love works in silence, hiding all the traces
    Of bitter conflict on the trampled sod,
And time shall show thee all earth's battle-places
    Veiled by the hand of God. '

INDEX

364 INDEX

Crook, Tree of, 13.
Crosses—
  Eccles, twelfth century, 261.
  Lilliard's Edge, 99.
  Peebles Town Cross, 32.
  Tweed Cross, 5.
  Wayside cross, Hobkirk, 183.

Darnley, murder of, 239.
David I.—
  Berwick made a burgh, 294.
  Jedburgh and Kelso abbeys founded, 73, 216.
  Lays siege to Wark Castle, 256.
David II.—
  Chief events in reign, 136-7.
  Lays siege to Wark Castle, 257.
  Marriage with Princess Joan of England, 315, 316
  Taken prisoner, Neville's Cross, 324.
Dawick, 18, 24.
Debatable Land between Sark and Esk, and freebooter dwellers entrapping Johnnie Armstrong, 146-154
De Brus, Princesses Marjorie and Marie confined in cages by Edward I., 134.
De la Bastie, cairn marking grave, 289.
De Morvilles, 248.
De Ros, Sir Robert and daughters, 257.
De Ros of Hamelak, 257.
De Venale, Sir Robert, death at Halidon Hill, 184.
De Vesci, William, 256.
Deil's Dyke in Galloway, 92.
Delorain, 48.
Denholm, 178.
Douglas, Archibald, murder of Darnley, 239.
Douglas, Archibald the Tineman, battle Halidon Hill, 184, 320, 321.
Douglas, Archibald, fourth Earl, Battle of Homildon, 263-4.
Douglas, Bishop Gavin, 226.
Douglas, Earl of Hotspur, and the

Pennon, ballad, 194-9.
Douglas of Drumlanrig, 167-8.
Douglas, James, Earl of Morton, builds Drochiel Castle, 28.
Douglas, Lord of Backhouse and ballad, 'The Douglas Tragedy' 58, 56, 57.
Douglas, Sir James, 26, 28, 66, 226.
  Death, 28, 321.
  Entraps English at Lintalee, 212-13.
  Exploits at Berwick — encounter with Neville, 307-8.
Douglas, Sir James—
  Meets Robert Bruce, 9.
  Recovers Roxburgh Castle, 134-5.
Douglas, William. Abbot of Holyrood, 136-8, 227.
Douglas, Sir William 'le Hardi,' 9, 299, 302, 303.
Douglas, William, first Earl. See Knight of Liddesdale.
Douglas Standard preserved at Cavers. 173-6.
Douglas tomb at Melrose defaced. 97.
Drochil Castle, 28.
Drummelzier, 17.
Drummelzier Haugh, 19, 20.
Dryburgh Abbey, 120.
  Sir W. Scott buried, 120.
Dryburgh Water and salmon fishing, 355.
  Scenery, 124.
Drycthelm, 95.
Drygrange, 117, 352.
'Dub', method of fishing a, 358.
Dun Hill, 35.
Dunbar, burning of, 215.
Duns Law—Town of Duns, church castle, 284-6.
Dye Water, The, 282.

Earlston (Ercildoune), 79, 84, 113.
Eccles, church and cross, 261.
Eddlestone Water, 31.
Eden, 244.
Eden Water, 245.
Edgar family and Wedderlie, 289-291.

Lothian, Marquis of, descended from Kerrs of Fernihirst, 129.
Lyne, Roman camp, 27 ; parish church, 29.

Maccus'wele or Maxwheel Fishery, Kelso, 140.
MacGibbon, Mr. David, quoted, 210.
Maid of Norway. *See* Margaret, Queen of Scots.
Maitland family, 104, 105.
Makerstoun and the Trows, 129, salmon-fishing, 357.
Malcolm the Maiden, King, 219.
Malcolm II. wins Lothian by right of conquest, 256.
Manor Water and various Castles, 29, 30.
March, Patrick, Earl of, 325.
Margaret, Queen of James III., 66.
Margaret, Queen of James IV., 66, 329.
Margaret, Queen of Scots, betrothed to Prince Edward, death, 226.
Mary of Gueldres, Queen of James III., 139, 249.
Mary Queen of Scots holds a court at Jedburgh, 221.
Maxton, 128.
Meldred, lord of Drummelzier, 22.
Mellerstain and Lady Grizell Baillie, 246-8.
Melrose Abbey—
  History of, 94-97.
  St. Cuthbert at, 106-107.
Merlin Emrys or Ambrosius, 21.
Merlin the Wizard and Drummelzier Haugh, 20, 21.
Mertoun Water, salmon-fishing, 355, 356.
Michael the Wizard. *See under* Scot.
Midside Maggie's Girdle, 111, 112.
Minto Crags, 178, 179, 181.
Minto Elliotts, descended from Auld Wat of Harden and the Flower of Yarrow, 179; rise of the family, 180-1.
Monk, General, 261.

Montagu, Sir William de—defends Wark Castle, 257.
Monteviot House, 191.
Montgomery, owners of Stobo, 25.
Montrose, defeated at Philiphaugh, 68-9, 71.
Moody, fisherman, 355.
Mordington, Cromwell's headquarters, 293.
Morebattle and church, 232.
Morton, Earl of. *See* Douglas, James.
Morton, Regent, 204, 224.
'Mosfenman or the Logan Lee,' 14, 15, 16.
Murray the Outlaw and James IV., 44, 45.
Murray, Sir Gideon, and 'Micklemou'd Meg,' 36, 37.
Mutiny Stones, 282.

Naesmyth, Sir James, 24.
Napier and Ettrick, Lord, descent of, 46.
Napier of Merchistoun, tragedy of, 67-8.
Napoleon, proposed invasion of England—Beacon warning on the Border, 252.
Neidpath Castle, 30.
Nenthorn or Naithansthirn, 248.
Nevill, Sir Robert de, encounter with Sir James Douglas, 308-9.
Neville's Cross, battle of, 138.
Newark Castle, 65.
Newton Don and its tragedy, 248-9.
Nicol, Rev. T., poem quoted, 36.
Norham Castle, scenes of splendour, passages from *Scalacronica*, 271-9.
North, Christopher, 55, 341.

Oakwood, 51.
Old Melrose, 94-5, 117.
'Old Q,' Duke of Queensberry and Neidpath, 30, 31.
Oliver Castle, 12.
Order of the Garter, origin of, 258.

ImTheStory.com